To Enlarge the Machinery of Government

Reconfiguring American Political History

Ronald P. Formisano, Paul Bourke,

Donald DeBats, and *Paula M. Baker*

Series Founders

To Enlarge the Machinery of Government

of Government

Congressional Debates and the Growth
of the American State, 1858–1891

Williamjames Hull Hoffer

The Johns Hopkins University Press
Baltimore

The Johns Hopkins University Press
2715 North Charles Street
Baltimore, Maryland 21218-4363
www.press.jhu.edu

Library of Congress Cataloging-in-Publication Data

Hoffer, Williamjames Hull.
   To enlarge the machinery of government : congressional debates and the
growth of the American state, 1858–1891 / Williamjames Hull Hoffer.
      p. cm. — (Reconfiguring American political history)
   Includes bibliographical references and index.
   ISBN-13: 978-0-8018-8655-3 (hardcover : alk. paper)
   ISBN-10: 0-8018-8655-4 (hardcover : alk. paper)
   1. United States—Politics and government—19th century.
2. Federal government—United States. 3. United States. Congress.
4. Debates and debating—United States. I. Title. II. Series.
   JK246.H84 2007
      320.97309′034—dc22   2006037746

A catalog record for this book is available from the British Library.

Contents

Introduction. "Badly in Detail but Well on the Whole":
The Second State   vii

Prologue. "The Great, Noisy, Reedy, Jarring Assembly":
The Capitol, Lawyers, and Public Space   1

1   A "Government of States": Sponsorship and the First Debate
on Land Grant Colleges, 1858–1861   8

2   "The Object of a Democratic Government": Sponsorship
and Supervision of Agriculture and Land Grant Colleges,
1861–1863   37

3   "A Government of Law": Sponsoring and Supervising
the Freedmen, Abandoned Lands, and Refugees, 1863–1865   63

4   The "Two Great Pillars" of the State: The Supervision
and Standardization of Education and Law Enforcement,
1865–1876   89

5   "To Change the Nature of the Government":
Standardizing Schooling and the Civil Service, 1876–1883   118

6   "What Constitutes a State": Supervising Labor
and Commerce, 1883–1886   144

7   "A System Entirely Satisfactory to the Country":
Standardizing Labor and the Courts, 1886–1891   168

Conclusion. "To Answer Our Purposes, It Must Be Adapted"   196

Acknowledgments   205
Notes   207
Essay on Sources   241
Index   249

"Badly in Detail but Well on the Whole"

The Second State

In a 1904 memoir Carl Schurz recounted a conversation he'd had with the minister president of Prussia and future architect of German unification, Otto von Bismarck Schonhausen, in 1868. Both were astute students of government, and both had seen its operation from the center of power. Schurz already had had a distinguished career in the United States. He had escaped the Prussian-ruled Rhineland in 1849 as a fugitive revolutionary and once in the States had served in state and federal government, as a general in the Union army in the Civil War, a civil service reformer, and an elder statesman of the German-American community.[1] He recalled that Bismarck "seemed to be much struck when I brought out the apparent paradox that in a democracy with little government things might go *badly in detail but well on the whole*, while in a monarchy with much and omnipresent government [as in Prussia], things might go very pleasingly in detail but poorly on the whole."[2] Schurz overgeneralized and likely couched his remarks to suit his audience, but his message could not have been clearer: Americans preferred the occasional incompetence of small government to the threatening competence of big government. The progressive agencies that proliferated in Schurz's old age had their place, but only as subordinate and closely watched dependencies.

Schurz was a brilliant and successful outsider, but other native-born observers shared his views. His observations on the character of American government were much in the mainstream of his generation's thinking. Autocratic bureaucrats and administrative agencies might get the details of government right, but, if they grew too intrusive, they would obstruct the progress of an energetic people. Writing on March 23, 1870, Horace Greeley—sometime politician, reformer, editor of the influential *New York Tribune*—responded to Mississippi federal judge J. Tarbell's suggestion that the U.S. Congress create bureaus of immigration to help rebuild the South.[3] Instead, Greeley recommended "good laws, thoroughly enforced. . . . Cheap and simple government, low salaries, light taxes. . . . Impartial justice to every one regardless of caste, or color, secured by an upright judiciary. . . . Making the state too hot for blacklegs, duelists, harlots, rum-sellers, etc." Above all, he cautioned, "avoid public debt."[4] This philosophy of "anti-institutionalism" went beyond the political groups Greeley might have been courting to the major political parties and all regions of the country.[5]

Schurz and Greeley enunciated with crystal clarity the central tenets of what may be called the "first state." Variously styled "Jeffersonian," "old democratic/republican," "Jacksonian," "limited government," or even "states' rights," the ideology had its origins in the founding era of the nation. Government was dangerous. It must protect liberty and keep order but not intrude too far into private lives or enterprise. Government was best that comported itself economically and responsibly to the people's wishes (albeit with the full recognition that all the people's wishes did not count equally). American government must not copy from foreign governments, for the United States was exceptional. Borrowing foreign political ideas would lead to tyranny at the top and slavishness at the bottom of society. American government must bow to federalism: the central government should not infringe upon states' rights.

Above all, the first state men such as Greeley were suspicious of bureaucrats, that is, professional government officials. Government was best that proceeded by committee, in deliberative rather than administrative fashion, arriving at ad hoc solutions to pressing problems. Expertise was suspect. Partisanship, though decried, was made welcome. Character and piety were the true, sure guides to probity and ability in office with political affiliation an acceptable surrogate. Last but not least, the courts had an important role to play in any kind of government action. The first state allowed their administrative activities.

All the more striking for the pride and the attachment Greeley and Schurz had to the first state was the fact that the nation had just passed through a most terrible test of that ideology and found it wanting. The Civil War had cost over a million casualties in dead and injured, destroyed much of the South, and called into question every basic American political value, from loyalty to the Union to personal liberty. Schurz and Greeley had seen all this firsthand and knew of their own experience that the powers that be had saved the Union and based the reconstruction of the nation upon a substantial, albeit temporary, expansion in the federal administrative apparatus. Without vast armies, themselves sprawling bureaucracies, hordes of administrators working in the multiplying offices in Washington, D.C., the systematizing of everything from the distribution of blankets to the troops to the issuance of new bond issues, the Union would have lost the war. Despite this experience, Schurz and Greeley's first state creed resisted change.[6]

But it did change. Consider a piece of a remarkable letter that Felix Frankfurter—like Schurz, an outsider (Frankfurter came to the United States from Austria at the age of eleven)—wrote to himself on the eve of his acceptance of a professorship at Harvard Law School in 1913: "All along the line we propose, determine, legislate—without knowing enough. . . . The problems ahead are economic and sociological, and the added adjustments of a government under a written constitution, steeped in legalistic tradition, to the assumption of the right solution of such problems."[7] Only an informed and professionalized government, one that respected expertise and administrative skill, could chart its way through modern public life. In short, Frankfurter's "Great State" must embrace its own expansion into ordinary life.[8] Frankfurter had no idea that a world war would make the United States the greatest power in the world or that another layer of administrative bureaus and agencies would enable the nation to prosecute that war. Nevertheless, he felt sure that the nation needed a regulatory, administrative regime and, furthermore, that legislation must work hand in hand with administration to solve problems.

Frankfurter had laid out the core concept of the Progressive Era's state, also known as the administrative state.[9] It grudgingly accepted the need for ongoing, trained, and semi-independent agencies to carry out an expanded mission. It welcomed new bureaus and commissions, so long as they fit the model of democratic responsiveness.[10] How did this about-face in attitude come about?

American history textbooks agree that something new and decidedly different marked the Progressive state, "Something astir in the country, something so important and pervasive that it altered the course of American history in the twentieth century." In this new age one would find "a shift in temper in American public life." There is some disagreement among historians and political scientists on exactly when this new era began and where its roots lay. Some chroniclers find precedent "in the effort to regulate and control big business" in the 1870s and 1880s, while others propose a later date: "As early as 1900 these reformers had set out to cleanse and reinvigorate an America whose politics and society they considered in decline." But all agree that the first, republican state gave way directly to its Progressive successor.[11]

This transition from the republican idea of the nation-state to the Progressive ideology, however, is difficult to fathom. They do not seem to go together easily. In fact, even at their edges, where pieces of one might be expected to fit into pieces of the other, one finds little overlap. One might simply attribute this leap from one set of ideas to the other to the "exceptionalism," the uniqueness, of American political culture. Part of that alleged uniqueness is Americans' ability to hold diametrically opposed ideas simultaneously. Another element of our self-congratulatory exceptionalism is our supposed pragmatism.[12] Unfortunately, this explanation does little to illuminate the process by which a political leadership dedicated to a largely antibureaucracy set of ideas created a strong, expansive, and dominating state, nor does it explain why and how these same leaders insisted on preserving the localistic, collective, antiauthoritarian character traits of the first state.

Like a celestial body whose discovery depends on its effect on other objects before someone could actually observe it, the very dissimilarity between the state of Schurz and Greeley and that of Frankfurter's hints that another state—a second state—lay between them. But where can one find evidence of that second, intermediate state? The usual sources of political history—private papers, published memoirs, newspapers, journals of opinion, and speeches—in the time between the Civil War and the Progressive Era provide little discussion about the nature of American government, particularly with regards to the administrative apparatus.

Where to look, then? Oddly enough, in the frequently quoted, huge, often unwieldy debates recorded in the *Congressional Globe* and *Congressional Record*, one finds a treasure trove of thinking about the nature and function of government embedded in the debates on particular pieces of legislation. There is little free-floating theorizing there, for most of the congressmen were not intellectuals in any sense of that word. Moreover, they came to their notions of a new kind of state not through abstract philosophizing but in the pressing and partisan contemplation of particular necessities. In short, they improvised, and all such improvisations gain a life of their own. The *Globe* and *Record* preserve a record of how and when those ideas began to appear, how the congressmen tested and modified, and sometimes camouflaged them; how party and interest, section and personal animus and alliance, shaped them. In these archives of living speech one can see how the second state resulted from the actions of a handful of men, not always fully conscious of what they were doing and rarely prescient about how the new ideas would play out over time. Reconstructing the dialogue within those pages profoundly alters our understanding of this period.[13]

Instead of finding a distinct moment or a sudden transition from the republican state to the Progressive state, when congressional remarks changed from that of limited government to a regulatory one, we find a distinct set of ideas developed in between. Even many in Congress who developed the ideas of the second state never really understood what they had done. They were not philosophers, only politicians groping their way toward solutions to their problems.

The seven chapters that follow reconstruct the debates on the Morrill, or Land Grant College, bill in 1858–59 and 1861; the Department of Agriculture and the Freedmen's Bureau during the Civil War; the Department of Education, the Hoar bill for national funding for common schools, and the Department of Justice during Reconstruction; the Blair bill and the Pendleton or Civil Service Reform Act in the Gilded Age; the creation of the Bureau of Labor and the Interstate Commerce Act that created the Interstate Commerce Commission; the discussions surrounding the elevation of the Bureau of Labor to a department and the Evarts, or Circuit Courts of Appeals, Act of 1891; and the Second Morrill Act. The topics—education, law enforcement, the staffing of the executive branch, labor-management relations, railroad regulation, and the courts—are representative of the broad range of activities that Congress tackled during this period, though any number of other topics would serve just as well. Taken together, they present a compelling story of intellectual change.

Certainly, the debates on these pieces of legislation do not constitute all of those affecting the ideas governing the shape of the national government. Nevertheless, they do reveal what changed and what did not in rhetoric, concerns, and perspective over this critical period from directly before the Civil War, through the Civil War and Reconstruction, to the convulsive industrialization of the nation during the Gilded Age. The debates on the U.S. military do not appear here because this work examines ideas about the civil administration— the traditional focus of government building for scholars—even though, in all probability, the debates on military matters developed along similar lines.

From mere sponsorship of education Congress agreed to serve that sponsorship with administrative organs. It then recognized that sponsorship required supervision and began to provide that as well. Because supervision without standards made all of Congress's efforts subject to the vagaries of partisanship and local resistance, standards and standardization followed. Reorganization of the federal courts was the capstone to this testing of ideas about the state, when the paradox of antibureaucracy ideas and administrative necessity found ways to compromise.[14] The debate on the Second Morrill Act makes plain the changes in congressional thinking. The three functions—sponsorship, supervision, and standardization—went beyond the mere monitoring and service functions of the first state. Each one presented its own difficulties despite the fact they were inextricably linked to one another.

Thus, the second state was not a physical entity so much as a state of mind, a way that members of Congress began reconceptualizing the powers and limitations of government and were willing to explore, in the debates on specific measures, how those powers and limitations applied to a series of increasingly complex and novel demands. In the years between the eve of the Civil War and the end of the Gilded Age, those demands proved the first state conception of government inadequate. Thus, the coming of the war, the need to help the freedmen and women, the unprecedented demand for regulation, and the unnerving spread of corruption drove the legislators. But events alone did not lead to the rise of the second state.

Nor was the invention of the second state the conspiratorial plot of a few nationalist centralizers—big government men yearning for expensive, extensive, professional administrative rule. True, some members of Congress were more receptive to the foundational ideas of the second state than others. But it is important to resist the temptation to regard the former as a band of visionaries, intellectually superior to their more conventional colleagues. These kinds of arguments about motive do not fit the evidence. Instead, the second state mentality also came about through a punctuated evolution of ideas, a series of questions whose answers led, bit by bit, to further and often unexpected explorations of old notions. Often, older terms gained new meanings in the course of the debates, and subtle shifts in political alignments produced new ways of looking at older assumptions.

The basis of this inquiry, then, lies in the over eight thousand pages of the recorded debates on these proposals in Congress, thousands of hours of debate.[15] Read closely this cornucopia of verbiage reveals that the period from just before the war, in 1858, to just before the rise of the Progressives, in 1891, represented an era of thinking about the national state in and of itself. By focusing on the ideas contained within, we can see how the earliest elaboration of the second state, its back edge, fit the first state approach and how the fullest development of the second state, its leading edge, fit into the Progressive Era. Step by step, congressmen conceptualized their own roles and that of the government in a new way: an antibureaucracy ethic that could create bureaucracies.[16]

A FEW REMARKS on the handling, sifting, and selection of the sources are in order here. To preserve the give-and-take of the debates—the context of the remarks—one must leave the arguments in their original order in the records. Necessarily, some of the discussions will seem disjointed, haphazard, and without a coherent structure. That was how the debate occurred. Most often, the logic appears just as tortured; it too reflects the debates' nature. These exchanges did not arise in an academic journal, and scholarly omniscience does violence to their historical quality. Although these qualities make the narrative more difficult to discern, the result rewards the reader with a more accurate understanding of this dialogue.

In some of these debates the issue of the role of government arose in the minds of congressmen from the outset. In debates on other pieces of legislation the issue of how to effect the will of Congress arose suddenly and sharply, without warning. All of the episodes built upon their predecessors, for Congress had a memory for its own precedents. The reader will find that the similarities in the debates become a kind of background, or gestalt field, to the differences in them. In the details of these differences of attitude and ideas lie both the source of the paradox and the remarkable ways in which the policy makers enabled the modern state.

Seen from this distance, over a long course of time, it might appear that the ideas about state development as posed here progress linearly, the first state leads to the second and the second leads to the third. Although a Whiggish interpretation of national government's growth has its appeal, and for many years was the orthodoxy,[17] the second state approach did not result from a universal agreement but from contestation. Consistent with the congressmen's backgrounds, professional practices, and context, they made the second state approach practical, grounded it in time and place, and cogently imposed it from above—from themselves. The long and complicated conflict between the exigencies of governing a great nation and the reluctance to confer power upon administrative agencies dominated these critically important moments in Congress's nineteenth-century legislative history.

Only an analysis of this public dialogue unearths these conclusions. While examinations of the manuscript sources and newspapers reveal other layers of the machinations behind the consideration of these proposals, they also divert our attention away from the implications of these arguments. The nature of this dialogue—public, both prepared and extemporaneous, governed by the rules of each house of Congress, from the congressmen themselves without the gloss of an observer—makes it necessary to view it without looking behind the curtain. Its performance alone carries meaning, a meaning otherwise missed. Neither a parliamentary history nor a series of statutory histories, this retelling of the history of a vital era in American political thought seeks an insight into the paradox of the American state's development through its avoidance of traditional material. It cannot do otherwise and retain its analytical power.

Although the elements of the second state were not entirely novel, the coherence and the interrelationships of these notions over time and the way this set of ideas became commonplace are both striking and a vital addition to our understanding of the American polity. The Congress created a leviathan, one that its members restricted according to their precepts, their ways of thought, and political exigency.[18]

To Enlarge the Machinery of Government

"The Great, Noisy, Reedy, Jarring Assembly"

The Capitol, Lawyers, and Public Space

In the year 1858 Congress assembled in an unfinished Capitol in Washington, D.C. Cranes and scaffolding loomed over the unfinished cast iron dome, and the chambers of the House and Senate were not quite complete.[1] In the meantime the members of Congress who lived in boardinghouses yearned to return home.[2] The road to the Capitol building, like all the other roads in the nation's capital, was pounded dirt. Dusty in summer, a river of mud in the spring, it was deeply rutted and humble, much like the federal government in 1858.[3]

Congress roiled that year in sectional animosity; bitter debates pitted North versus South and Republican versus Democrat. A pall of violence hung in the air. Southerners sensed affronts to their honor and threats to their institutions, and northerners grew testy at the sight of so many slaves in the streets. Who could tell if the nation itself would survive the increasingly bitter debates surrounding "Bleeding Kansas" long enough to see the building project completed?

The great national forum, the focal point of representative government, the Capitol had seen giants walk its corridors and fill its halls with immortal oratory. Now, with the nation looking on as Congress debated the future of the nation and the shape of the federal government, the House and Senate chambers took on even greater importance. Set in the center of their respective new wings, the chambers were spacious halls with the speaker's or presiding officer's rostrum at the front and an array of desks in a semicircle facing the front of the room.[4] Because they were at the center of their respective wings, there were no windows. Illumination came from skylights in the ceiling and gas lighting.[5] Many members complained about the air quality, especially in the Senate chamber, where the vents improperly let in the stench of basement mold, mildew, and rot.[6] The acoustics in both rooms were poor, and the voices of speakers often could not carry above the din on the floor. The walls created various dead spots.[7] Some modern commentators have traced the decline of congressional oratory to the effects of the new halls.[8]

The additions had cost millions and had already consumed several years of intermittent progress. By the close of the construction project, the architect and the chief engineer would no longer be on speaking terms. Their sole communication took place through subordinates and the charge and countercharge relayed by their respective champions in the House and Senate.[9] In a final irony Jefferson Davis, a man who would be the leader of the cause to dismantle the union, was the prime mover behind the project.[10]

Surrounded if not comforted by the grandeur of their new home, senators worked at their desks on the floor of their chamber. They franked their speeches and wrote their correspondence, while others waxed eloquent a few yards away.[11] More than one foreign visitor to the Capitol in the early 1860s gazed on these two bodies of men who embodied the ways and legislated for the republic, disbelieving that the institution functioned at all. The oratory itself, although done with great "fluency," was often accompanied by bizarre hand gestures, pacing, and poor elocution.[12] During a member's speech other members would be clapping their hands to get the attention of the pages, who would then be "running about the floor, ministering to the members' wishes," carrying petitions, water, delivering letters, and "running with general messages."[13] At their seats congressmen had trouble hitting the spittoons with their expectoration, and tobacco smoke filled the air. As one observer wryly complained in 1876: "There is . . . an increasing hum of conversation as the session progresses, and a uniform circulation from one part of the Chamber to the other. . . . Members stand up and talk to each other in the aisles of the hall during the disposition of every kind of business. They send for books, they post letters, buy postage-stamps, and in a word do everything that could be done in a smoking-car except smoke cigars and play cards."[14]

The procedures for the debates themselves confounded even the most expert legislator, and the exchanges on the floor alternated between benign indifference and brawling free-for-alls and everything in between.[15] A visitor to the House in 1862 noted of one meeting, "The scene looks like a lecture room where the class is paying no attention to the lecturer."[16] For journalist George Alfred Townsend, covering Congress for the *Chicago Tribune,* "the great, noisy, reedy, jarring assembly which reminds you, at the first peep, of some temple once honoured by worship, where they are now selling doves."[17] The Senate was usually quieter, "a grave, sparsely attended assembly, where voices seldom rise to oratorical pitch," a French visitor remarked in 1864.[18] Given that much if not most of the business of Congress took place in committee, many members were said to have used the House chamber only to write letters and deliver the occasional speech.[19] Some congressmen memorized their speeches and delivered them in a schoolboy manner. Others were famous for their lively style of delivery.

But in their fashion the activities that made the floors of the House and Senate so lively revealed the essence of American democracy. It was a republic of words, a nation that loved the spoken word, whose politics still featured the stump speakers and whose orators were honored like today's movie stars. Congressmen such as Daniel Webster and Henry Clay might not wield the power of party managers or ever hold the high office they so much desired, but they were worshiped as demigods when they took the floor. (One might say, with much justice, that even the written culture was a reflection of oral traditions—storytellers such as James Fenimore Cooper, Nathaniel Hawthorne, Washington Irving, Herman Melville, and Edgar Allan Poe had simply become men of letters.) In any case one cannot help but be repulsed, amused, and awe-struck at the vast profusion of words uttered in the Congress.[20]

Even more important, of all the "public spaces" in which words were spoken and heard in the nineteenth century—the arenas in which ideas were tested and refined—Congress was the foremost.[21] The "great debates" in its halls from the Missouri Compromise to the end of the century, which were reported in the newspapers, became or reflected the debates that framed the national political agenda.

Of course, some of these "debates" never really occurred. They were manufactured after a fashion. Some speeches were ghostwritten. Others were not spoken but were added to the *Globe* or *Record.* Some were altered and some deleted from the records entirely by crafty opponents. As one correspondent bitterly complained in 1874, "the Congressional Record is a fraud, covering about seventy pages per day. The real debates in Congress are not contained in it. Whenever there is anything interesting in the way of an exchange of observations, the remarks are 'withheld for revision.'"[22] Political spite, in large measure, motivated many of these complaints. Editors and correspondents were political actors and exercised "a power in their own right."[23] They did not seek objectivity, much less neutrality. They too were partisans. And, following them, one might conclude that all of the debates were about party and personal pique. The Congress of the newspapers is all about party and full of foible.

Yet one cannot read the *Congressional Globe* and the *Congressional Record*, the officially disseminated version of remarks made on the floor of the House of Representatives and the Senate, without experiencing more than a little awe. Even if they were never a word-for-word transcription of the exchanges on the floors of both houses, even if members often submitted their remarks without actually delivering them, and speeches uttered could be amended after the fact to delete substantial portions of the text as well as provide new sections, even if Congress and contemporaries lamented the corrupted nature of what is supposed to be an impartial record,[24] one cannot dismiss the obvious effort, occasional eloquence, and intellectual content of the congressmen's remarks.

While the conventional approach might derogate the speeches and repartee in *Congressional Globe* and *Congressional Record* as mere bombast and posturing, a sideshow outside the big top where the real action was, it is a mistake to dismiss the congressmen's words or reduce the speeches to mere reflections of party and personality. Congressmen might have ulterior motives for what they said, but they were careful not to speak against their larger beliefs or to offend their constituents. What is more important still is the fact that the contributors to the *Globe* and the *Record* believed in their wider impact. The participants in these debates well knew that their words could influence other audiences than the ones in the galleries, including newspaper readers receiving a choice quote or constituents getting the reprint of their remarks through the franking privilege accorded to members of Congress. They took ideas from their mail and from newspapers. They conversed incessantly with one another in the boardinghouses where they lived, ate, and spent their leisure time. There was no congressional staff to speak of, no speech writers, no researchers. Only committee chairmen had a clerk until 1884, when senators received one clerk each.[25] Unlike in the Congress of more recent decades, congressmen themselves created the words in the *Globe* and *Record*.

Most important, the words associated with congressmen and directed to particular matters of state afford critical insights into the minds of the creators of the U.S. state because they formed the precedent, the public discourse, on the problem and prospects of adding or subtracting from the national state's administrative apparatus. If one were to analogize the Congress to a court (much as the Parliament in England is a court), then the published exchanges (not the spoken or back room or private correspondence) could be like judges' published opinions. For the purposes of this analogy it would not matter what the politics or the personal backgrounds of the congressmen might be, just as it does not matter what the politics or the personal backgrounds of the judges might be. It is their published words, connected to particular issues just as the judges' opinions are tied to particular cases, which create the precedent.

The analogy to a great court is not as far-fetched as it may seem (at least in light of the conventional fashion of reporting these debates). The United States Supreme Court and courts in general in the twentieth century have relied on these very legislative records to derive congressional intent, so this oftentimes less-than-accurate account generates substantial comment from justices, judges, law scholars, and historians concerned with the evidentiary value of these critical documents.[26] Many of the members of Congress had reputations as excellent speakers. More important, almost all of those who took key roles in the dialogue over the shape of government, as we will see, had experience as legal pleaders. Although judges, justices, and legal commentators derided statutes in comparison to the common law, it is not surprising that congressmen cared enough to prepare their remarks and enter into exchanges with their colleagues in the *Globe* and *Record*.[27]

The fact that many of the congressmen in these pages were lawyers with varying degrees of courtroom experience, or that some had argued cases before the Supreme Court, also plays a vital part in understanding how the second state's discourse within the government was framed.[28] As the French visitor Alexis de Tocqueville wrote in the 1830s, "lawyers are called upon to play the leading part in the political society," and "the government of the Union rests almost entirely on legal fictions" that lawyers understood and manipulated.[29] De Tocqueville was more interested in the way that courts, judges, and juries functioned than in legislatures and statutes, but he understood that being a lawyer was more than just practicing law.[30] These values included the celebration of the objectivity and elevating power of words by the "lawyer statesman." Founding fathers such as

John Adams, Alexander Hamilton, Thomas Jefferson, and James Wilson were all able practicing lawyers whose professional work taught them how to use words in the framing of the new nation.[31]

As Felix Frankfurter saw, looking back, the lawyers were "the coordinator, the mediator."[32] The lawyers' habits of speech and thought of the key debaters were crucial—for to a remarkable extent these were conversations among lawyers. Whether they had been successful or not, whether they went on to hold offices in the legal system, to teach in its schools, or simply used their legal contacts to vault into politics, the lawyer-congressmen came to understand that the only safe foundation for enlarging the state was in the close attention of lawyers to the framing and management of those additions. That lawyers' principles, allegiances, and argument styles had a disproportionate influence should also come as no surprise. After all, U.S. litigiousness, intellectual proclivities, and legalistic conceptions are notorious.[33] Behind the otherwise bewildering words of our political leaders, the foundation of our modern state is the result of this lawyers' encoding process: both in terms of the restraints upon it and the outcome of the American paradox.[34]

By training, experience, and preturnature, the lawyers of later generations privileged their words in debates on public policy. They had a powerful sense that the lawyer could see the principles of republicanism in clearer fashion than others—what two recent students of American legal culture have called the nineteenth-century lawyers' "Ciceronian" faith in their own perspicuity.[35] They also understood the limits of lawmaking because they were lawyers.[36] Many had no doubt learned the principles of hermeneutics from the works of Francis Lieber, the widely read Columbia University law professor who had immigrated to the United States from Germany. This legal theory taught a method for reading texts in order to discover their intended meaning which was particularly suited to lawyers. That method required close attention to the manifest (expressed) intent of the speaker or writer. Hermeneutics spoke to private law as well as public policy—for example, the intent of the parties was vital in determining whether an exchange of promises was an enforceable contract.[37] This and other claims to preeminence in fashioning laws might well have had a special impact in the high-turnover and especially heavy lawyer congresses of the nineteenth century as opposed to the more careerist, institutionalized, and lighter lawyer congresses of the twentieth century, the usual focus of the roll call studies that dispute the lawyers' impact.[38]

It is true that there were many kinds of lawyers sitting in Congress. Some had extensive practices (which sometimes called them away from D.C. during the debates), while others had largely abandoned the practice of the law. Some grew rich from law; others never were successful at it. Yet the legal culture in which they learned the law and practiced it imposed on them certain ways of seeing and hearing, of using words.[39] Equally important, that legal culture featured a kind of administrative apparatus—the courts and the lawyers together—which would become the model for the reluctant leviathan that the congressional lawyers ultimately constructed in the second state era.

The crucial common element in the experience of learning and practicing the law, whether or not the lawyer in Congress went on to a lucrative practice, was the administration of estates. Every lawyer of whatever rank became adept in this area—the management of property of the deceased for the surviving family members, the administration of a business that had failed, or keeping together a farm or plantation in the face of the demands of the creditors. Administration of estates required a light touch, for the property did not belong to the lawyer. He acted for others. He could and was expected to sponsor various projects for the good of the estate; he could and was expected to supervise the assets' use to ensure that they were not wasted; he could and often did arrange with the court (which supervised him) to standardize various kinds of property in the estate, that is, to eliminate the danger of misuse of the assets. Play this same scenario on the screen of congressional action—as Congress faced new demands and opportunities; as the nation itself grew; as war, economic innovation, and industrialization posed new problems—and think of the "estate" as the commonwealth, and one sees in a flash how lawyerly habits of mind, training, and experience infused the second state even as early as 1858, when our story begins in the "great, noisy, reedy, jarring assembly" that was the Congress of the United States.[40]

CHAPTER ONE

A "Government of States"

Sponsorship and the First Debate
on Land Grant Colleges, 1858–1861

In hindsight the congressional session of 1858–59 was a watershed. Behind it lay two years of roiling debate over acceptance of Kansas's pro-slavery constitution; the *Dred Scott* decision that had split the nation; and the bitter recriminations of antislavery congressmen such as William Seward of New York and Henry Hammond of South Carolina, whose stark intransigence laid bare the sectional division over the expansion of slavery—a Congress so riven by section and party that it could not choose its own speaker and whose members carried weapons into the Capitol. Ahead of the session lay the John Brown raid on the Harpers Ferry federal arsenal; Senator Jefferson Davis's call for a federal slave code; and growing sentiment in the South for the reopening of the Atlantic slave trade and in the North for personal liberty laws. Ahead lay the most divisive presidential election in U.S. history and secession. Ahead lay a Civil War.

Into this maelstrom its supporters brought the Land Grant College, or Morrill, bill of 1858–59. Students of American higher education have celebrated the proposal. Students of the nation-state have dismissed it. A closer look reveals the opening act of a long conversation in Congress over the limits and powers of the federal government, and American state building itself. For, in this proposal to sponsor higher education through the sale of federal lands, advocates saw glimmerings of an active nation-state, led by its legislative branch, fostering the national good through the sponsorship of education. They characterized this plan not as the first step toward a centralized administrative state but as the natural extension of goals as old as the nation itself. Because the idea of government aid to higher education was rooted in fundamental republican values and ensured that an educated citizenry would save the democratic republic from its own partisan excesses, because the agrarian purposes of the land grant colleges spoke to the old ideal of the yeoman republic, the Morrill bill should have had wide support in Congress. It should have brought the sections and the parties together. That the very opposite in fact occurred—that the bill was viewed in sectional and partisan terms—should not surprise students of this troubled era. But in the ongoing give-and-take of the arguments of supporters and opponents, more than sectional and party differences surfaced. The debate over a "government of states" versus a government that sponsored, supervised, and standardized had begun.

In retrospect one can see the Morrill bill debates as part of a significant change in the Congress's thinking about the U.S. national state, a process that continued through the Civil War and into the decades beyond, but that effort was never fully conscious of its implications. Its advocates saw that second state as a form of sponsorship rather than administration, a vision linking it to earlier adumbrations of republican governance as well as European innovations.[1] Opponents of the act deployed a critique of any attempt to expand the national state which would prove remarkably enduring as well as highly serviceable over the next fifty years.

In their effort to answer this critique, advocates of the bill hesitantly began to explore its wider implications. They did not fully understand where these explorations would lead, however, and couched them in language ill suited for coherent policy making, much less as a rationale for changing the nature of American government. Many have seen the final version of the act, passed in 1862, as a significant turning point in American administrative history and philosophy, but, as the early legislative debates reveal, it did not seem so pivotal at the time.[2]

Land, Government, and Education

The first state, antibureaucracy mind-set that most Americans then shared had a long and tangled pedigree. Its roots went at least as far back as the struggle that local elites had waged against British officialdom at the end of the colonial era. The colonists preferred their own brand of administration—committees of their assemblies, grand juries and local court officials—to the placemen the empire had sent to America. During the crisis and the War of Independence the revolutionaries' preference for ad hoc committees of legislators and local, amateur, partisan (or at least highly politicized) administrative agencies such as committees of safety continued the colonial antibureaucracy tradition. The revolutionary heritage of decentralization of power and collective rather than unitary direction of government circulated throughout the new state governments and the confederation. The same heritage of thought and deed explains why the federal government, created in 1787, did not establish elaborate federal administrative agencies.[3]

Under the Constitution Congress was empowered to set up postal and customs collection apparatus and armed forces, and the executive branch had its departments. The secretaries of the latter and the organization of the former lacked staff organization. Posts were filled not by disinterested experts but through political patronage. Regardless of whether the system lent itself to corruption in particular cases, throughout the early nineteenth century, the administrative apparatus of government was dominated by party and run on the cheap. The few exceptions—Alexander Hamilton's plan to create a stable, professional cadre of federal administrators, the Judiciary Act of 1801, George Washington and John Quincy Adams's dream of a national university, and the like—invariably ended with failure or capture by partisans.[4]

The incapacity of the federal bureaucracy elicited celebratory speeches from Jacksonian Democrats as proof that government belonged to the people. The Jacksonians were right to this extent: in the national political culture the absence of administrative discretion was seen as a triumph over tyranny.[5] Nationalist writers de-emphasized the key role of the French, British blunders, societal discord, and the general incompetence of divided government during the Revolutionary era in favor of a story of inevitable victory from Republican virtue and American superiority.[6]

The antibureaucracy, antiprofessional thinking dominated congressional rhetoric throughout the early nineteenth century. This did not mean Americans abandoned plans for national government aid to various causes, particularly education and agriculture. From the founding of the republic, leading Americans such as George Washington, Thomas Jefferson, Benjamin Franklin, and Noah Webster fought for institutions to aid agriculture and learning in general, but they did not agree on the best way to create such institutions. Gentlemen farmers in the Northeast had come to the conclusion that wasteful, ignorant agricultural practices had needlessly decreased the fertility of New England soils. Many believed that it was only a matter of time before this sterility reached other regions of the country.[7]

Some of these reformers looked abroad for inspiration. They found kindred spirits in the societies and universities in Europe. Agricultural society journals, books, and letters went from Britain to the United States; students from the United States crossed the Atlantic to study in the European universities that offered curricula for agronomy, forestry, and geology. They returned to the United States inspired by the heady science of agriculture and the solutions that government sponsorship of agricultural innovation seemed to provide. Noting that all the universities and research stations they wished to copy came from monarchies, they attempted to modify the transplants to remove the taint of authoritarian government and bureaucracy; in short, the agricultural reformers sought to transplant institutions of learning suitable to the prevailing political climate in the United States.[8]

Given that the most apparently successful efforts at higher education came from one of the most autocratic of systems, the kingdom of Prussia, this sanitizing effort constituted a nearly impossible task. After all, the German universities served the monarch's need for developing land, manufacturing, timber supplies, and provided the bureaucrats for his governing apparatus. They served him, increasing his power and wealth. Antidemocratic thinking underwrote all that even enlightened despots did.[9] How could one separate the educational administration that enabled these foreign institutions to flourish without importing the antidemocratic elements of these institutions of higher learning? The answer returned was to promote European-style agricultural trade schools for the American yeomanry without the bureaucrats, using the decentralized system already in place in the United States and to embrace a federal rather than a centralized system and call for sponsorship rather than close supervision.

Early attempts to accomplish this hybridized reform varied sharply by region. The campaign for agricultural reform through education exhibited a sectional character, with strong advocates in New England and the upper Midwest. In New England, with its long history of public support for education, the states issued charters and voted funding for agricultural colleges, agriculture professorships in existing institutions, and research stations appended to planned universities. New Englanders migrating to the Midwest carried their public financing policy agenda with them, in the 1840s reproducing their programs in Illinois, Ohio, Michigan, and Iowa.[10]

Southerners, whose commitment to agricultural reform had once been as potent, held back. Southern states lagged behind, despite Jefferson's plans for public education and agricultural reform in Virginia, although agricultural societies in the South lamented the perceived depletion of eastern soils from cotton's empire, and private efforts in border states such as Maryland had some success. The concern was that agricultural reform not undermine the authority of slaveholders over their bondmen and women.[11]

The agricultural reformers who wanted government sponsorship of their programs found allies in educational reformers who had taken part in the formation of large-scale state educational systems, in part inspired by European examples. Some had traveled to Europe and reported back about the schooling programs of the enlightened monarchies of Prussia, Bavaria, and the Austrian Empire. Once they returned to the United States, they wanted to translate the European system of higher education for their native land.[12] From the 1830s to the 1850s reformers such as Horace Mann, Calvin E. Stowe, Cyrus Pierce, and Henry Barnard came to the conclusion that the common school system needed more than simple sponsorship; the schools required supervision and standardization.

Borrowing what they believed to be the best elements of their model system from the kingdom of Prussia, the state educational reformers pushed for centralized state control, teacher certification and training colleges, graded classrooms, and compulsory education. Their reports circulated through education journals, most notably Henry Barnard's *Journal of American Education*. They founded the National Education Association.[13] Like their counterparts in the agricultural reform movement, the New England leaders of the state educational reform cadre carried their ideas with them as they moved west. The result was a series of colleges whose professors and administrators joined their colleagues in the East, creating a network of educators.[14]

The network thrived even though their creations struggled to attract applicants, recruit faculty, and, most important, attain the necessary funding. Thus, the educational reformers, like the agricultural progressives, turned to the national government for assistance. Unlike the latter, the educators saw the value of professional, expert administration, and they would have added a measure of these qualities to sponsorship. Newly minted national lobbying groups such as the National Teachers' Association agitated for support, combining their efforts with the agricultural lobby and like-minded nationalist education advocates to spur Congress to action.[15]

Yet the Congress was hardly an advocate for its own expansion. Instead, it was home to suspicion about expanding the nation-state's operations. One might attribute this to the influence of the South in Congress, something the opponents of slavery dubbed the "slaveocracy."[16] There was more than a little truth to this in 1858 because many reform roads seemed to lead to abolition of slavery.[17] But southerners did not oppose federal government intervention on behalf of southern interests, even when it required considerable expenditures or the elaboration of a federal administrative activity—for example in the Mexican-American War or the laying of rail lines through the Southwest. Again, interest might override ideology, as when southern congressmen who had, as recently as 1850, argued for states' rights strongly supported the vast increase in federal power over state sovereignty in the Fugitive Slave Law of 1850.

The ideological aversion to state building was shared by North and South, a legacy of the Revolution and very much alive in the politics in the 1850s. Part of the legacy was the fear that all governments, unchecked and unwatched, could become arbitrary in their use of power, which marked the origin of tyranny. Some Americans devoutly opposed any kind of state action in certain areas. Defenders of a regime of laissez-faire denounced government involvement in the economy; the laws of the marketplace were not to be undermined by government action.[18] Other Americans did not mind some intervention, as long as it "released energy" or promoted the most profitable use of property. These individuals might oppose legislative enactments but support the intervention of courts or (in some cases) prefer the actions of legislatures to the restrictions that judges imposed. In short these anti-statists were results oriented.[19] There were also those who believed, with Jefferson (before he authorized the purchase of the Louisiana Territory), in a government that cost as little as possible. Governments that spent money were more likely, in this thinking, to be corrupt. A substantial national debt was a "death sentence."[20]

In addition, there was the federalism-based objection to the growth of the national government. The federal Constitution recognized the sovereignty of the states. While this "dual federalism" was limited by the Supremacy Clause and other provisions of the Constitution, in particular the enumeration in Article 1 of certain powers that belonged only to Congress, the debate over the construction of enumeration (that is, between a "loose" and a "strict" construction) periodically erupted.[21]

If similar-sounding aversion to a comprehensive central government united the representatives, the Morrill bill debates introduced a harmonic variation: might not simple sponsorship be an acceptable extension of federal power? Federalism as ideal and federalism as existing law did not prevent state governments from regulating many segments of economic life. Federalism merely enjoined the national government from acting in coherent fashion. Nevertheless, exigency and opportunity did lead to some sporadic federal actions in this, the first state approach to government.[22] These efforts included internal improvements, the addition of agencies for pensions and Indian affairs, and other initiatives, one of which was the provision of land for schools.[23]

Beginning with the Articles of Confederation, the national legislature had sponsored education through land grants. The one-sixteenth provision of the Northwest Ordinance of 1787 had set a precedent, and several million acres had gone to the states and individual institutions out of the public domain as the nation reached the mid-century mark. Land grants became so common that they could be divided into several categories. Marsh lands, salt lands, and timber lands all went for specific purposes in pieces of legislation known as minor appropriations.[24] While the national road in the Washington administration, the Gallatin infrastructure plan during the Jefferson administration, the Henry Clay program for the "American System" of national infrastructure and tariffs for manufacturing, President John Quincy Adams's much-derided proposal for national observatories and institutions of higher learning, and the Smithson bequest (the origin of the Smithsonian) all lost out to what most writers have labeled either federalism or sectional rivalry,[25] many unambitious proposals that did not draw on the general treasury succeeded.[26]

Reformers who looked to the federal government for aid focused on the only means assured of passage—the land grants. But they needed a standard-bearer in Congress. While the exact provenance of the land grant college idea remains controversial, what is not in doubt is that Justin Smith Morrill, a representative from Vermont, became its leading national champion.[27]

Morrill and Land Grant Colleges

Morrill was born April 14, 1810, in Stafford, Vermont, the son of a blacksmith and tool maker.[28] To his later regret his straitened circumstances meant that his formal schooling ended in his fifteenth year. Apprenticed to Judge Jedidiah Harris at the general store, young Justin learned firsthand the intersection of politics, law, and shopkeeping. The general store was more than just the vendor of life's necessities to farmers and workingmen and women; local store owners, tavern keepers, and mill operators practiced politics with a small and a capital *p*.[29]

Morrill adapted well to his commercial and political clerkship and eventually entered into a partnership with Judge Harris, a local Whig Party leader. Morrill traveled extensively throughout the northern part of the United States to fill orders and establish commercial ties with regional suppliers. In 1848 he sold the shares of the stores he had acquired and retired from business life, but Morrill never stopped borrowing, purchasing, and reading books to fulfill his almost insatiable need to learn.[30]

In the meantime his political career blossomed. In the 1840s he cultivated the role of an intelligent, well-read, and patriotic New Englander. He had found a political voice consistent with the Whig program of free soil, tariffs, and public support for internal improvements. To that program he added a personal distaste for the southern Democracy. Writing in his journal in 1841 while on a trip to Washington, D.C., he noted caustically, "Southern jealousy, and southern cupidity, refused the northern granite" for the construction of capital buildings.[31] Northern granite, northern enterprise, northern values of hard work, and northern free labor were thwarted by unappreciative southerners.

In 1854 Morrill easily gained a seat in the United States House of Representatives. Although he worked hard on appropriations matters, he spoke only once in his first term. He seemed to friends a reliable pro-tariff moralist with strong antislavery views. His only public stands were protection for Vermont wool and the struggle to bring the Mormons in Utah under federal authority.[32]

This much was also clear: Morrill was not an advocate of big government. He cautioned against government spending as an inducement to dependency and insisted that the national government should be frugal in all its endeavors. Morrill's advice to his country thus represented two of the strands of antibureaucracy thinking in the first state mentality. One might even suggest that his politics were still local and his perspective still that of the Yankee storekeeper. Yet on one subject he saw a little farther than the Vermont hills. In 1858 Morrill reintroduced his bill to provide federal funding for institutions of higher learning for agriculturalists and machinists.[33]

A not so distant mirror to his commitment to building the national capital with New England marble and granite was his campaign for national support for higher education for the "industrial classes."[34] A year before he reintroduced his bill, in 1857, Morrill had joined the fledgling Republican Party, which for him represented the interests of the free farmers of the North.[35] But there was more to Morrill's proposed education program than just a political deal to wed farmers to the Republican Party. Morrill's mail (he kept meticulous records as a means of polling his district) shows a considerable desire for access to general education. Although so-called book farming had negligible appeal for his constituents, Morrill himself had attended the United States Agriculture Society meeting in 1856 and heard discussion of plans for land grant technical schools. By the time Morrill began his agitation for land grant colleges, several states had sent resolutions to the U.S. Congress asking for land grant school monies.[36]

Morrill's land grant education proposal of 1858 was simple on its face but complex in its ramifications. It allotted twenty thousand acres of public lands per congressional representative to each state to establish a fund for the support of institutions for the teaching of the liberal, mechanical, and agricultural arts and sciences. States without any federal land, most of the East, would receive scrip for an allotment that they could then use to select available parcels for sale to the public. The money could go to an existing institution or to found a new one. The vagueness of such a large appropriation left a great deal of leeway to the states in the actual use of the money.[37]

The only federal bureaucracy involved, the General Land Office, had been performing this kind of transaction since 1812.[38] Not noted for its incorruptibility, tremendous resources, or expertise, it had a tremendous amount of power but little discretion to use it, even less knowledge to do so, and employed several hundred administrators to operate across and to administer a territory the size of western Europe. The office's proclivities and debilities were typical, one might even say inevitable, given the first state antipathy to bureaucracy.[39]

The land office relied on the apparatus that one scholar has dubbed the state of "courts and parties."[40] What little enforcement there was centered on federal courts and the U.S. marshals who were attached to them. This proto–police force was composed of appointees from the area. Their salaries came from the bounties placed on arrests, fees for the execution of any particular task, and the revenue garnered from whatever cases were at hand. There was no training, no organization, little supervision, meager compensation—and, as one might guess, the institution was of limited effectiveness. The marshals could form posses of local citizens and possessed some common law and equity powers as officers of the court, but mostly they had to negotiate their way around local officials and political squabbles.[41]

Morrill's proposal reflected a states' rights and fiscally conservative perspective, but the land grant colleges bill of 1858 departed considerably from its predecessors in its vision, method, and implications. For the first time since the Northwest Ordinances, the national government would be sponsoring a national education agenda. Although enforcement would be lax, the legislation specified a certain kind of educational institution: the practical curriculum and more open enrollment of a German-style university. In addition, the funding allotment scheme distributed monies based on population, not the usual per-state formula. This favored more densely populated eastern states. Finally, one might, and many did, believe that the bill would give to the national government a power to shape the course of higher education in the United States which government did not have before. As the debates surrounding the Morrill proposal of 1858 show, many congressmen quickly found all of these implications for sponsorship, supervision, and standardization in the bill.

On April 20, 1858, having run afoul of the House Committee on Public Lands for reasons that became apparent in the subsequent debate, Justin S. Morrill had to do an end around the usual path for legislation, bringing up the "Agricultural Colleges" bill as a separate point of order.[42] The United States House of Representatives at this time had already developed its own particular structure and process. Although the original House rules came from Jefferson's compilation in the 1790s, additional rules embellished the highly complicated manner in which the House chose to manage its now 237 members.[43] The speaker of the House, chosen by a majority (occasionally a plurality), determined who gained the floor to speak and the chairs and composition of the standing committees, whose number had reached 37 by 1858, as well as substantially influenced what legislation would reach the floor for a vote.

Fortunately for the supporters of the land grant college bill, Nathaniel P. Banks, a Republican from Massachusetts, was the speaker.[44] Unfortunately, in the Thirty-fifth Congress Morrill's Republicans had 92 votes, the Democrats 131, and others, including the American Party (or "Know-Nothings"), had 14.[45] With this composition any obviously Republican piece of legislation could not be promoted in straightforward fashion.

To gain Democratic votes, Morrill cast the measure not as a sectional one or a party one, and certainly not as one to promote a more powerful national government, but as a boon to farmers all over the country, a good investment for capital, and an essential tool to keep the American farmer ahead of his European competitors. He called his measure an act of public justice, "just politically, just to all the States, and just, above all, to the manhood of our country."[46] Above all, he hid his and its New England twang.

Morrill was well aware that regionalism was stronger then than it is today. New Englanders not only spoke with a different accent from southerners, they looked, thought, and saw things in a different way. The differences were culturally determined and of long standing. Some of them were fabricated in the nineteenth century; some went all the way back to the radical Protestant reformers who settled New England. New Englanders who traveled outside their region were conscious of their difference from other Americans and tended to look down upon the latter.[47]

Morrill spent most of his limited speaking time on the floor of the House pushing the legislation's beneficial effect on agriculture. His argument had three main points. First, all states of the Union needed a scientific agriculture to counter the inevitable depletion of the soil. Second, the United States depended on agriculture for a favorable balance of trade with Europe. The Europeans threatened this export market by their sponsorship of agricultural colleges in their own territories. With scientific exploitation of the land, Europeans could outstrip those older states already experiencing diminishing yields. Third, agriculturalists bore the brunt of federal taxation while providing the bulk of the country's exports. In return they should receive their fair share of the federal government's largesse.[48]

The basic assumption of the importance of education lay deeply embedded within these points. Morrill's comments professed a fervent faith in education—more specifically, education's ability to improve any person's life. This belief had its roots in the New England colonies' commitment to literacy. It was essential to participation in the radical Protestant Church to be able to read the Bible. This original conception had mutated through the American Revolution into a commitment to an educated populace that could fully engage in the republican institutions the new nation required.[49] Here it met and married the Enlightenment faith in science and human progress.[50] Morrill's assumption that applied science could improve American farming captured an entire worldview in a nutshell. As he stated unequivocally, "Scientific culture is the sure precursor of order and beauty."[51]

Morrill anticipated his opposition's likely arguments. First, he grounded the allocation of federal lands in prior actions consistent with a due regard to constitutional authority. The colleges at West Point and Annapolis served as two examples of the sponsorship of education through the use of the "necessary and proper" clause. Schools for the deaf, the dumb, and the mentally ill had all gotten endowments from congressional grants of public land.[52] This power derived from article 4, section 3, clause 2, "The Congress shall have power to dispose of and make all needful rules and regulations respecting the territory or other property belonging to the United States; and nothing in this Constitution shall be so construed as to prejudice any claims of the United States, or of any particular State."[53] As long as the grant improved the land, the Congress could dispose of it as it chose, he argued.[54] In short, Congress could, should, and must sponsor education.

Although couched to appeal to the widest segment of the House membership, Morrill's views immediately came under fire. Williamson R. W. Cobb (D-Ala.), chair of the Committee on Public Lands, made a motion to lay the bill on the table, in effect to kill it. Although Cobb's motion went down to defeat 114 to 83, signaling the measure's likely passage, despite his committee's negative recommendation, he succeeded not only in delaying consideration but also in gaining the floor.[55] There his counterarguments presaged the rest of the debate.

Cobb was not only opposed to Morrill's bill; his life course was in many ways as distinctly Deep South as Morrill's was northern New England. Born in Tennessee in 1807, Cobb's family took up cotton planting in Alabama in 1809. After a brief foray as a clock peddler, then at the mercantile exchange, he became a planter himself. He had served two years in the state legislature before he began his seven terms in the U.S. House of Representatives in 1847. For the three Congresses preceding the thirty-fifth, he had chaired the Committee on Revisal and Unfinished Business. His views reflected his allegiance to the Democratic Party, his place as a representative of southern interests, and his experience as a cotton planter and slave owner.

Cobb saw a plot behind Morrill's bill, and he wanted everyone in the chamber to know what that plot was. "But two members of the committee voted for the measure." The rest had agreed to an adverse report on the bill (a report he wrote), introducing the reading with a dire warning: "The bill proposes an inauguration of a new system, the result of which no man can foresee. Certain it is that the result will not be a good one."[56] Contrary to Morrill's assertion that the bill followed a long line of precedents, Cobb claimed that it was entirely unprecedented and that once Congress launched such a policy it would become accepted practice. Sponsorship was the first step down the primrose path to tyranny.

The committee report Cobb authored made the fundamental concern obvious. "The patronage [under the bill] would be fatal to the independence of the States; with patronage comes the power to control, as consequence follows upon cause."[57] This overarching fear of creeping, insidious, centralized power appeared repeatedly in speeches southerners made in response to any federal action that would have barred slavery from the new states and territories.[58]

Cobb also maintained that the bill would distribute the lands according to population, unfairly benefiting the older states.[59] Cobb did not say so, but the free states' population was growing much faster than that of the slave states (because of German and Irish immigration and the three-fifths compromise limiting the number of slaves who could be counted for representation). Thus, the bill favored the free states even more.

Cobb continued that once a bill such as Morrill's passed, there would be no stopping on the slippery slope to tyranny from the center of power, reiterating that, "if this bill passes, the people of every State will have a right to ask Congress to provide for their common schools and other local institutions. The poor will have a right to come and ask Congress to grant lands to aid in the erection of buildings to shelter them from the inclemency of the weather."[60] Ridicule, hyperbole, and dire warnings were drawn from the anti-statist grab bag, mixed and well shaken, to which Cobb had added a specifically southern spice.[61]

With some adept maneuvering by Morrill, Speaker Banks, and their allies, the supporters of the bill managed to override several attempts to postpone action. In order to get the floor for the bill, Morrill had made a motion to recommit. He now asked that his supporters vote down his own motion, which they did by a vote of 105 to 93. That accomplished, Morrill proceeded to get a vote on the measure. and the House approved it by the same tally.[62]

The Senate and Its Lawyers

Because the U.S. Senate's operating procedures, structure, and style varied significantly from those of the House, debates in the two bodies usually took different forms. While a determined though small majority could, with friendly leadership, bring legislation to a vote relatively quickly in the House, the Senate presented a different set of problems to any bill's passage. With a smaller number of members—only sixty-four by May 11, 1858—a more collegial ethic prevailed. Having to work with one another on a more intimate basis for a longer period than their colleagues in the other house, senators operated with "courtesy"—meaning they extended privileges to one another in debate, appointments of officials, and consultation and expected the same in return.[63]

The presiding officer of the Senate was Vice President John C. Breckinridge of Kentucky. If the vice president was absent, the president pro tem, the most senior member of the majority party, presided. In the Thirty-fifth Congress this was Benjamin Fitzpatrick of Alabama.[64] Like the House, the party system provided a governing structure—standing committees, with the majority party getting a majority on each committee.[65] For the Thirty-fifth Congress the Democrats had a comfortable majority of thirty-six seats to the Republicans' twenty, with eight votes belonging to neither party.[66] Although Webster, Clay, and other luminaries no longer graced Senate debate, Senate speeches were still longer, more ornate, and more extensive than those in the House. A number of senators—for example, Charles Sumner of Massachusetts and William Seward of New York—were superb orators.

On May 19, 1858, the Senate engaged in discussions about whether or not to debate Morrill's bill. Senator Charles E. Stuart (D-Mich.) initiated the exchange with his motion to consider the bill. Unlike Morrill, Stuart was a lawyer. In 1835 he had left New York State for Michigan, where he served in the state legislature before two nonconsecutive terms in the House and what would be only one term in the Senate. Appropriately for someone who represented what had been, until quite recently, a frontier state, he chaired the Senate's Committee on Public Lands. His motion appears the result of either courtesy or some command (the state legislature may have instructed him on the matter) because in it he announced that he was "under obligations to bring up this bill." George E. Pugh (D-Ohio) raised an objection to a hurried consideration. He anticipated that the bill would be "debated at great length" and wanted "a test vote."[67]

Michigan and Ohio farmers would benefit from land grant schools, and northern Democrats well knew this. At the same time, the Democratic Party had a strong southern wing that would, like Cobb in the House, raise objections. Pugh was Cincinnati-born with a degree from Miami University in Oxford, Ohio. He had studied law, entered private practice, then served one term in the state legislature before becoming city solicitor in 1850. After a stint as state attorney general, in 1855 he gained his place in the Senate. Cincinnati lay on the edge of the slave South, runaways from Kentucky passed through its streets on the way north, and a number of infamous cases had come to Ohio courts.

Party concerns and sectional animus to one side, the bill was now in the hands of lawyers. Not every one in the upper house had practiced law to be sure, but everyone who weighed in on the bill was a lawyer. As the debates would prove and the participants reveal, the Morrill bill raised as much concern about the nature of federal law—the shape and role of the national state—as it did about promoting agriculture and sponsoring education. Where others had seen the benefits and perils of sponsorship, the lawyers worried about supervising. Sumner, Stuart, and Pugh were all lawyers, trained to see into the very fabric of texts. Long hours of reading law and the pervasiveness of the legal culture had left an indelible mark on these men. Laws were no different from contracts, statutes the same as bills of sale. Lawyers studied their implications, the tracery of their language.

Most lawyers learned their craft in this day not in law schools but in other lawyers' offices, "reading law."[68] Even those who attended law schools such as Harvard and Litchfield, in Connecticut, had similar training: a steady diet of St. George Tucker's Blackstone's *Commentaries*, New York chancellor James Kent's *Commentaries*, treatises from Joseph Story and Simon Greenleaf. There were no exams and no degrees. The only advantage might be a few years cut off the clerkship or apprentice requirement before the oral examination for admission to the local bar.[69]

Even the brightest of students found the work hard. As Story, the greatest jurist and law teacher of the first half of the century, recalled at the end of his career, "After trying it [reading law in an office] day after day with very little success, I sat myself down and wept bitterly." It was an apprenticeship of copying documents, learning the rules of pleading, and attentive listening. In court the ability to speak well and long, to respond quickly to shifts in the opponents' logic and evidence, were the skills of a successful advocate. The entire system depended upon the adversarial pose. The orator might swell uncontradicted on the stump circuit; in court one had to be a debater. But the joys of mastery of the law changed the student and buoyed the practitioner. Story continued: "I went on and on, and began at last to see daylight, ay, and to feel that I could comprehend and reason upon the text and the comments. When I had that I breathed a purer air, and that I had acquired a new power."[70] It was a transforming, even an arrogant, power that the lawyer gained, and he brought it with him into politics. Lawyers were in "the ascendancy" in antebellum politics and carried the conversation with their peers begun in the courtroom into the legislative chamber.[71] Indeed, the highest goal of the lawyer was public service, whether on the bench or in the legislature.[72] While their impact as individual lawyers varied, the field of law achieved dominance in political culture by the 1840s.[73]

And being a lawyer made a difference. Popular images of lawyers suggest that no one had any difficulty telling a lawyer from a nonlawyer by their carriage, language, and aura. Lawyers were accused of misusing common language or twisting what ordinary people said, in effect corrupting speech itself.[74] Paradoxically, at the same time that Americans were targeting lawyers for abuse, they were embracing a commitment to the rule of law which placed lawyers center stage. This commitment elevated constitutions above all other forms of political writing, made law courts secular temples of justice, and made legislatures the pure voices of the people. In effect the lawyers became the natural governing class, an elite entrusted with the fabrication of an impartial republican governmental machine.[75]

With the lawyers at the controls, H.R. 2 survived this "test vote," twenty-eight to twenty-four. It had universal Republican support and some aisle switching, for example by Stuart. Pugh voted with the minority, suggesting that his purpose had been to ferret out some preliminary allegiances.[76] Lawyers shared a concern for the bill but did not agree on its value.

On February 1, 1859, well into the abbreviated second session of the Thirty-fifth Congress, a fourth lawyer, Republican Benjamin Franklin Wade of Ohio, made a motion to consider the agricultural colleges bill once more.[77] Born in Massachusetts in 1800, he received no formal education, but after teaching school he studied for and was admitted to the bar in 1825. In and out of private practice he became a county prosecutor, a state senator, then a judge of the Third Judicial Court of Ohio. Elected as a Whig to the U.S. Senate in 1851, he later helped found the Republican Party in Ohio. "Bluff" Ben Wade had already earned a reputation as a pugnacious, occasionally profane, and quick-witted public speaker.[78]

Wade expounded only briefly on the merits of the bill as he saw them. Basic fairness, he reasoned, demanded that the national government do something for agriculture. After all, "the military arm of our Government has its West Point; the naval has its Annapolis; the commercial its Coast Survey; but the agricultural interest of the country seems to be almost entirely overlooked."[79] Each interest, he suggested, should receive some service with an attendant program in the executive branch. Wade articulated a national theory of representation which was the polar opposite of his colleagues' across the aisle. Instead of the Madisonian concept of factions countered by other factions, Wade's ideal of republican government would accommodate all interests. A more cynical phrasing might call it the open-trough policy, in which every substantial interest gets to feed. A positive phrasing might be that, in addition to general policies favoring the whole of the nation, the national government should promote significant groups with more targeted programs. Wade saw government as a sponsor, perhaps more.

Wade held his hand close to his chest. It surely included the supervision card, but he dared not play it. Wade noted that the bill's "friends understand its provisions perfectly well, and are ready to act upon it; and it need not, therefore, consume more than a very small portion of our time in its consideration." The measure had received the backing of the House and the agricultural societies and deserved Senate consideration. After close votes of thirty to twenty-six, then twenty-seven to twenty-six, the Senate began debating it in earnest.[80]

The Senate Debates

Senator Pugh rose to make the theoretical basis of his objections plain. His argument rested on two points: first, that the grant would harm the financial position of the national government; second, that the Congress had no authority to make such an allocation. This was "a proposition that proposes to alienate an empire, and for purposes wholly beyond the limits of the authority of this Government." With little alteration this would be the opposition Democrats' primary ground for objection throughout the debate. Democrats who opposed central authority based that opposition upon a close and strict reading of the enumerated constitutional powers of Congress. The framers of the land grant bill had tried to avoid this objection by tying it to the territorial power. To buttress his point, Pugh placed President Franklin Pierce's veto message of a similar measure for insane asylums into the *Congressional Globe*, which merely recapitulated Pugh's own position.[81]

Pugh saw into Wade's hand. He saw a federal government that would supervise state education. His fundamental principle, federalism, dictated separate spheres of activity for the national government and the states, with the states having the preponderance of the power. As representatives not of the nation but of the sovereign states, "it is just as much a violation of our duty to invade the province of the State government under the head of donations as it would be to invade it by force and violence."[82] This equation of a legislative funding action with a physical act of war sounds extreme except when one considers the fact that pro- and antislavery forces had been waging a genuine war in Kansas for the past five years. Democrats could easily argue in this heightened state of anxiety that any action that took place outside of the established understanding of the Constitution exacerbated an already tense standoff. Jumpy senators who had only just concluded their investigations of this possibly vast conspiracy continued to be on edge.

With reasoning worthy of the old oath ex officio—refuse to take it and you are in violation of the law, take it and you will be found guilty of perjury—Pugh insisted that new programs have limited means (small expenditures and few bureaucrats). In effect, he denied any federal program the wherewithal to supervise the outcome of its operations. Opponents of the programs then objected that the innovations would never work or that land speculators would take of the lack of enforcement apparatus to corrupt the entire process. Whatever the bill's proponents did, Pugh could find fault. Either they were unauthorized, or they served corrupt interests. H.R. 2 survived Pugh's motion to recommit by a single vote.[83]

James M. Mason (D-Va.) furthered Pugh's case. He described the legislation as "one of the most extraordinary engines of mischief" to have come before the Senate.[84] Mason, like his fellow southern Democrats, endorsed strict construction when it came to policies they did not favor. The federal government could not simply give away public lands or sponsor education because there was no explicit clause in the Constitution allowing such largesse. But Mason had helped write the Fugitive Slave Law, a part of the Compromise of 1850 which extended the reach of the federal government into every free state and funded new officials and courts to assist slave catchers bring home their prey.[85] In short, as a good lawyer, he advocated his section's interest with zeal. There was an explicit provision in article 4's Rendition Clause for such legislation, but Mason had added to that general authorization provisions for supervision.

Born into a Virginia planter family that could trace its ancestry to the Cavaliers who supported Charles I, Mason had the extensive education and breeding of one born to privilege. He looked down on what he considered to be the corruption of the North, with its many immigrants and lowborn politics. With his imposing height, salt-and-pepper mane, homespun clothes, and powerful speaking style, he nevertheless felt himself and the way of life he defended under siege.[86] Educated at the University of Pennsylvania, with a degree from the law department of William and Mary, he had practiced law, served in the Virginia House of Delegates and the House of Representatives, and had been in the Senate since 1847.

The source of the enemy's forces was obvious to him. H.R. 2 created that same corrupting influence nationwide which he saw in the "New England free schools." "That system of social organization" would now spread through federal "alms" to the rest of the country. This would "destroy that peculiar character which I am happy to believe belongs to the great mass of the southern people." In other words, the South was the last true bastion of the first state. Reining in what might have amounted to an incipient paranoia—after all, the bill under consideration hardly constituted the vanguard of national control over education—Mason qualified his statements. "Now, sir, this is not to see too far ahead. Unconstitutional howsoever it may be, the bill may be harmless, except that it is the basis for future superstructure."[87] Sponsorship was not superstructure, but supervision, looming behind sponsorship, bore a different cast.

In the bill's defense its sponsors noted that the federal government already supervised a military academy at West Point, a naval academy at Annapolis, the land set-asides in the Northwest Ordinance of 1787, and Congress's other territorial mandates for education. Yet Mason was not concerned with precedent. A good common lawyer, he knew when an advocate had to abandon precedent (when it went against one's case) and argue doctrine. From the time, in 1828, that John C. Calhoun secretly authored the South Carolina Exposition and protest, states' rights lawyers had constructed their own brief on the nature of the good state. The state protected private property but did not reallocate it; fostered economic growth but did not manage or regulate it; and, above all, stayed out of the private lives of gentlemen.[88]

James Harlan, a former Free-Soil Party member and now a Republican from Iowa, joined the conversation to counter the Democrats' characterizations of the bill as the opening wedge of a vast centralizing conspiracy. Harlan emphasized the precedents of the academies, the completely voluntary nature of the proposal, and its laudatory purpose of aiding the laboring classes both rural and urban. He rejected the notion of a conspiracy against southern rights. "If I were disposed to go into an investigation of this subject, I think I could show conclusively that it is mind that rules the country and rules the world."[89] What harm could there be in education?

Harlan knew. He stated unequivocally, "It may be that it is a blessing to Virginia that she is now more largely represented by adult white people who are unable to read and write, in proportion to her population, than any other State of the Union; it is a blessing, however, that the people of my State do not covet." Harlan himself had a common school and college education, later teaching and then serving as Iowa City's superintendent of public instruction. He next studied law and gained bar admission in 1850. He served as president of Mount Pleasant Collegiate Institute, now Iowa Wesleyan University, until he became one of the Free-Soil Party's senators in 1855. A lawyer and teacher himself of middle-class background, Harlan argued that "the masses, on whose shoulders have been imposed the burdens, shall participate in the enjoyment of some of the advantages of Government."[90] Perhaps the politicians of this age were spoilsmen too; perhaps corruption went everywhere in the Congress; and perhaps many of the words of the congressmen recorded in the *Globe* hid more than they revealed, but Harlan's advocacy of the land grant bill was fully reflective of his own rise to prominence. We must conclude he meant what he said.

Harlan and Wade were groping toward a vision of a second state—one based on sponsorship and supervision. Harlan did not advocate the enlargement of federal power or a coercive role for government but framed the matter in a way consistent with the Federalist, then Whig, conception of internal improvements, protective tariffs, and bounties to encourage economic development.[91] The act of framing the policy in a limited, positive light embedded within the legislation the compromise with the fears of a bureaucratic government but included elements of sponsorship and supervision.

Unimpressed, more Democrats queued up to point out the dangers present in any expansion of federal government activity. Missouri's James S. Green only saw the evils to come. Asking where it might end, he queried "Must we, in consequence of that, make appropriations to establish law schools; must we make appropriations to establish medical schools; and other schools for science and for agriculture and for manufactures?" Where would the representation of classes end? He characterized the federal government as "this limited association of States" which could not go beyond its set purposes for any reason—the objection to more government founded on old-style federalism.[92] The republican, first state should not be altered.

John P. Hale (R-N.H.) replied in his typical fashion. Hale had refused to support the Mexican-American War and was driven from his seat by the pro-war regular Democrats in his state legislature. On the Free Soil ticket he had run for president in 1852, and by 1856 he was a Republican. Hale had gone to Bowdoin College in Maine, gained admission to the bar, practiced law, received Andrew

Jackson's appointment to be a U.S. attorney, and served in his state's legislature. A fierce defender of civil liberties, his maverick reputation and his skills as an attorney went hand in hand. His present term dated from 1855, when he had regained office.[93] His style tended toward the combative.[94]

Hale prepared for the debate the way he would for complex litigation. Apparently with an index of federal statutes before him, Hale cited numerous grants Congress had made to "seminaries of higher learning." Pugh chimed in that no acres had been given to Ohio for a seminary of higher learning. (It is a truism that all politics is local.) Continuing with his reading from the index, Hale cited the twenty-five thousand dollars for Columbia College in Washington, D.C., a deaf and dumb asylum in Kentucky, and one other in Connecticut.[95] With the flourish of precedents, Hale made his argument like a lawyer before an appellate court.

Occupied as they were in the arguments coming to the floor, the Senate was well on its way toward justifying its reputation as the debate club of Capitol Hill. Mississippi's Jefferson Davis, chairman of the Committee for Military Affairs, took this moment to enter the fracas with the opinion that the deaf and dumb asylum in Kentucky was a bad precedent.[96] He spoke often in debate, with much force. Davis could not deny that a precedent was a precedent—or, rather, Davis, no lawyer, had little use for precedent. He saw with different eyes—pale, scarred, and partially blind from illness—a world in which law took second place to honor.[97]

This time Davis did not speak at great length. A military man himself, he confined his remarks to Hale, Wade, and Stuart's reliance on the military academies' similarity to the land grant college bill. He argued "the cadets were part of the Army; the midshipmen are a part of the Navy." The academies fit under Congress's power to raise armies and navies. He added that this policy choice should be supplemented with training by experience in the field if the United States had a larger army. "Such is the perfect system adopted in Governments of a more strictly military character than our own."[98] He spoke from both practical experience as a serving officer in both the Black Hawk War and the Mexican-American War and, later, as Franklin Pierce's secretary of war.[99] The character of governments, he implied, resembled the character of the military. Good government lay not in institutions or policies but in people's nature. Honorable men, like those with whom he had served, were the best governors of the people. He had only a rudimentary conception of the state, although he had served the federal government in a variety of capacities. He remained, in the end, a Mississippi planter and former infantry officer with a local view of national needs.

The rest of Davis's contribution to the exchange reveals the contrast between what may be somewhat oversimply called the "New England style" of thinking and that of other parts of the country. The proponents' claim to aid the agriculturalist was, Davis said, "delusive, not to say fraudulent." After all, "agriculture needs no teaching by Congress."[100] The farmer best learned his trade by practicing it, picking up local methods, and being left alone. Davis gained his knowledge about cotton plantation agriculture not from his attendance at several academies in Mississippi and Kentucky, and Transylvania University, but from his father. The idea that he might benefit from education with regards to farming imposed the New England way on the proud, independent South. For a son of the South education at the higher levels provided a veneer of refinement, comradeship with other members of the same social strata, and a training ground for public life.[101] Southern higher education for Davis had not offered opportunity but merely confirmed it.

But no one, not even a planter/officer, could ignore the legal question the bill raised. "The States are sovereign." Hence, "this Government cannot coerce a State."[102] The enforcement provision of H.R. 2 required the federal government to oversee the use of the funds granted. If a state refused to account properly for the money, the federal government would have to take legal action against the state. State sovereignty, codified in the Eleventh Amendment, meant that state governments had a form of sovereign immunity; they could not be sued without their consent. Davis's implicit dismissal of the Supremacy Clause was portent. He and his ideological compatriots favored the notion that the federal government was powerless in the face of a state's opposition.[103] He did not argue the law; he merely announced his view of the law.

By contrast, Jacob Collamer (R-Vt.) saw the proposal squarely from the legal perspective. Collamer had been a superior court judge in Vermont and had an undergraduate degree from the University of Vermont in Burlington. After volunteering for service in the War of 1812, he had become a lawyer. "If Congress has the power to pass the law in question, the court says it is constitutional," he reminded Davis. Then Collamer, the former state circuit judge, donned imaginary judicial robes, examined the Constitution, and found that it gave Congress "a simple, unqualified, unlimited grant of power to dispose of the public lands." The sponsorship of education by the federal government did not encroach on local needs or wishes. Collamer's strong support of the bill serves as another reminder that its advocates shared the fundamentally decentralized, antibureaucratic ethos of the bill's opponents but not their states' rights reading of the Constitution. In his own words, "That is a great advantage and leading feature of the bill."[104]

James S. Green (D-Mo.) contested Collamer's reading of the phrase *dispose of* and ended up driving home the point that more was at stake here than just education, the public lands, and agriculture. He argued the cession in the ordinance had been for a specific purpose; it could not be read as a general precedent. Congress had to adhere to the original intent of the agreement under the Articles of Confederation. What was more, "there is a vast difference between political action as a political body, as we are, and the action of such tribunals as a court." Because "they decide only such questions as come before them" and Congress "take[s] the whole range of right and wrong, or constitutional power and expediency," Congress could not decide what was constitutional in the same way.[105] Green's argument represented a serious disavowal of federal power, a reliance on the unwritten understanding behind the Constitution, one that limited its actions and how it could carry out that effort.

Equally important, Green denounced any attempt to analogize the Congress to a court, legislation to administration, and administration to bureaucracy. That is exactly what was happening before his eyes, as the lawyers on the other side of the issue made their case. And, having disavowed the analogy, he proceeded to reason as if he were a high court judge giving an opinion in a constitutional case. "Each state will fix its own system of education." The allocation of federal funds in any form violated this division of tasks. Once Congress crossed this line, opening Pandora's box, "it is the introduction of a swallowing-up system that will conglomerate every power in the Government, gather it all in one common focus, and every farm will belong to the Federal Government, every manufactory will belong to the Federal Government." Passage of the land grant college bill was akin to "saying he [the farmer] needs a guardian in the person of the Federal Government."[106]

Green had seen the lighted face of what Mason only glimpsed in fleeting shadow. His anticipation of the consequences of the bill was more acute and his sense of its logical conclusion more astute than many of its advocates' (at least than what they admitted aloud). For Green knew that "medical schools" and "schools for science" would not be far behind. He was right. Morrill Act funds would go for these institutions in coming years. What, then, so worried Green? Was he opposed to healing and experimentation? Some antebellum thinkers did reject these symbols of modernity, but Green's objection lay not in reactionary fears of modernity. He wanted a small federal government—cheap, simple, and unable to exert any authority on slavery save to protect it.

Harlan insisted that the land grant scheme was akin to the distribution of federal lands for internal improvements. It was nothing new; no one need fear it. Congress had sponsored many improvements in the past. The Congress was not coercing the states to improve themselves. They could take it or leave it. The grant was "a trust" that each state supervised as trustee, and "this is the whole of the assumed attempt to coerce the States to educate their people."[107]

Harlan's reference to a trusteeship would be familiar to any lawyer who had practiced estate law. Trusts were equitable devices—that is, they were found in equity courts, not law courts, wherein the creator of the trust put assets into a fund managed by trustees for the use of the beneficiary. Here the trust was not a loose term or an analogy but a genuine "constructive trust" whose beneficiaries were the nation's children. The idea of the government as a trustee went all the way back to the first state constitutions and would reappear periodically throughout Congress's deliberations (for example, in the Freedmen's Bureau debate, discussed later).[108] But the idea of government as a trusteeship for the benefit of all the people had many implications, not the least of which was the way in which judges in the South wishing to honor the last wishes of deceased slaveholders had used the idea of trusteeship to free their slaves. Maybe Harlan was referring to this kind of trust as well.

This was sarcasm, surely, and a measure of the advocates' frustration, but Harlan's offhanded rebuke suggested that the proponents had an ulterior purpose: to encourage all the states of the Union to provide higher education on a broad scale. Pugh now renewed his motion to recommit the measure to the Committee on Public Lands (months before he had warned that this kind of exchange would occur). Before the yeas and nays could be taken, Hannibal Hamlin (R-Maine), who would be Abraham Lincoln's running mate in 1860, moved that the Senate consider other business. In a brief statement, the *Globe* recorded that Pugh's motion passed and the Senate then adjourned.[109] Its opponents had once again derailed H.R. 2.

Further Consideration

On February 3, 1859, with Stuart of Michigan in the chair, William M. Gwin, a Democrat from California, followed the instructions of his state's legislature and moved to reconsider the land grant colleges bill. In two close votes, twenty-seven to twenty-six and twenty-eight to twenty-seven, Wade managed another round of floor debates on the measure. With Wade's concurrence Stuart gained an exemption for mineral lands from the allocation.[110] A series of amendments followed, reflecting the importance of special interests—localism triumphant, even in the midst of a discussion of national power.

Pugh then struck again, this time seeking to omit the enforcement clauses of the legislation, sections 4 and 5. Pugh argued that the enforcement sections represented an "attempt by Congress to assume control over the legislation of the States." He either unintentionally confused a voluntary assumption of a restricted grant with a mandate or he intentionally mischaracterized the situation in order to sway the suspicious members against a grant he opposed for other reasons. He called for the yeas and nays on his motion to force a vote that could make the bill an unenforced grant to aid college education. He intended to vote no regardless, but this amendment in effect constituted an admission that the supporters had the votes to pass the measure.[111]

James A. Bayard Jr. (D-Del.) seconded Pugh's comments with some of his own. He reiterated Jefferson Davis's point that the federal government could not enforce its grant against the states, but he accepted the idea that the grant was a form of trust in which the states were the trustees: "It is better to make it a gift broadly, without attempting to restrain the States." The increased powers the federal government would have to assume in order to monitor the grant violated the spirit of federalism in which the national government could operate only within a sharply delineated sphere. Moreover, foreshadowing the preeminent contention of future members of the Democracy, he saw "that it threatens to increase that corruption which is spreading fast over this country."[112] His meaning here might have been anything from the increased willingness to stretch federal powers to promote activities such as the railroads or commerce prevailing over some halcyon republic to simply a perception that links between certain industrial interests and Congress were overcoming more public-spirited notions.[113] Pugh's motion narrowly failed, twenty-five to twenty-seven.[114]

Clement C. Clay (D-Ala.) now invoked senatorial courtesy to postpone the vote. Clay was the son of former senator Clement C. Clay. With an undergraduate degree from the University of Alabama at Tuscaloosa and a degree from the law department of the University of Virginia at Charlottesville, Clay had been a state representative, a county court judge, and an advocate for states' rights as a senator since 1853. He would leave the capitol in 1861 to become a member of the Confederate senate. He wished to speak, but "the condition of his throat" temporarily prevented him from doing so. Wade and others viewed this as a subterfuge but soon apologized, after Clay protested.[115]

On February 7, 1859, the Senate resumed consideration of H.R. 2. Clay's oration partook of a long senatorial tradition in which great men took the occasion of a contested measure to expound on the nature of the United States government. More important than the immediate effect on the bill of the speech, Clay probably believed that he would have another, larger, more distant and appreciative audience than the Senate. The end of the four-year cycle of stump oratory, hand shaking, tub thumping, and fire eating that marked the democratic excesses of presidential election years was fast approaching. In these critical times differences of opinion grew into chasms, and sectionalism was the talk of the nation. Every occasion was ripe for the senators to appeal to the state legislatures that elected senators.[116]

For Clay the federal government was one of limited powers to be interpreted strictly. The allocation of public lands for an unconstitutional purpose bribed the state to do what it might not do if not so tempted. It would "enable greedy capitalists to monopolize large bodies of the public lands" keeping them from adding to the prosperity of the states. This, in turn, upended the balance between the states and the federal government in the federal government's favor. This threatened local institutions as well as individual freedoms. It "will be a long step towards the overthrow of this truly Federal and the establishment of a really National Government."[117] How pregnant the term *overthrow* would become, but here only sensed. If the federal edifice came down, Clay hinted, it would be the doing of the advocates of measures such as Morrill's.

"Just as the Devil tempted the Saviour" within a more national government, the "honest tillers of the soil" would become "your clients," "wards," and "tenants at will," Clay predicted.[118] For him the moral intersected with the political in a latter-day jeremiad. It is not difficult to come to the conclusion that Clay was really talking about the demise of his South, the South of courtly manners and loving, obedient slaves, the South supremely confident and in control of its own destiny—his South, crucified by the capitalists, the moneychangers of the North.

Clay concluded his oration with an attempt to distinguish the Morrill bill from centralizing legislation that he favored—the Fugitive Slave Act of 1850, for example. "Sir, this is not a Government of precedents, but of a written constitution." The Rendition Clause of the Constitution seemed to beg for a Fugitive Slave Act. George Washington, Thomas Jefferson, and James Madison would not have supported Morrill's bill even though they had endorsed similar proposals in their lifetimes. They would have seen that public lands for colleges "are hostile to the reserved rights and the true interests of the States."[119]

John Bell, a Whig from Tennessee (the Whig Party was no longer a national force, but there were still Whigs), spoke against Clay, Pugh, and Mason's interpretation of the land grant college proposal. He described the allotment as "a pittance of six million acres, for a generous, noble object." His own interpretation of the Constitution did not preclude this kind of grant. He argued that the distinction between giving away and disposing to improve the value was "a mere pretext."[120] Bell's career had led up to this Whig train of thought. With a degree from Cumberland College in Nashville, he had studied law, entered politics, and served in the Tennessee legislature and U.S. Congress before becoming secretary of War under the brief presidency of William Henry Harrison. He had been in the Senate since 1847 and had voted consistently with H.R. 2's supporters. His run for the presidency in 1860 under the Constitutional Union Party would fail, but it signified that there could be a southern alternative to fervent states' rights policies, though Bell himself could not carry the South with it.

The senators were tiring. Everyone knew where everyone else stood; all the arguments seemed to have been made and repeated. The final word came from Davis, a Cato of the first state. He rested his argument on his conception of the bargain through which the states had yielded their land claims to the confederation and then its successor, the federal government. By now the lawyers' language had so permeated the debate that he simply adopted it. "The Federal Government has violated its trust and exceeded the powers conferred upon it."
It was a fair enough contention. His disagreement with the proponents of H.R. 2 could be construed as a local versus a national one, though this would neglect the localism of the proponents. The formulators of the land grant college bill created a measure that could be interpreted in both a nationalist and a local orientation. Mason, Clay, Davis, and Pugh, among others, saw it as a national program. Others such as Bell, Stuart, and Collamer saw it as a locally centered program. Both views were equally valid. Consequently, the final victory of H.R. 2 in the Senate by a vote of twenty-five to twenty-two was seen differently by the two sides.[121] Creeping sponsorship and self-deprecating supervision had won a modest victory.

A Temporary Setback

Fortunately for the opponents of the bill, President Buchanan sympathized with their position. His veto came on February 26, 1859. Like his predecessor, Franklin Pierce, who had vetoed similar legislation (in that case the lands would address Dorothea Dix's plea for more asylums for the insane), the seriousness with which he considered his action becomes obvious from the fact that the veto message was substantially longer than the legislation itself.[122] His message's six points duplicated the sum total of the arguments that the bill's opponents had proffered in the House and Senate. Namely, the allocation of federal lands would deprive the federal government of substantial revenue; Congress's new role in sponsorship would unbalance the division between the two "spheres" of government; the funding formula would injure the new states by giving more to the older ones and placing lands in the hands of "wealthy individuals"; the colleges' contribution to agriculture and the mechanic arts was "dubious" at best; the new schools would interfere with the existing colleges; and Congress did not possess the power to give away lands, only to improve them. He closed with a saying that might have been the motto of his administration: "'sufficient unto the day is the evil thereof.'"[123]

The message, the cautious (one might even say fearful) ideology behind it, and the political calculation that accompanied it fit his presidency's ultimately disastrous policy of appeasing the more radical southerners at the expense of the northern Democratic moderates in order to forestall a break.[124] In a vote on Morrill's motion to overturn the veto, the House failed to provide the requisite two-thirds majority, 105 to 96.[125] If the bill's supporters needed any further reminder that they needed a friendly voice in the Executive Mansion, this vote provided one. The division between those who felt threatened by what they feared to be the opening wedge of federal aggrandizement from a sectional and partisan interest and those who had not intended to extend the power of the government or introduce another bureaucracy, but who did not see a danger in sponsoring education, appeared clearly in the debate over Morrill's land grant bill. It was the first but not the last proposal to raise the implicit issues of sponsorship and supervision, but the division should not obscure what both sides agreed on: the state could be no more than the sponsor of improvement. Neither side wanted a state that actively supervised its own sponsorship, not yet at least.

THE LAWYERS on both sides had learned something valuable. Law and government were closely tied even when the subject of governance was not the legal system itself. The very act of legislating for these men involved vital ideas about how law worked, which, as the Morrill bill debates shows, then touched foundational concepts of government, in particular its purposes and its limitations. Harlan and Hale's use of precedent, Harlan's analogy to trust doctrines, and Collamer's judicial reading of the Constitution suggested ways in which lawyers could finesse the issue of limited government. Yet their adversaries cited their own precedents, their reading of the Constitution, and their equity doctrines that centered on states' rights. In the end the proponents of the bill might not concede but surely could see that its opponents were right to this extent—sponsorship without adequate administrative provisions might vitiate educational, or any other government, initiatives. They were ready to take the next step when the presidential election of 1860 altered the political landscape.

CHAPTER TWO

"The Object of a Democratic Government"

Sponsorship and Supervision of Agriculture and Land Grant Colleges, 1861–1863

The Congress that considered non-war-related proposals to expand the national government during the Civil War scarcely resembled the one assembled in the winter of 1859 to hear the debates on the Morrill bill. The Thirty-seventh Congress had only forty-nine senators. Of these, thirty-one were Republicans, ten were Democrats, and eight were unaffiliated with either party.[1] The situation they faced had also changed dramatically.

The secession of the southern states forced the U.S. Congress to answer Jefferson Davis's assertion that the United States government could not enforce its will upon a state should the state decide to resist. The crisis was many things, but at its core was a legal question: how could a government with powers limited by strict construction and federalism compel sovereign state governments against their will? The Republicans' answer was the fabrication of a wartime state that violated many of the strictures of their ideology of governing. Pushing their wartime powers to the limit of the Constitution, and sometimes beyond, they eventually established an income tax, a national banking system and a national currency, instituted a draft, imprisoned disloyal persons in the border states, confiscated property on a massive scale, and raised an army that would rival the world's largest.[2] It was sponsorship and supervision on a novel and colossal scale. But the concepts of the second state lagged behind its deployment.

When the Congress met in December 1861, at its first regular session, the first Battle of Bull Run, or Manassas, had already demonstrated their fight for the Union would be long and hard. Wade and several other congressmen had already begun sparring with President Lincoln by creating a Joint Committee on the Conduct of the War. Wade was its hard-charging chair.[3] Almost as a side note, in January 1862 they turned their attention to the program they had been unable to enact under James Buchanan.[4]

The Morrill Act remained part of the Republican Party's agenda. Although not mentioned in the Republican Party platform of 1860, land grants for colleges remained a popular talking point for Morrill and the agricultural and education reformers. With the exit of the entire Deep South contingent from Congress, most of the opposition to the land grant college legislation had evaporated. The war, ironically, provided its own obstacle. Congress concentrated its energies on military necessities. Another kind of sectionalism slowed the bill's progress now: the Committee on Public Lands's suspicion of any land grant bill that would favor the East over the West stymied Morrill's proposal in the House. In the meantime Congress turned to a measure that was even more forward than Morrill's in terms of increasing the scale and scope of the national government: the creation of a department of agriculture. It was all part of the hesitantly evolving congressional effort to sponsor and supervise "the object of a democratic government."

Conceptualizing a Clientele Department

The proposed department of agriculture represented a significant step beyond the Morrill bill, for it was the first of what a later scholar called the "client-oriented departments."[5] Although Congress created the department in the midst of the Civil War, most see it not as a wartime policy but as the foundation for a more expansive state in the Progressive and New Deal eras. In fact, the conceptualization and realization of the department did not anticipate the Progressive state at all. Instead, it embodied the ideals of the second state.

One does not find in these debates the language of desperate exigency and high-flying moralism of the debates on war measures. They constitute a calmer, almost more natural coming together of themes in thinking of the proponents of the Morrill bill, freed from the need to propitiate states' rights southern

Democrats. The congressmen began to explore openly, albeit tentatively, a state that did not stop with simple sponsorship of improvements but considered how that sponsorship could be serviced—in other words, what kind of administration best promoted the nation's farm interests.

True, one administrator in the federal government had been performing certain service tasks for the farmers since 1836, when Henry Leavitt Ellsworth was appointed commissioner of patents. Ellsworth began a program on his own initiative of gathering information, disseminating reports, and gathering and distributing seeds to interested parties. In 1839 Congress formally recognized his activities with a separate appropriation of one thousand dollars from the Patent Office Fund, the proceeds from patent fees, for "the collection of agricultural statistics, and for other agricultural purposes." By 1861 the Maryland Agricultural Society, the Massachusetts Board of Agriculture, the U.S. Agricultural Society, Horace Greeley's *New York Tribune* and other northern papers, Lincoln's secretary of the interior, Caleb Blood Smith, and Lincoln himself, in his first annual message to Congress, had asked for a separate bureau or department to manage this burgeoning endeavor.[6]

In order to understand what happened to the proposal for a department of agriculture after 1861, we have to look at the composition of the House in the aftermath of southern secession. Secession left the Republicans in overwhelming control of the lower house. There were 105 Republicans, 43 Democratic representatives, and 30 who were unaffiliated with either party. Republican Galusha A. Grow of Pennsylvania became the speaker.[7] Grow's parents had moved from Connecticut to a farm in Pennsylvania, and he had become a pugnacious proponent of homestead legislation. (He and Representative Lawrence Keit of South Carolina had initiated a brawl over the matter on the floor of the House in March 1858.)[8] But, unfortunately for Grow's commitment to agricultural service, the Republicans were divided in their thinking about the shape of the state they hoped would emerge from the Civil War. These divisions become apparent in the debate, changing a conversation about farming into one about governing.

Congress first took up the issue on January 7, 1862, during consideration of the civil appropriations bill for the coming year.[9] The war was showing signs of becoming a protracted, expensive struggle, and the stress of the war effort did nothing to reconcile existing divisions within the ruling party. One must recall that the Republicans began as a coalition of antislavery Democrats, "conscience" Whigs, Know-Nothings, and abolitionists. Now some were "radicals," others were "moderates," and yet others were "conservatives." Republicans, even with an insuperable numerical majority, divided into several distinct groups on any given issue. Their goals might be the same, but they differed about the particulars.[10]

Once again, lawyers, not farmers, immediately became the leading figures in the discussion. What is more, as one follows the debates, it becomes clear that the conversants were genuinely trying to figure out what kinds of service the government ought to provide and how that service ought to be delivered. Old concerns, and the revered republican creed of fiscal sobriety and the dangers of corruption, still framed much of the debate, and other continuities linked it to prewar ways of thinking about government.

John Hutchins (R-Ohio), chairman of the House Committee on Manufactures, moved to amend the appropriations legislation by striking out the Patent Office's agriculture program. He reasoned that "in the present state of the country it ought to be dispensed with." The amount in question was sixty thousand dollars in a budget of nearly a half-billion dollars.[11] The lawyer from Ohio nevertheless argued for fiscal stringency. Like other lawyers, he felt capable of learning any subject, then applying that knowledge as an expert. Lawyers in this era were general practitioners. They did not turn away business and thus had to be quick studies on subjects ranging from contract and property to personal injury and insurance. Sixty thousand dollars appeared a princely sum when viewed on the level of civil litigation.

William S. Holman (D-Ind.) objected to Hutchins's amendment because "it would be taken as a bad indication in the country if Congress were at this time to abandon this whole enterprise."[12] Dumping this project might be perceived as an act of weakness, a sign that the Union was straining under the weight of suppressing the rebellion. In this conflict of will with the South, the posture of foreign governments as well as the morale of the North depended to a considerable extent on the perceived fortunes of the combatants. If the Union looked weak, foreign recognition and support for the Confederacy could combine with disenchantment in the North to destroy the Union.

Holman suggested the appropriation be cut to thirty thousand and the experimental garden program absorb most of the shortfall. After all, in his opinion, "the country at large would receive very little benefit" from these gardens. Known to his colleagues as "the Great Objector" for opposing appropriations for items other than prosecuting the war, he too was a lawyer and had served as a probate judge, judge of the court of common pleas, prosecuting attorney, and a member of the state house of representatives. Because he felt himself to be "a little more identified with the agricultural interests of the West than my friend from Ohio," he felt entitled to render a judgment on the value of the gardens.[13]

Agriculture had its defense attorneys too. Samuel Sullivan "Sunset" Cox (D-Ohio) spoke out against curtailing the budget of what he called "this agricultural department." The war demanded the redirection of the expenditure, not its reduction. The Union needed to replace the cotton and sugar supplies from the South with homegrown crops, "to adopt the plan of France, and raise our own sugar." A graduate of Brown University in Providence, Rhode Island, one-time lawyer, author, and journalist, his efforts to keep northern Democrats Unionist made him the de facto minority leader. His appointment to the American legation at Lima, Peru, which he could not take up due to illness, might explain his reference to the "Peruvian cotton" notices in the newspapers. His suggestion demanded a link to the war effort for all expenditures. His only disagreement with Holman rested with his different estimation of the value of an agricultural bureau. He seconded his fellow Democrat's point that there should be no expenditure on "sending out seeds which are of no value, not worth looking after when they have been distributed," only an expenditure on the promotion of cotton and sugar cultivation.[14]

Fiscal conservatism, a philosophy not limited to Democrats, had a strong hold on the minds of many congressmen.[15] The war's great expenditures, the revenues to maintain those expenses, and the apparatus to administrate the whole enterprise were viewed as temporary expedients. This was not just a relic of antebellum political economy. It was part of a larger vision of republicanism which the war's exigencies did not erase. According to this view, a small government had to be a fiscally limited one. In theory expenditures and expansion of government powers went hand in hand. The agricultural program's minimal impact was both its primary asset and its critical flaw—too small to have a large effect and too small an effect to receive more resources. The first state was alive and well in the minds of these legislators.

A determined group set out to break the support for agriculture out of this limiting ideological box. Illinois Republican Owen Lovejoy had grown up in Maine, where he graduated from Bowdoin College, studied law, and became a minister, before escaping poverty by settling in Illinois with a landed widow and becoming a successful farmer. A committed abolitionist and at the same time a supporter of Lincoln's gradualist approach, he had complained vociferously since he came to Congress in 1857 (after several terms in the Illinois legislature) that the federal government had not done enough for the agricultural interest. Along with his pivotal support for homestead legislation and the land grant colleges bill, he championed what he believed to be agriculture's need for a cabinet department to sponsor its development.[16] He attempted to offer an amendment creating a department for agriculture, but Horace Maynard got there first. Maynard, a Unionist from Tennessee, wanted not only to increase the allocation, but "so far from confining the operations of the Department to mere clerkships in the Patent Office, I would make an independent agricultural bureau." His proposal represented more than just an organizational rearrangement; it stemmed from a larger vision of what government should do and how it should do it. Maynard argued that "the American people are to a very great extent an agricultural people" and this "species of industry" should find support within the confines of the government and its budget.[17] As with the concept behind the land grant college bill, Maynard thought the government should assist the agricultural interest.

Its service to the farmers, Maynard said, would make the United States unique among all the "other civilized Government[s] in the world."[18] This view resonated with an exceptionalist tradition in contemporary political speeches and writings. The roots of this powerful story of the nation's messianic mission reached all the way back to the Puritan "city on a hill" ideal. The United States could avoid prior republics' dissolution and European tyrannies through its unique institutions, situation, and spirit. In particular, the independent yeoman classes immunized America to the decadence, decay, and despotism that flourished across the Atlantic.[19]

Lovejoy protested that this economy was to be practiced solely upon the minimal requirements of agriculture. He referred to the secretary of the interior and the president's request for an agricultural bureau. Abuses had probably occurred "in every Department of the Government," but only this appropriation received attention. Holman interjected that he favored an agricultural bureau too, but, he added, "I do not think that now is the proper time when we are engaged in a war of vast proportions." With this tangle over thirty thousand dollars, the House suspended discussion on the civil appropriations bill. A few moments later it gave unanimous consent to Lovejoy's introduction of a bill to establish an "Agricultural and Statistical Bureau" and referred it to the Committee on Agriculture.[20]

Thus far, the proposed "bureau" did not offer or require a thorough rethinking of old bromides of limited government. Isolating the debate over the measure from the background buzz and hum of the early wartime Congress's lawmaking, as though we could use modern electronic devises to lift a single conversation from the noise of a crowded room, we can see that significant continuities linked it to the prewar debate. But the administrative exigencies that the prosecution of the Civil War in 1862 imposed on Congress, and the experience of the war at its doorstep, taught Congress that government must supervise; it could not merely sponsor. It must be active, not passive. Passivity would lead to the dismemberment of the Union.

A Half-Step Forward in the House

Redrafted into a bill to establish a "Department of Agriculture," Lovejoy reintroduced House Bill 269 and the Committee on Agriculture's report on February 17, 1862. Instead of having a "secretary" at the helm of the new department, the bill provided only a "commissioner." A secretary would be a member of the cabinet, whereas a commissioner would not. It was a symbolic distinction intended to answer objections to a new cabinet post. Lovejoy hoped that, "as they have nothing in about the negro, I hope that they will be listened to,"[21] a sly reference to the far hotter debates about confiscation of confederate slaves. There was laughter in the chamber, but Lovejoy's jocular aside to the issue that had occupied the Congress's attention since the beginning of the war and would continue to bring forth the most perfervid rhetoric throughout the war suggests exactly the point I am making. In a sense the war was a tangent—to be sure, an immensely important tangent—in the longer course of the evolution of ideas about the American state.

But the laughter was uneasy, for these extraordinary concerns could absorb days and days of debate. Lovejoy was pointing to the gap between the Radicals who favored abolition and equal rights and those who, like President Lincoln, wanted a moderate course to appease the border states, their Unionist sympathizers in the North, and the anti-secession Unionist populations in the rebelling areas. What was more, Democrats were not averse to using the race card to embarrass Republican candidates in the 1862 election campaign. Lovejoy and those who wanted service for the agricultural interests tried to sidestep this controversy.[22]

The first section of the bill stated the purpose as well as the mission of the proposed department: "to acquire and to diffuse among the people of the United States useful information on subjects connected with agriculture in the most general and comprehensive sense of the word, and to procure, propagate, and distribute among the people new and valuable seeds and plants." It was the same mission that had begun in 1836 in the Patent Office; this time it would take place in its own department. The program would no longer be under the secretary of the interior. The committee report spelled out the reason for this move: "Agriculture clad in homespun is very apt to be elbowed aside by capital attired in ten-dollar Yorkshire. Every Government in Europe, your committee think, without exception, has an agricultural department connected with it."[23] Congress, as it did with many other measures, had looked abroad and wanted to act in response to a perceived rival effort that could endanger American interests.

The jockeying within the majority now began. With the cooperation of Speaker Grow, Lovejoy monopolized the floor, only begrudgingly entertaining any changes. With Holman looking for any opening to kill the bill, Lovejoy could not yield for amendments or he would lose control of the debate. Ultimately, he had to accept several changes from the floor, reducing the commissioner of agriculture's salary from five thousand to three thousand dollars, and specified the procedure he had to use to hire the specialists in chemistry, biology, and botany needed to engage in agriculture research. Cox's attempt to demote the department to a bureau within Interior fell by voice vote. Divisions over war policy and what to do with slavery neither paralyzed the House nor delayed the vote, though Grow's artful use of the chair's authority to make rule determinations and recognize speakers surely helped. The bill passed the House 122 to 7.[24]

Avoiding the Slippery Slope: Formal Consideration in the Senate

On April 17, 1862, the heavily Republican Senate heard James F. Simmons, a Republican from Rhode Island and chair of the Committee on Patents and the Patent Office, introduce House Bill 269. After he accepted some amendments that included a clerk and reporting requirements for the new department, he explained his views on the matter: "It is simply a compliment to the great leading interest of industry, who have been desirous of having some recognition by the Government of their peculiar pursuit."[25] If he had any intention of increasing the federal government's role in the largest occupation in the country, he kept it to himself.

In fact, he argued the opposite. He mentioned his membership in his state's agricultural society for some forty years, though his boyhood on his father's farm and career in manufacturing yarn inclined him to indifference to the Patent Office's agriculture program. He labeled the elevation of the activity to department status as "merely a compliment" and "this little boon, if for nothing else, merely to gratify their pride." The movement of the activity from the Patent Office would not affect its operations and would demonstrate the United States's recognition of "the pillar of the national strength—agriculture."[26] He cast the bill as a harmless symbolic action. This strategy defused any potential opposition based on the limited government philosophy. But the manufacturer from Rhode Island oversold his product.

Joseph A. Wright, previously a Democrat but now a member of the Union Party from Indiana, offered a substitute bill. While Simmons had spoken briefly with little punch (the silence-is-golden tactic of the Morrill bill proponents in the later stages of that debate), Wright vigorously presented a case strongly derived from his experience. Born in Washington, Pennsylvania, he had worked his way through the state seminary in Bloomington (which would become Indiana University) by doing odd jobs such as ringing the school bell and serving as the librarian. In school he studied law with a local judge and then entered private practice in Rockville, Parke County.[27] A loyal Democrat, he served in the state house of representatives, the state senate, one term in the House, and two terms as governor of Indiana. Buchanan appointed him envoy extraordinary and minister plenipotentiary to the German kingdom of Prussia, where he stayed until the Civil War Senate expelled Jesse D. Bright and Wright, now a Unionist, took his place on February 24, 1862. As he had successfully advocated as governor and worked as a diplomat, his substitute bill would have created four bureaus to carry out the same functions as those outlined in House Bill 269.[28]

Wright had seen the future of sponsorship, and it spoke in supervisory bureaucratese. He pointed out that the success of the war effort depended on the nation's continued exports of foodstuffs to "fill the warehouses of Liverpool, Havre, and Bremen." House Bill 269 did nothing to further the "science and practice of agriculture" because it lacked a statistics-gathering, analyzing, and reporting bureau. The new department had to have research bureaus in other sciences to prevent infestations, cultivate better varieties of crops, and help farmers replace the cotton and sugar lost with the South's departure. Even more important, the United States had to compete with the kingdoms of Germany, Britain, and Napoleon III's France, all of which were conducting agricultural research to great effect. The situation demanded action. Without "scientific investigations into our nation's resources," he prophesied, "we shall gradually sink into a mere dependency of Europe." He added, "It is evidently the duty of that *public machine*, which we style Government, to take the matter up and carry it through."[29]

Wright had introduced into the debate the same transatlantic concerns as motivated the educational reformers. Science could serve agriculture and produce wealth, employment, and progress, but only with ongoing, expert government involvement. Wright's arguments were both cosmopolitan and nationalistic at the same time. With due regard for objections based on the need for fiscal restraint, Wright maintained that his version would cost no more than the current allocation of sixty thousand dollars. Above all, government had to pursue these goals actively. "It may be said that private individuals will do this. We all know that private enterprise has failed to do it." Any person familiar with the periodic disasters that came with the absence of a government-led effort in banking, commerce, medicine, and education understood this point, he implied. Wright urged his colleagues on: "Let the people know what we are doing, so that the great farming interest of the Government may not be in the hands of dupes and at the mercy of incidental information utterly unreliable, when we have it in our power to keep them accurately advised."[30]

When the Senate took up Wright's amendment on April 22, 1862, Simmons briefly informed the body that he and his committee had considered this proposal and believed, contrary to Wright's arithmetic, that it would cost more than the original. "The committee did not think we were just now in a situation to make that outlay." It would be best to add those "colleges" after the war was over.[31] Simmons, however, did not dispute Wright's musings on supervision. This army had passed in the night.

With Charles Sumner (R-Mass.), Wade, and Collamer voting with Simmons, aided by fiscal conservatives such as Maine's William Pitt Fessenden, Wright's substitute went down to defeat twenty-three to twelve. None of them shot down Wright's frank call to link supervision to sponsorship. Instead, Simmons said, "We thought we could wait a little while before we put them [the bureaus] in," which implies a permissible future action. Wright's substitute made the heads of the delineated bureaus appointees of the president to be approved by the Senate.[32] In fact, even more was going on than met the ear.

Wright's glaring omission of "Prussia" anywhere in his presentation, despite its obvious relevance and his firsthand knowledge, is telling. He referred to "Great Britain," "Holland," "France," and "Germany," but not to the kingdom where he had spent several years as a special envoy.[33] His fellow senators knew of his appointment and recognized that Wright's proposal resembled the strong executive bureaucracies of that German state. Simmons's use of the word *colleges*, instead of *bureaus*, may indeed have been a deliberate attempt to avoid a connection between the new department and anything present in that unpleasant kingdom in northern Germany.[34]

Silently, Simmons and his cohort had conceded what Wright demanded even if they voted against his formulation of the proposal. The real challenge came from Lafayette S. Foster from Connecticut. He wanted a mere bureau within the Interior Department. His proposed "Bureau of Agriculture and Statistics" would, in addition to performing the tasks for agriculture, carry out the decennial census. The president, with the consent of the Senate, would appoint the commissioner, whose salary of three thousand dollars would be the same as under House Bill 269. Foster's principal argument was the need for fiscal restraint in the time of "a struggle for national existence." He did not object to the idea of ongoing supervision but suggested that the original measure constituted a slippery slope into great expenditures. "If we make it a Department, there will be a necessity for a greater amount of expenditure," he predicted. Natural ambition would lead to additional demands. "The head of the Department of Agriculture will naturally consider himself somewhat slighted if he does not have a salary equal in amount to that of the other heads of Departments." This will lead to additional requests, for "there will be, of course, a much greater number of clerks in order to keep up the rank and dignity of the position."[35] (Here, in 1862, is a line of reasoning which anticipated modern entrepreneurial bureaucrat theories.)[36] The fear of where any proposal might lead resembles Mason and Davis's apprehension of federal government power before the war. In any case the slippery slope rhetoric remained a critical element in some lawmakers' thinking.[37] But Foster did not object to federal sponsorship or supervision in principle.

Foster, a graduate of Brown University, a lawyer, and a Whig, gained election to the Senate (his first full term began in 1855) in a deal with Free-Soilers. In 1862 he was a Republican, but deep down he remained an old Whig. "The Department is really not under the control of Congress as much as I think it ought to be," he argued. Congressional supremacy was a Whig article of faith. The reports should go to Congress, not the president. He elaborated, saying, "I think we are the more appropriate tribunal to refer the reports of this Department or bureau to than the President." He considered the Congress in the old parliamentary sense, a supreme body of law and judicature. What was more, he asserted, "we do not want a fancy Bureau of Agriculture."[38] Still, referring perhaps more to Wright's concept than House Bill 269, he expressed the second state's concern for tying supervision (albeit congressional rather than presidential) to sponsorship.

On May 2, 1862, Simmons offered a few words on Foster's amendment. He argued that the change "is no essential improvement of the present system." Desiring to delay the vote until more of his supporters were present, Foster countered that there was no quorum present. When Sumner contradicted him, he pled for additional time to make further remarks. Simmons had to wait until May 8 to get his vote. Simmons began by inserting into the *Globe* a petition from "the National Agricultural Society" calling for the new department: "I know of no class of people, no great branch of industry that have importuned Congress so little. . . . They lean upon the handles of their plows rather than upon this Government for supporting their families." He continued, "Sir, I am astonished at the opposition made here to a mere recognition of that class."[39] He stuck to his strategy of outfitting this measure in the clothing of the simple husbandman and farmer rather than the cotton and silk of the D.C. bureaucrat.

Hale was having none of Simmons's soft-pedaling. Hale claimed to venerate agriculture as much as Simmons or Wright, but he did not value any government involvement, however slight: "that great art, communicated from the divine Author of our being to man when He made him and placed him on the globe, and subjected the earth to his use and made it his lot get his living from the earth, by the good providence of God had thus far been kept out of the hands of politicians." He traced the holy nature of farming from Abel to the tillers of the United States. They asked for nothing but "'for God's sake, let us alone.'" Repeating Foster's warning, he prophesied, "If you make a separate Department of this, you will have it with a Cabinet minister before long."[40] In fact, the Department of Agriculture only became a cabinet-level institution in 1889, under President Grover Cleveland, but Hale was more concerned about bureaucratic dynamics than timing.[41]

Simmons countered Hale's slippery slope argument: "If Congress has a mind to extravagantly waste the Treasury of the Government in creating new establishments hereafter, it will not be the fault of the bill."[42] Simmons did not see the danger in any particular label for the head of the new department. What was in a name? But Hale, an old Democrat, set great store by names. Names were not mere words; they were things. Behind this brief interchange of rhetorical arms lay a much deeper divide over perceptions of government's role in everyday life. Simmons trusted government; Hale did not. Neither man questioned the value of sponsorship. The ship of state had sailed this far.

Some in Congress refused to accept this tacit framing of the second state. Pennsylvania Republican Edgar Cowan took issue with both Foster and Simmons. A successful defense attorney and prosecutor as well as a graduate of Franklin College in Ohio before entering the Senate in 1861, he opposed not only a department of agriculture and a separate bureau but also the appropriation for the gathering of seeds and the study of agronomy. He favored a strict construction of the Constitution. He quoted from Justice Joseph Story's *Commentaries on the Constitution* on reading the language of the Constitution and found no rule that would support such a broad reading of congressional authority. His philosophy of government came down to a basic function, which he described as follows: "to protect the people, furnish to them security in their lives, their liberty, and their property, so that every man may have what he earns and may be enabled to keep it after he has got it; and the less government meddles with it the better." It was Jeffersonian republicanism pure and simple. The United States had no need of the agricultural schemes of Europe because its population did not exceed the land resource.[43]

Fessenden's heart lay with Cowan, but his head told him the second state had come to stay.[44] He asserted that opposition to the legislation should not come from the question of legislative construction (he viewed that question as settled) but from the deeper question of how far they "ought to go." He backed Hale's view that farmers did not care at all about whether or not they had a department set aside for their occupation. The lobbying, in Fessenden's estimation, came from "certain gentlemen of position and wealth and reading" who tried to speak for the farmers. The motivation was "that certain gentlemen would like places [in government service]." Their scrounging ambition would drive the expenditure ever higher. "We shall have recommendations at once for a little more science here and a little more science there," he predicted. The Department of Interior secretary's report had asked only for a bureau, and that was more than sufficient.[45] As chair of the Finance Committee, a lawyer who excelled in debate, a politically astute tactician, and an indefatigable worker, Fessenden spoke infrequently, but when he did it carried much more weight than it might first appear.[46] While these concerns came from solid Republicans from Maine, Pennsylvania, and New Hampshire, they indicated a current of feeling that ran throughout the Congress.

In the face of this onslaught, Simmons made a final attempt to assure those straddling the line between department and bureau that Hale, Fessenden, and Cowan's austere view of the objects of government was consistent with the legislation as written. They could, after all, reduce its appropriation at a later date. When Wright called for the yeas and nays on Foster's substitute, the Senate divided evenly eighteen to eighteen. With that lukewarm reception, the Department of Agriculture bill came to a vote. By a vote of twenty-five to thirteen the Senate gave its assent to the amended House Bill 269. Fessenden, Cowan, Harlan, Lane of Indiana, and Wright joined the dissenters, for differing reasons, to be sure.[47]

THROUGH A MANEUVER that made a vote on a motion to lay the amendments to the bill on the table a vote on the bill, Lovejoy managed to secure the House's approval of the Department of Agriculture by a vote of ninety to fourteen on May 13, 1862. Two days later President Lincoln signed it into law. Its immediate effect was extraordinarily limited, but it did lay a foundation for broad-based federal sponsorship of agriculture. Time and the progress of science was on the side of the second state advocates—the Department expanded bit by bit, becoming the active service agency that Hale, Cowan, Fessenden, and Collamer feared, but its creation owed little to the inchoate promise the second state fulfilled.[48]

A Senate Compromise on Higher Education

Even with the Deep South's Democrats gone, Morrill had to maneuver around a recalcitrant Committee on Public Lands in the House to revisit his plan for colleges. Once again, he let Wade take the lead. On May 21, 1862, Wade brought S. 298 to the floor of the Senate. The approval of the land grant colleges bill was assured, but the attitudes of the congressmen in 1862 demonstrate how the ideas of sponsorship and supervision were linked. Some of the earlier concerns still echoed in Kansas's James H. Lane's complaint that the bill "will exhaust all of the valuable lands within the State of Kansas." Its operations, if not amended as he proposed, would "take the lands of Kansas and give them to the States of Massachusetts and New Jersey, and by and by to the States of South Carolina and Alabama and Georgia." This would be unjust, of benefit not to Kansas but to "speculators."[49]

Lane's plea echoed his distaste for the remote, eastern, monied, faceless investors caricatured as "capitalists" by the antebellum Democrats. The perception that corruption had followed land grants as surely as pigs to the trough was widespread and had much proof.[50] State-centered thinking was still so universal that even the legislation's wartime proponents argued in those terms. Although secession was excoriated as an excess of states' rights philosophy and law, the primary political attachment of the vast majority of representatives and senators from all the states and in all the parties was to their state.

Lane subscribed to this logic not just because he represented a western state, not just because he was a partisan, and not just because he lacked the advantages of a formal education, foreign travel, and broad interests (though all of these were true of him). But he had journeyed far in other ways, from Indiana to service in the Mexican-American War, to Congress and Kansas in its bloody heyday. He had moved far in politics too, from being a supporter of Stephen Douglas to becoming a staunch Republican, indeed the leader of the Republicans in Kansas. He became president of the Topeka constitutional convention and lobbied, poorly, for its adoption in Washington. He returned to Kansas after a speaking tour on behalf of the antislavery cause in the North and helped frame the antislavery Leavenworth Constitution in 1857. In 1861 he gained election as a Republican to Kansas's first U.S. Senate contingent. Nor was his dislike for speculators evidence of narrowness in other ways. For example, he would become an advocate of African-American rights—by 1864 calling for the franchise for African Americans.[51] But his advocacy of energetic action by the federal government in prosecuting the war did not extend to changing the nature of American government. Again, listening to him on this subject instead of following his views on the war itself, in effect stripping the noise of war from the quieter, long-standing discourse on creating new agencies and functions, shows how strong the anti-statist continuities remained.

Lane's amendment would have limited those states receiving scrip because they did not have enough public land within their own territory; the amendment would limit them to scrip outside the boundaries of any existing state. Most of the scrip, then, would be for lands not likely to be worth very much for some time. Wade opposed this western-oriented limitation on the legislation, but, being cognizant of the time restrictions, commented, "I do not wish to debate the subject; I want a vote, if I can get it."[52]

The division between the newer states of the West and the older states of the East threatened to undo Republican unity. James W. Grimes (R-Iowa) tried to reconcile Lane and Wade. He pointed out that Kansas had received more acreage for its public schools than had other states, including Iowa. His description of these actions as "pretty liberal" treatment, however, did not carry much weight.[53] There was reason for adherents to first state tenets to be suspicious of Grimes. Despite what his tenure as governor then U.S. senator from a western state might indicate, Grimes hailed from Deering, New Hampshire, Hampton Academy, and two and a half years at Dartmouth College before becoming a lawyer and moving west at the age of twenty.

Morton S. Wilkinson (R-Minn.) opened the second day of consideration in this round over land grant colleges, on May 28, 1862, with the corruption theme.[54] Without a sophisticated allocation plan and the means to administer it, Congress could not properly police the use of the scrip. The classic double bind that had appeared in 1858 and 1859 played on the minds of the senators in 1862. If anything, the phenomenon was more apparent due to the Congress's recent exposure of corruption in the War Department.[55]

To avoid large government departments with their corresponding large budgets, the sculptors of new policies had to economize on the administrative mechanism. The alternative, what today would be termed "privatization," lent itself to opportunities for "speculators" to misuse the funds. Wilkinson condemned this "pernicious system" and the "vampires" who profited from it in the strongest terms. He would vote against this scheme regardless of whether Lane's amendment passed. Closing consideration for the day, Lane suggested he might be conciliated if states were limited to one million acres in any one state.[56]

On June 10, 1862, Wade renewed his efforts to take up the bill. Instead of fighting Lane's amendment, Wade consented. He alluded to some prior agreement and labeled the amendment not "unreasonable," choosing to "leave it to the Senate" to decide.[57] Localist xenophobia was one of the most pernicious issues, for it was often the vaguest (hence hardest to refute) but most potent objection to foreign inspired additions to American government. Perniciously suggestive terms such as *outsiders, bureaucrats,* and *speculators* had different implications, but all served this line of thought. As they indicate, there was a deep reservoir of suspicion that could be deployed in a wide variety of situations. One can glimpse the same suspicion, sometimes amounting to paranoia, in the attack on the science-based, university learning that Morrill, Wade, and others valued so highly.[58] Under the older ideas of a limited government, no lawyer barred consideration of sponsorship and supervision, so much as jousted for a place in their midst, creating a kind of hybrid of the two systems and giving the debate a layered quality.

Wilkinson stated his position firmly: "I do not want to see large quantities of the public lands pass into the hands of a single individual."[59] His enforcement mechanism, placing purpose and names on the front of the scrip, grew out of his legal experience. Lawyers' practices were filled with disputes over endorsement of promissory notes, bills of exchange, and bonds. His plan could work if there were private suits in the courts or state actions for fraud. Someone using the scrip in violation of the restrictions might face fines, jail, or, in civil cases, substantial monetary liability. Thus, the courts would serve as a cheaper alternative to more substantial policing. Wilkinson not only was a lawyer but had also been a register of deeds, a legislator, and a member of the board that had drawn up a law code for the territory of Minnesota. He was well acquainted with how laws actually worked at the ground level, often against the interest of the small farmers he favored. More important perhaps, endorsement of the scrips permitted a kind of supervision that every lawyer understood.

Samuel C. Pomeroy (R-Kans.) seconded Wilkinson's amendment. The concern about speculation had other advocates in the western states. Pomeroy wanted scrip labels comparable to land allotments to soldiers for their service in wartime. Otherwise, he argued, speculators would accumulate large blocks without congressional knowledge "to the public detriment." This had happened in other wars, most notably the American Revolution. Wade countered that this safeguard was "unusual." After all, Congress had not seen fit to make railroad grants in the same way.[60] Here two lawyers used the common law tactic of arguing by analogy. Like a court, Congress had instituted a rule in a prior situation; therefore, it should adhere to the same concept in analogous circumstances.

Besides, Wade continued, the land involved in this bill amounted to no more than a "drop in the bucket," comparatively speaking. He had hoped that the bill might progress "without the embarrassment of further amendments." James R. Doolittle (R-Wis.) opined that the "amendment cannot operate with any peculiar hardship." He further reasoned that the states would, naturally, keep an account of the sale which would enable them to enforce Congress's strictures quite easily. Fessenden interjected that "the States could not sell it [the lands] in a body."[61]

Tinkering, juggling the details of a dense deal at the same time as they juggled the core values of the first and second states, the legislators inched, crablike, toward a fuller understanding of the implications of sponsorship and supervision. Practical considerations spurred Doolittle to spell out his position. He argued the states would get more for small lots "than . . . [they] will if the States take it all and throw it into Wall street, in the city of New York, and sell it all at once."[62] Doolittle was firmly anti–Wall Street, anti-city, anti-outsiders. He had switched his affiliation from the Democratic to the Republican Party after the Kansas-Nebraska Act undid the Compromise of 1850. He, too, had been a lawyer, judge, and legislator before his state legislature selected him for the Senate in 1857. He did not need Wade to explain how the act would work.

Wade and Collamer both took runs at this lingering suspicion, forgetting for the moment their desire to move debate along to a vote. Wade posited that the amendment would in fact reduce the value of the grant. Collamer added that the grant amounted to a pittance. Timothy O. Howe (R-Wis.) interjected that the grant amounted to "nothing at all to anybody" and merely added a burden to "one portion of the country." His complaint did not address the power of the Congress to make the grant nor the policy of aiding education. Rather, he believed that the grant was so small that the colleges would derive little or no benefit. One million acres would go to outsiders rather than local farmers or new migrants (under the recently passed Homestead Act). The legislation "made the whole Northwest and the whole West but little more than a province of New York."[63]

Howe's distrust of the East may seem to derive from and express the same attitude toward governmental expansion which Pugh, Mason, Clay, and Davis expressed in 1858 and 1859, but his remarks differ from theirs in one important respect. He stated in no uncertain terms that, "if you want to ingraft a new kind of education upon the educational system of the country, I am ready for it."[64] Sponsorship was good; supervision necessary, even if dominance of one region by another was bad. This evinces a substantial shift in prevailing views toward federal powers, federal involvement, and national policy. It shows that even the measure's detractors accepted the legitimacy of national sponsorship of what was traditionally a very local activity.

Howe had been a circuit and, for one year, chief justice of the Wisconsin supreme court. He had received a degree from the Maine Wesleyan Seminary before he studied law and moved West. He and the other lawyers had spoken. Although they disagreed on the basis for funding, they agreed that, in law, the federal government could assume the role of sponsor of higher education and supervise its largesse. Filled with qualifications and asides—support for agriculture, for farmers, for the nation's role as producer, for progress—the legislation moved ahead. Behind it was a still inchoate but gradually defined ideal of sponsorship along with the minimal supervision of the second state.

The Devil in the Details

As in the debate over the Department of Agriculture, the concept of supervision, of how to administer the grant—in this case how to label the scrip—lingered. In a largely sectional vote with the radicals Wade, Sumner, and Collamer on the losing side, Wilkinson's amendment became part of the bill, twenty to nineteen. James Dixon (R-Conn.) moved to reconsider the vote, and Fessenden called for the yeas and nays. Dixon explained that he had mistakenly voted in the affirmative and wished to change his vote.[65] Dixon was another lawyer—a graduate of Williams College who had studied law and entered state politics in his home state of Connecticut. Dixon supported the bill. Fessenden had cleverly called for the yeas and nays to keep the debate going while the bill's supporters gathered their forces.

Wade now made more extensive arguments against the Wilkinson amendment, but they added little to the debate. Namely, "to clog and encumber it [the grant] with a condition that will defeat it and destroy its value, is, I think, impolitic, illiberal, and unjust." The land belonged to "the General government," and its disposal rested solely with the will of the Congress, but it should not be used to the "detriment of the people of the new states." In his opinion Senate Bill 298 fulfilled this obligation as much as any grant did.[66]

A stark truth about the process of adding to the American state lay underneath this divide between the West and the East, between radicals and conservatives, between the Free-Soil Democrats and the Whigs. Both sides argued about the legislation's effect while assuming or neglecting the question of its enforcement. Both sides agreed that government should tread really lightly, but they could not agree upon the shape and size of the boot that did the treading. The removal of the southern fire-eater faction ended the open opposition to federal action, only to have it surface in the debate over regional allotments, scrip, speculation, and Wall Street. Wilkinson bowed to the inconsistency of large grants for railroads but not for colleges. "I think this Government ought not to grant lands for the benefit of railroads. I believe that the principle is wrong, essentially wrong." The dislike for "monopoly" trumped the desire to sponsor development.[67]

Grimes attempted to stem this tide of rising revolt against this necessity of some kind of explicit supervision of sponsorship. There had to be rules and someone, somewhere, to enforce them. He expressed support for the community of interests that bound the states together. He was in favor of the amendment not to kill the bill but to ensure that the future states in the territories grew up as strong as their older compatriots.[68] Essentially, he conceived the land grant college idea as an individual state-building policy. Each new state in the Union got the chance to develop alongside the older ones. Grimes had introduced a new concept, albeit without the name: a kind of cooperative federalism, in which the national government orchestrated a program for the benefit of all the states. Cooperative federalism did not require extensive central services or a large bureaucracy in Washington, D.C., because the states would run their own variants of the program. It was a brilliant solution to the problem of servicing grants and ahead of its time, which was perhaps why his colleagues did not recognize its formulation.

Pomeroy, speaking for the opposition, certainly did not endorse this view. He still conceived of the situation in state-versus-state terms. Wade's logic fell apart, Pomeroy insisted, because the railroad grants were "confined to the line of the road," whereas the scrip represented "a new feature in disposing of the public lands." Howe went even further than Pomeroy. To the detriment of his side, he insisted upon using the arguments that might well have sprung from the absent senators from the South. "I do not believe the time has come when the people of the United States are prepared to charge the work of public education upon the United States." To be fair to the senator from Wisconsin, he used the phrase *United States* to refer to the national government. This indicates a shift in terms from the federal or general government language to a more general concept of the nation—while not a sea change, it was the beginning of a discernible change. Howe, after all, did consider a general bequest out of the Treasury to be "equal, undeniably equal" and, therefore, better.[69]

Iowa Republican James Harlan, who had spoken in the first debate on the land grant college bill, countered Howe's assertions. He found it odd that anyone would object to the legislation on the grounds that it did not serve their people. "This body is a body of lawyers," he noted. "There are very few gentlemen here who are not professional lawyers." That they should resist doing something that would meet with the general approval of the rest of the country seemed counter to democratic government, rule by the people.[70] Lawyers were supposed to serve the best interests of their clients in the most effective and expeditious manner. They were given to bombast certainly, but only to further a practical cause. Harlan knew more than this, and so did the other debaters. The representatives of the people not only do not resemble them—an overabundance of lawyers skews the proportions—but the representatives' thinking was powerfully influenced by their professional experience as lawyers.

Howe rose once again to press home the point that the burden of the allocation, due to its land per congressman formula, fell heavier on the less-populated western states than those of the East. "Hence you do not offer the same value, but you impose the same burden on each of the States."[71] This was a fair point, but now Howe's plan met with no serious consideration. The lawyers had worked out a deal. As lawyers, they understood that government would still be limited, but it could service its sponsorships.[72] Nevertheless, Howe persisted with his particular plan for block grants. He wanted the federal government to sell the land and give the money to the states directly. This, he asserted, despite Wade's prodding that it would be impracticable, "is equal; this proposition is not."[73]

New Jersey's John Ten Eyck challenged Howe's notion. He countered that the older states had subsidized the newer states from the beginning. Land grants improved their common schools, built railroads, and provided cheap plots for easy settlement. Moreover, the populations had "intermixed, we are intermingled." A community of interest existed between the birth states and the future homes of this surplus. Ten Eyck captured one part of Grimes's cooperative-born federalism. He was a native born New Jerseyan who had spent his entire life in his state. While others may have left, he stayed to study under private tutors, practice law, enforce the law as a prosecuting attorney for Burlington County for ten years, then enter politics with a stint as a delegate to the New Jersey constitutional convention of 1844. In 1859 he entered the Senate, where he voted his Republican affiliation. He plead his case as an advocate might to the jury before him. He reminded the reluctant senators from the West, the representatives of the newer states, "as they know the disposition is to continue that feeling towards them, they might yield their opposition to this bill." Ten Eyck argued what everyone might have suspected; they might "yield their opposition to it in the way of proposing amendments which may embarrass it or render it less valuable for the purposes that are designed."[74]

Howe did not feel the same way. He and Henry M. Rice (D-Minn.) continued to argue that the current formula still unfairly favored the older states. Kansas's Lane joined the fray to ask Ten Eyck to put himself in the shoes of a representative of Kansas. Would he still favor the measure? Ten Eyck replied cleverly that the people of New Jersey had done as much throughout Kansas's history, "mourning with her in her difficulties, and rejoicing with her in her triumphs." Lane responded that he thought "the Senator from New Jersey overrates the magnanimity of his State in this respect."[75] The rivalry between sections still existed. A catastrophic war that had resulted from just such a mind-set was not enough to dislodge these affinities.

As if to buttress this point, Howe continued his refutation of Ten Eyck. "I have told the Senate why you did those things. It was not to benefit Wisconsin; it was to benefit yourselves." Most likely, without realizing it, he slipped into making his opponents' argument for them. "It was not to benefit Iowa, it was to benefit the nation. You wanted to strengthen the nation, and you took the best means to do it." Howe's inadvertent point put, at the very least, a neutral spin on what James M. Mason had postulated in the first debate: the land grant college bill instituted a national policy, albeit one based on a New England–inspired approach to higher education. Howe also subscribed to Mason's resentments. "You granted lands for railroads; and New York and Boston and Philadelphia own them to-day." He continued to state bluntly that "it was to sell it to improve your lands."[76]

Ten Eyck, nonplused by this deep-seated animosity, thanked Howe for his frankness. Now the public would understand that all the older states had done they had done "through a spirit of gain." Rice interjected to place a more positive spin on the situation. His summation reflected a pragmatic appreciation of the situation: "Not only has the land been a gift, . . . but in addition the old States give us settlers and they give us money to build our roads, and I, for one, think it has been a gratuity, and a most noble one."[77] Rice expressed a second component of Grimes's cooperative federalism. Land policy, economic growth, and now a common struggle linked the interests of both West and East, and the role the federal government played in servicing that link.

Grimes and Lane dominated the final exchange. With several safeguards now in place, Lane of Kansas had become the legislation's champion against Grimes's continued, strident opposition to Lane's amendment. Grimes did not pull any punches in his opening flurry. "I believe that it [the amended bill] will be disastrous to the Territories," he proclaimed. Further, "I predict that if it is enacted into a law we have seen the last one of the agricultural Territories come into this Union." He reasoned that Lane's amendment limiting the acreage in any one state to one million would in effect relegate the rest of the lands to Nebraska and Dakota territories. Lane took issue with Grimes's numbers. By his calculation he found only five million acres had to be located in the territories, not Grimes's eight. Grimes rejected this approach and pushed his argument based on an assessment of the probable value of the land available.[78]

The dispute over the numbers and quality of the parcels suggests another substantial factor in the formation of congressional attitudes toward the question of servicing the grants. Without a detailed report on the topic at hand, congressmen had to rely on their personal experience, their instincts, and communications they may have received from friends, constituents, or organizations with an interest in the matter. Early second state approaches were information-poor, which put an additional burden on an ideology favoring them.

Grimes had to dig back into the reservoir of impressions, memories, and judgments he had formed years ago as an attorney in the "Black Hawk Purchase," the future site of Burlington, Iowa. Pushed by Rice to explain why anyone purchasing land would want to hold onto it for an indefinite period, Grimes informed his listeners about the speculators who had purchased large tracts and held on to them to prevent the formation of territorial governments. The speculators' aim was to dominate the future state, all in a concerted effort to maximize the sale price of their parcels. In so doing, they deprived the would-be state of revenue, aggrandized their own power, and drove away all but the most well-off settlers. But Grimes's protests were in vain. Although his interlocutor, Kansas's Lane, ultimately voted with him and five others, thirty-two voted in favor of passage, including Howe of Wisconsin.[79] The problem of information gathering lingered in the shadows, a brooking omnipresence that would soon become a central issue.

In the House Anew

On June 19, 1862, Morrill received recognition from the speaker and moved to take up Senate Bill 298. A recalcitrant minority of Democrats might try to derail legislation, but this was not the Senate. A determined House leadership could bulldoze opposition. John F. Potter (R-Wis.) objected to Morrill's motion. He wanted the bill referred to the Committee on Public Lands, of which he was chair. Not a chance. The speaker ordered the tellers on the motion to suspend the usual order of business to consider Senate Bill 298. With a vote of fifty-six to thirty-eight, the land grant college bill arrived on the floor. Now it had to survive a Potter motion to commit to his committee. Most likely, this was an attempt to bury the measure in committee once again, a move Wade's maneuvers in the Senate had early avoided. Potter argued that "this bill has never been considered in committee." He implied that it violated all fairness to consider a proposal that had not gone through the usual process of committee examination. Morrill countered that in fact "it has been five years before the country, and is essentially the same bill that has repeatedly been before the House." In effect the House had considered it for some time.[80]

Potter's opposition to such a popular proposal was not only a personal matter (he had been ignored and his committee slighted); it was a matter of procedure. Potter was not a major player in the great debates of the first Civil War Congress, but he was a lawyer and a stickler for good form. A Maine man transported to Wisconsin, where he studied law and was admitted to practice, he served as a judge, then in the state assembly, before election to the House. Indiana's Holman, who had opposed the Department of Agriculture, called for the yeas and nays on Potter's motion. By a solid majority of eighty-three to thirty-one, Senate Bill 298 survived. Potter now tried a series of delaying tactics including adjourning the House, postponing the vote, and having the bill read. Only the last one succeeded. It was traditional to have the bill read at least once before a vote. Potter asked the speaker for the opportunity to present some amendments. But Speaker Grow would have none of it. Debate was not in order. Holman called for the yeas and nays on passage of the legislation. With a vote of ninety to twenty-five, Senate Bill 298 passed the House to be presented to the president.[81] Its long, arduous journey had at last reached an end. Although the curtailed proceedings of the House of Representatives did not allow the members a great deal of talk, their speedy actions spoke volumes. Here was a proposal to add to the American state which could receive the approval of the leadership as well as a sizable majority of the representatives.

ON JULY 1, 1862, with President Abraham Lincoln's signature, the Morrill Land Grant College Act came into effect. Its impact was as diverse as the states that received its benefit. With no federal supervision some of the worst fears of the western opponents came to fruition. While what became Cornell University benefited tremendously from the exploitation of Wisconsin pine lands, elsewhere higher education struggled.[82] What was more, the farmers did not benefit as much as the railroad companies. The glut of public land combined with the states' already hard-pressed finances during the Civil War to constrain any efforts to establish colleges.[83]

But the final act of the debate on the Morrill Act, like the debates on the Department of Agriculture, proved that out of the back and forth of debate, pressed on by the needs of a wartime nation, congressmen could think the unthinkable and approve the novel. The act encouraged all states to found agriculture and mechanical arts colleges. From that foundation sixty-eight universities arose, providing the United States with a substantial system of federally aided, state-run higher education facilities that later became the most open and vibrant educational industry in the world. Those results would emerge, however, only after considerably more money, time, and effort were invested and substantial economic and social changes had taken place.

In the coming years, and often without thorough debate over their implications, the exigencies of war created the impetus for the creation of other additions to the national state, including the empowerment of the Office of the Controller of the Currency to regulate national banks, the formation of the Internal Revenue Service to administer the new taxes on income, and, in the final days of the Lincoln presidency, the establishment of the Secret Service Division of the U.S. Treasury Department. The Secret Service was an example of the expansion of the American executive apparatus regardless of congressional action. If Congress would not expressly consider additions, events would proceed anyway.

Without express congressional authorization, the solicitor of the Treasury Department, Edward Jordan, on his own authority to enforce the Legal Tender Act, established the Secret Service on July 5, 1865, by swearing in William P. Wood as its first chief. After a checkered career during the war littered with extralegal actions, Wood staffed the new agency with émigrés from the War Department's wartime provost marshal national policing force as well as former private detectives and even former counterfeiters. Like the U.S. marshals, the Secret Service agents were appointed, without training, and had to use local authorities to carry out their functions of safeguarding the currency. The wartime experience created an entrepreneurial spirit that filled in the gaps Congress had left in the enforcement provisions.[84] This process of quiet, discretionary administrative growth recurred frequently, exercising a powerful influence on the practices of U.S. law enforcement agencies. This lack of oversight amounted to a tremendous grant of power to these small, underfunded bureaucracies, a seemingly contrary result to the antibureaucracy approach to enlarging the state.

The consensus view is that measures such as the founding of the Secret Service along with the National Banking Act and the unprecedented powers the federal government assumed during the war reflected the free labor ideology's compromise with wartime necessity.[85] But we can see that, in the debates on the

Morrill Act of 1862 and the creation of the Department of Agriculture, the old ideas retained their potency while newer conceptions of service burbled beneath the surface. Lawyers on both sides continued to invoke precedent, argue the niceties of phrasing, and quote from law treatises. Harlan's outright recognition of the lawyers' dominance only underscored the point that legal arguments and legal procedures continued to shape the discussion.

At the same time, the Congress struggled with its newfound relevance. Ultimately, these wartime exchanges might have been dismissed as quickly as the conscripted armies. The debate over the exact course of the U.S. state, however, did not stop there. The novel demands of the war and even more compelling questions that arose at its end—in particular, the overwhelmingly complex question of how to help the newly freed slaves—forced Congress to continue its consideration of the nature of the U.S. state.

CHAPTER THREE

"A Government of Law"

Sponsoring and Supervising the Freedmen,
Abandoned Lands, and Refugees, 1863–1865

One might assume, after reviewing the actions of Congress during the Civil War, that in its wake Congress would accept the idea of active and expensive administrative governance by a much expanded and much more intrusive federal government.[1] Surely the problems of physical reconstruction of the national economy alone would require such devices. Added to this, the need to assist millions of newly freed slaves would demand far more than sponsorship and minimal supervision through courts. After all, by the end of the war Congress had declared that freedom for the slaves was to be an irreversible outcome of the war in a draft amendment to the Constitution, the Thirteenth Amendment, whose importance cannot be underestimated.[2]

Congress did in fact take steps to assist the freedmen and women, but these efforts were framed at the outset by a lingering commitment to the republican ideal of limited government. What was more, they were confined within a pervasive attitude toward their intended beneficiaries which in some cases was overtly denigrating and dismissive.[3] When viewed within our context, however, the Freedmen's Bureau debates illustrate second state thinking.[4] For the first time Congress explored the need to add overt, comprehensive, and extensive supervision to its administrative agenda. Discussion of how this supervision was to function—its housing within the existing frame of government, its operation on the ground, the means by which it would be staffed and how and to whom it would report—then laid the groundwork for additional Reconstruction legislation.[5]

Once again, law, legal culture, and the question of legal enforcement were foremost in the debates over the Freedmen's Bureau and subsequent Reconstruction legislation such as the Civil Rights acts of 1866, 1870, 1871, and 1875 and the Fourteenth and Fifteenth amendments. Lawyers naturally took a lead, bringing to them their concerns over the enforceability of law, protection of judges and other court officers acting within the scope of their duties, and the relation between federal courts and state courts. What is important for this essay was the way in which the lawyers' approach to the Reconstruction measures continued the second state notions expressed in the earlier debates on sponsorship. Not recognizing the role that the second state ideas had played in framing the Morrill Act and the Department of Agriculture, one might mistakenly assume that the lawyers' part in inherently legal issues of Reconstruction simply grew out of the subject matter of the latter, rather than including an ongoing and vital interest in the shaping of American government—specifically, "a government of law."

THE AGITATION for a freedmen's bureau originated outside of Congress, in 1863, when the War Department created the three-member American Freedmen's Inquiry Commission.[6] Its report and its recommendations reflected the tension between Radicals' ideas regarding equality and their conception of a limited government. Like-minded members of Congress recognized that it would take a considerable effort to sponsor and supervise a free labor system in the South, but, at the same time, they shared concerns about authoritarian, centralized, and bureaucratic government.

The compromise was a proposal for a temporary agency that would have only limited functions. The model was not the War Department or the federal judiciary but the Civil War Sanitary Commission.[7] Although they were called "Radicals," even the most ardent advocates for African Americans in the Congress did not envision a fundamental rethinking of the national government.[8] Congressional leaders only gradually broadened their goals to a full reconstruction effort in the South.[9]

From the beginning of the war the U.S. Army had to deal with the so-called contraband populations of runaway slaves who increasingly flooded Union positions. Federal troops handled their charges in a piecemeal fashion according to the commanding officer's predilections. While some treated African Americans as little more than children, others recognized their perilous condition and sought to help. A smaller group treated them as fully capable human beings with rights. African Americans within Federal lines had a considerable role in changing attitudes of reluctant army officials away from condescending caretaking.[10]

Flooded with requests for instructions, Congress belatedly took up the issue in 1864. From the reception of the report of the Freedmen's Commission, the would-be Freedmen's Bureau became caught up in a jurisdictional dispute between Representative Thomas D. Eliot of Massachusetts, who favored a War Department bureau, and Senator Charles Sumner, also of Massachusetts, who favored the Treasury Department.[11] There were also familiar obstacles: fiscal conservatism, an ineluctable reluctance to create additional agencies, and the ideology of limited government. The debate on the original Freedmen's Bureau bill reveals in telling detail how far the planners were willing to take the implication of the second state approach.

A Bureau for the Freedmen

On February 10, 1864, Eliot introduced his committee's plan to deal with the persons he and others now labeled "freedmen."[12] Over the objections of Democrats Holman and Cox, whose resistance to the Department of Agriculture and the Morrill Act had never faltered, Eliot related the nature of the problem and how House Bill 51 would deal with it. Eliot had been a lawyer since 1831, when he was admitted to practice in New Bedford, Massachusetts. In between he had practiced a stint in the Massachusetts legislature and one term in the U.S. House as a Whig. Like many other so-called conscience Whigs, he was opposed to slavery and joined the Free-Soil Party in 1855, then the Republican Party. He returned to the House in 1859 and became chair of the newly created Committee on Freedmen in 1863 under President Lincoln's Emancipation Proclamation.

The need for this new bureau, Eliot argued, stemmed from the freedmen's impoverished condition. Exigency demanded action. Freedmen had not yet "learned to be free." Hence, the federal government had to teach them basic entrepreneurial skills. Eliot believed that, with the proper schooling, the freedman was capable of achieving the status of a citizen in the republic. The years of enslavement had not permanently damaged him, only denied him the perquisites to handle life outside of his master's control. Furthermore, Eliot stated that very little was required to give freedmen these skills. A temporary government agency "in the charge of able and administrative men" would suffice. In addition, he asserted that the freedmen would quickly pay the rents for the farms the bureau would give them from confiscated lands. Thus, the government would not have to appropriate a single dollar that would not be paid back with interest in the form of hardworking, law-abiding new citizens.[13]

It was the Republican ideal, New England style: give a man a farm and teach him to read and write, and the rest would take care of itself. But government had a vital role to play, and sponsorship and supervision were inseparable. The United States had incurred a moral obligation to help those whom slavery had debased and Union arms had freed. Eliot's intertwining of religious faith and political theory was a staple of antebellum public speech, but for him it was genuine. Eliot was also aware of European efforts to aid those who had been slaves after emancipation. Although this was not quite the same as the school reformers borrowing of European pedagogical initiative in the Morrill Act debates, it nevertheless demonstrated that the same process of using European models that applied to education and agriculture was appropriate to the lifting up of the freedmen.[14]

Eliot knew, however, that any provision for aid to the freedmen must not exceed the narrow bound of sponsorship and supervision Congress had already drawn. The Freedmen's Bureau was to be the freedmen's "parent or guardian or friend," but only temporarily. Its "superintendents" would aid them in their training period then disappear.[15] Eliot minimized the effort involved, its expenditure, and its impact on the large course of American government. Despite the fact that this bureau would be in charge of settling up to four million former slaves on several million acres across the conquered South with a personnel and budget allocation smaller than that of the land office, the Bureau of Freedmen's Affairs would not constitute a fundamental reworking of the United States federal government.

Even with these acknowledgments of Congress's fiscal conservatism, distrust of executive agencies, and reluctance to do anything that might backfire, his argument stirred concern on the other side of the aisle. Brutus Junius Clay, a Unionist Democrat from Kentucky; Holman; Robert Mallory, another Unionist Democrat from Kentucky; and Anthony L. Knapp (D-Ill.) objected. Three of the men—Holman, Mallory, and Knapp—were lawyers. The inner debate over the second state retained its sectional component. All four critics were from a border state or were raised in and represented a district just across the river from one. Holman's Aurora, Indiana, sat across the Ohio River from Kentucky. Knapp's Jerseyville, Illinois, looked out across the Mississippi River to St. Louis, just a few bends south. Their concerns did not center on the scope of this proposed agency but on the legislation's impact on Unionist landholders in the border states and the South. Despite Eliot's repeated assurances that only lands held by conspirators in rebelling states were affected, the Democrats made plain their objection to the confiscation of Rebels' property.[16]

The connection between the practice of law and the objectors' reasoning was clear. Most lawyering in the heartland involved land disputes—titles, mortgages, contracts for sale, boundaries, and the like. Kentucky land disputes in the early republic, for example, had been particularly contentious.[17] Confiscation for wealth redistribution purposes ran athwart all of the values that the owners of property associated with land. Lawyers for the landowners heatedly opposed legislative efforts to take land under the eminent domain doctrine.[18]

Had this not been enough, all these men suspected the Republicans' plan for postwar reforms, for, if the freedman landowner became a voter (even if the right to vote was not mentioned in the bill), he would vote Republican. Republican plans for reconstructing the South through a freedmen's bureau suggested that the Republicans were trying to ensure Republican dominance of state and national government for the foreseeable future. Mallory, Knapp, and Clay, with Holman prodding in the background, made their party's tactic clear: refocus the Congress's attention on the loyal southern whites and away from the debased former slaves.[19] One way to do this was to talk about the right to property, though there were other, equally effective strands in the argument they wove. The most important among them was that emancipation had been acceptable as a war measure to cripple the rebellion. It should not become an engine to fabricate a new kind of state.

In the negative report on the measure prepared by a minority of the committee, Democratic representatives Knapp and Martin Kalbfleisch, from Brooklyn, New York, raised more objections to the new agency. First, they alleged that Congress did not have the express power to undertake such an activity (the same argument that opponents of the Morrill Act had made, unsuccessfully). Second, the agency would have too much control over their charges, a situation ripe for abuse. This argument was astute for the two objections went to the heart of the proposal. With muffled oars the majority was rowing toward more sponsorship and supervision. But, applied to the freedmen, the measure seemed to contradict the formative ideology of the Republican Party. The Democrats tried to drive a wedge into this opening. The Republican mantra of free soil, free labor, free men, bespoke a rugged individualism, a faith in the capacity of ordinary men.[20] An uncharitable reading of the bureau implied that either the freedmen were not really men, that they were children and needed special help—a view that most Republicans did not accept—or the core values of the Republican Party were a sham.

The two Democrats also warned that every official entrusted with a degree of autonomy would aggrandize and/or abuse his position. This was always a danger in supervision—who could supervise the supervisors? Finally, Congress did not have to act because the judiciary constituted the proper forum for the adjudication of any traitor's guilt, claims to their property, and any and all disputes concerning the freedmen.[21] The last touch was the nicest—for it played to the lawyers' professional pride. If you want to protect the freedmen's rights, do not add administrative agencies to government; merely go into the courts and bring suits.

Eliot responded to these questions—questions that concerned the very nature of federal administration in the second state—with what would be called today a liberal credo. First, the president and Congress's war powers gave explicit sanction to remedial enterprises. Second, the proposed bureau would give authority to a very limited number of people, whose selection would weed out anyone of bad character. Third, Christian charity demanded a swift response to the destitution of the South. He made the very vagueness of the bill's administrative apparatus a virtue. In point of fact, he maintained, "a detailed system of government embodied in the organic law would be unwise and prejudicial to all the interests concerned."[22]

Implicit in this rejection of a more defined agency was a concession that no one in Congress knew exactly what this agency would do, how it would perform its tasks, and how to staff it. At the very least its superintendents would function as educators, real estate agents, attorneys for both the government and the freedmen, social workers, relief aid disbursers, adjudicators of competing claims, and keepers of the peace in what was most likely to be a hostile environment. In an age before professionalization a temporary emergency could justify the creation of a temporary officialdom with plenipotentiary powers.

Consideration of the measure continued on February 17, 1864. Cox, the Ohio Democrat and de facto minority leader, spewed forth a mixture of virulent racism, antiauthoritarian rhetoric, and pseudoscientific pontificating.[23] In a long, convoluted, at times rambling diatribe, he blasted this vast "confiscation system. . . . This eleemosynary system for the blacks, and for making the Government of the United States a grand plantation speculator and overseer, and the Treasury a fund for the helpless negro," which would ultimately lead to unfettered interracial breeding. This, in turn, would lead to the death of the black race because physiology tells us that "the mulatto does not live; he does not recreate his kind; he is a monster."[24]

Cox made the connection between race and expansion of the state clear: "When the party in power, by edict and bayonet, by sham election and juggling proclamation, drag down slavery, they drag down in the spirit of ruthless iconoclasm the very genius of our civil polity, local self-government."[25] Race relations has to be the sole responsibility of local authorities. Why? Because a national majority enacting its will on a locality is tyranny. Why? Because localities must always trump national will to maintain true democracy.

Cox's take on Jeffersonian principles was not exactly news in the House. He did not overtly support slavery (he absented himself when the vote on the Thirteenth Amendment took place) or the Confederacy (he supported the war and opposed the peace Democrats). His bigotry was mainstream. He had gone to Brown University, graduated with honors, and returned to Ohio in 1846 to study law and practice for two years in Cincinnati before he took over a Democratic newspaper as a prelude to a political career. On his honeymoon he traveled to England, France, Germany, Switzerland, Rome, Naples, Venice, Sicily, Greece, Turkey, and Smyrna, after which he wrote a best-selling travelogue titled *A Buckeye Abroad*. Like many other Americans who visited Europe, his travels reinforced his love of American institutions while confirming his opinions about the superiority of European peoples over non-Europeans.[26] As much as Cox's attitudes toward race might figure in his assault on the bill, they were in one sense mere window dressing. Cox had a genuine attachment to states' rights ideas of governance and a genuine dislike for innovative administrative instruments.

Representative Kalbfleisch spoke on the measure on February 19 and repeated Cox's aversion to expanding the state without explicitly mentioning race. In addition to the standard assertions of states' rights, Kalbfleisch added two more arguments to the minority leader's scattershot foray. He maintained that the project would require a massive expenditure employing a vast number of officials for which the bill made no provision. The bureau's very task, he said, made it "an exercise of power more despotic than the imperial Government of Russia within any portion of its territory."[27] He referred here to the autocracy of the Russian Empire, with its single head of state with virtually unlimited powers. (This is a caricature of Russia rather than a conception based on extended study. Russian politics at this time included Tsar Alexander II's liberation of the serfs, education and legal reforms, and the strengthening of local elected governments.)[28] Russia manqué, however, served well as a stand-in for the very opposite of what Americans held dear.

Kalbfleisch's second point about the inevitable result of this agency's creation centered on the open-endedness in the bureau's mission. "If Congress possesses the power to provide in this manner for these emancipated slaves, where, let me ask, is the power to end?"[29] While he acknowledged the benevolent mission, he pointed out that a bureau aimed at helping one group could easily oppress another. Bureaus cannot be trusted with power. Kalbfleisch could claim firsthand knowledge, having received his education in his native Netherlands and emigrated to the United States at the age of twenty-two in 1826. Swarms of bureaucrats, their power unchecked—the nightmare of the first state mind-set.

While Kalbfleisch worried aloud about legions of bureaucrats, Representative James Brooks, a Democrat from New York City, returned to the racial issue. Supporters of the measure favored the black man over the white. They had the New England virus. "I know her inexorable, unappeasable, demoniac energy," the Maine born and educated refugee intoned. Why did the New Englanders do this? He linked black racial inequality and Republican greed: "The whole scheme is one of money-making; the whole scheme is one for the use of the black race by northern masters." Brooks saw blacks as the witless tools of Republican financial power in the North generally and in New England particularly. Abolition and aggrandizement of the government went hand in hand. The ultimate victim would be the liberty of the people—by definition white males. He warned his country, "Do not abandon this beautiful theory of States, and convert this Government into a consolidation and centralization, solely for the money-making purposes of this bill."[30]

Brooks, though he studied law, made his living as the owner and editor of the *New York Daily Express*. He spoke as he wrote (or rather wrote speeches as he wrote partisan editorials), in spurts of partisan vitriol.[31] By allying with the masses of freedmen, the Republicans would set loose chaos. Brooks's references to the excesses of the French Revolution as the source for this plan hinted at the dangers of placing the fate of the republic in the hands of the inheritors of the reforming fanaticism of Robespierre and Marat.[32] Charles Dickens's *Tale of Two*

Cities was a best-seller, and Brooks could rely on it "conjuring up the imagery of intolerance, fanaticism, madness, the mob let loose, disorder, the rabble in control, terrorism, violence, mass executions in the name of 'the people' the destruction of all checks and balances within the government."[33] But there was another theme in such references that ran deeper than best-sellers. The United States was better precisely because it was unlike other nations. It rejected central authority; it suspected unitary leadership; it eschewed networks of entrenched bureaucrats. The United States was exceptional.

On February 23 Eliot responded to the Democrats' first day's concerns about the overexpansive scope of the bureau's duties by amending his bill to cover only freedmen and lands confiscated from Rebels.[34] William D. Kelley, a Republican from Philadelphia, took Eliot's cue. His lengthy peroration elaborated the Republican position on new agencies, although not necessarily to his side's advantage. Six foot three, with a "lean frame, deep-set eyes, and florid complexion," Kelley identified with the radical Republicans.[35] He was a man above corruption, dying as poor as he was born. He was also seen as a fanatic, never varying in his course. And on the floor "his cry is that of the plaintive, pathetic, yet powerful in-lungs perambulator." His oratory, according to another correspondent, was from the school of "thunderous flatulency."[36]

Kelley ardently endorsed Thaddeus Stevens's view that the South was an alien nation and should be treated as such. Federal supremacy was incontrovertible, while congressional power to do all that the radicals required of it rested with the Guarantee Clause of republican government.[37] The policy of the nation, he posited, must be consistent with "the great eternal laws of justice, right, and truth" and must adapt when need be to ever shifting circumstances. His concept of changing institutions based on immutable principles was an alternative American credo to the Democrats' outright rejection of new agencies. Furthermore, Kelley asserted that modifying institutions to suit the times brings "the order of society into harmony with nature's laws, and thus secure the prosperity and peace of the people."[38] Kelley implied that prosperity and security lay not with a stagnant approach to governing, but with continuous changes to the apparatus to reflect new needs—all within fixed and uniquely American principles, to be sure. Long before pragmatism became well established as a formal philosophy, Americans of a progressive bent recognized the need for an experimental, evolving state.[39]

While he wore his sentiments on his sleeve, his motives were not so obvious. He was a former deputy prosecuting attorney for the city and county of Philadelphia and judge of the court of common pleas, but there is nothing explicitly legalistic in his plea. More to the point was his own experience. He had been born and bred in Philadelphia but traveled to Boston for his education. There his "foster-mother" had provided libraries, lyceums, and scholars for his development as a person and citizen.[40] His experience left him with the opposite impression of the Bay State than Brooks or Cox, both of whom openly derided the state's preeminence in the war effort. More to the point still, in Kelley's view government served as a benefactor, a provider of schools, means of transport, and policeman of the public order. Kelley saw the positive creative potential in active government sponsorship and supervision.

This did not mean Kelley took a wholly egalitarian approach to the proposed bureau. He analogized the position of the freedmen to those of "orphan children": "They need such guidance and assistance at the hands of the Government as a faithful guardian would bestow." He diminished their independence, agency, and capacity further when he asserted, "all that they need is guidance, fair play in the battle of life, and fair wages for fair day's work."[41] He fell into the trap decades of bigotry and Brooks's cleverness had set for him. He could not advocate aid for them without lamenting their condition, and, when he did so, he had to admit to their inadequacies as citizens.

Although Kelley tried to place all of the blame for the freedmen's ignorance, lack of formal marriages, and general poverty on slavery, he put blacks into a special category that reinforced their difference from other poor denizens of the South.[42] The project of servicing their needs required supervision precisely because it could so easily go wrong. What was more, Kelley presumed a period of tutelage in which the federal government would treat the freedmen in a way similar to its treatment of the Native American tribes—as wards of the state.[43] Without a broader appeal to both whites and blacks, an appeal based on opportunity for all, Kelley's self-described "revolution" in political life would apply to a sharply circumscribed space and time. He was unwilling to make the jump to a full-blown national state that could reallocate land, provide schools, and guarantee the civil rights of all Americans. He portrayed the bureau as a one-time investment that would pay off in a population of taxpayers and consumers of northern products both agricultural and manufactured.[44]

On March 1 Knapp turned to two points essential to the supervisory state: how this agency would be staffed and its scale and scope. He pointed out, correctly, the patronage system would govern recruitment to the Freedmen's Bureau. He noted, exaggerating the case that "the head of any constitutionally governed country upon earth to-day has not a tithe of the patronage which is this day vested in the Executive of the United States."[45] For so long dominant over the executive branch, Democrats recognized the danger when the opposing party had control over appointments. Knapp thus denounced the partisan plan behind the Republicans' creation of new bureaus. The Republican president would appoint his people to the new positions, and they would use their offices to recruit votes and money for the Republican Party. The larger national state under Republican presidents could dominate the country for the foreseeable future. New bureaus were, to his partisan mind, reduced to weapons in the battle for votes.

Knapp's second major point in reference to supervision leaped ahead to a more abstract notion: the kind of society—its feel—which would result from the existence of such a bureau. "The measure, in my judgment, proposes such extensive and important changes in the whole social economy of so large a portion of the laboring population of a part of the United States" that it warranted special scrutiny. One should note his use of the term *social economy*. Knapp's propositions recognized the interrelationship between government agencies and the general structure of human relations. Today the social economy is a term of art meaning those employers in neither the private nor the public sphere—community organizations, voluntary associations, and the like. It is a term of approbation in a growth area of modern employment. In some sense the Freedmen's Bureau anticipated the modern definition. That is not what Knapp meant: his characterization of the result of this agency's presence was entirely negative. "The gentleman in effect asks that the Government shall become the great patroon, the great landlord, the great lord of all of these people; that they are to become the vassals of the Government," he posited. This "feudal system" was contrary to the very essence of a democratic society.[46]

Inadvertently, Knapp had conceded the abolitionists' point. The role the government was to assume with respect to the freedmen would be the same one that the previous owners of slaves had held. The federal government became a surrogate parent. Slaves could hire out their services; now the bureau would ensure that they performed their duties under contracts to their employers. Did not governments in slave states, barring manumissions, limiting what slaveholders could do with their slaves, present the exact same problems of overreaching and tyrannous discretion that the new agency might exercise? Ultimately, Knapp and his fellow Democrats could not escape this contradiction in their logic. His points about the threat posed by additions to the state and patronage, however, would linger. Would-be supporters of new agencies did not have an answer to the staffing question yet.

They did have a strong motivation to act, however, for the danger to the freedmen was grave, the time was short, and the problem had to be solved. Hiram Price (R-Iowa) understood both the potential and the limitations under which the Republican planners operated at this time. He brushed aside constitutional objection on the grounds that this was a situation without precedent. Waxing eloquent, he stated, "This wicked rebellion, forced upon us against our will, and in violation of all law, both human and divine, has upheaved and unsettled the very foundations of society, and thrown its component parts into chaotic wildness, and forced upon us the necessity of reorganization."[47]

For Price the agency was temporary, limited, and nonthreatening because its charges were ready for full participation in the life of the country. "The negro has learned to live with and copy the virtues as well as the vices of the white man," he opined. "He is careful, kind, and affectionate in his disposition." Furthermore, just like whites in the North, "he seeks a fixed habitation, he accumulates property, he grows rich, he builds churches and school-houses, and he feeds, clothes, and educates his children as the white man does." He is unlike the Indian, who "is of a roving and unsettled nature, not domestic in his habits."[48] But how exactly to sponsor and supervise this end? Free labor ideas did not, as the war proved, actuate themselves.[49]

Price closed his remarks with a hopeful prediction. "The industrial energies of the nation will be set in motion, and good will be achieved." Government does not create; it sponsors and supervises. It does not direct; it indicates the direction. Supervision is exercised only lightly and briefly. Only "a proper exercise of vigilance on our part will work from the important events now transpiring around us the great problem of man's political salvation."[50]

By a majority of sixty-one to forty-six the House seconded the question and moved toward a vote. With the outcome predetermined, Eliot allotted the remainder of his time to George H. Pendleton (D-Ohio) to present the Democrats' last word on the project. The bulk of Pendleton's argument concerned the unconstitutionality of the enterprise, but he found time to state that the freedmen "long for the repose and quiet of their old homes and the care of their masters; that freedom has not been to them the promised boon; that even thus soon it has proven itself to be a life of torture, ending only in certain and speedy death." The "enormous powers" given to the agents of the bureau would corrupt not only the personnel but would soon aggrandize into a department that "will last as long as the Government itself."[51] Pendleton had attended the University of Heidelberg in Germany before studying and entering the practice of law in 1847, but his exposure to the centralized German states did not lead him to an affection for national government's growth.

William H. Wadsworth of Kentucky took up the cudgels of the opposition when he asserted that the bill "aims at swallowing up people and States." Federal government supervision constituted an impermissible task in and of itself. He gave full vent to his suspicions, stating, "These bureaucrats, these negro-catchers, meddling with the inhabitants of States, would find their road a hard one to travel."[52] His use of the term *bureaucrats* marks one of the first times this pejorative entered into congressional discussions of the state. From here on, it was a staple of those who would not concede any of the second state contentions.

Aided by a narrow majority, Eliot got the bill to a vote intact. It survived the House by two votes, sixty-nine to sixty-seven. Morrill and Lovejoy joined Eliot, Kelley, and Price, among others. A cadre of second state advocates had formed a party within a party. With an official name change from the Bureau of Emancipation to the Bureau of Freedmen's Affairs, House Bill 51 moved to the Senate.[53]

Sponsorship Requires Supervision

On June 8, 1864, Charles Sumner, chairman of the select committee on slavery and freedmen, presented his committee's substitute for House Bill 51. It closely resembled Eliot's bureau, with two critical exceptions. First, Sumner and his committee placed the bureau within the Treasury Department instead of the War Department. Sumner explained this change as appropriate because "it appears that there is now an organization under the Secretary of the Treasury, and also a system, both of reasonable completeness, to carry out these purposes."[54] In effect the switch was an easy answer to the lingering problem of staffing. The Treasury agents had promulgated regulations for the tending of abandoned lands. Being most familiar with the situation in the conquered areas, they were entrusted with its care.

The second change to the measure countered the objections that Democrats and Unionists had raised in the House over the discretion of assistant commissioners. Sumner reported that he and his colleagues had added safeguards to prevent any abuse. "Here is a safeguard against serfdom or enforced apprenticeship [of freedmen] which seem to your committee of especial value," he asserted.[55]

The alteration showed that the committee was influenced by abolitionist thought. Unfortunately, this admission that the staff needed legislative restrictions opened the floodgates to additional changes to the bill.

Sumner's impressive height, melodious voice, and extensive preparation for his important speeches made him the leading light of Senate debates. But his focus on principles more than the mechanics of any specific legislation, combined with his maverick, arrogant personal demeanor limited his effectiveness. He was a lawyer who had never experienced great success in the courtroom, and one could see why. As debates wore on past his scripted remarks, he often found himself tongue-tied and prone to defective responses.[56]

Sumner urged swift Senate action on this measure as a "charity and a duty." The freedmen were "adrift in the world, they naturally look to the prevailing power." He reassured nervous colleagues that the new bureau would exist only for the "transition period." While the expansive and significantly original mission of the agency might disconcert its opponents, its limited duration and benevolent purposes mitigated its potential for mischief. Sumner confidently concluded: "I am not aware that there is to be any debate about it. Indeed I was not prepared to expect any extended debate on this question."[57] Whether disingenuous or not, Sumner had badly missed the mark. His colleagues had no intention of acting quickly.

William A. Richardson (D-Ill.) marked the divide between the Republican radicals and the Democratic Party, a gulf opened in the House debate. He asserted, "This whole Government is being run to-day on the question of making all interest yield to that of the negro." The program to provide equal treatment and protect the liberties of every American regardless of race was inextricably linked in his logic to the building of the national state. "The thought forces itself upon my mind often that all this effort to keep the negro before the public is for the purpose of attracting attention from the effort to overthrow liberty and establish despotism in this country."[58] He compared the Republican effort to the regimes of Oliver Cromwell and Napoleon I.

Coming down from the rhetorical heights, his specific complaint was with the bill's procedure for confiscating Rebel lands. Richardson maintained that "the object and intention is to have military tribunals to take the place of the courts. You intend to overthrow the judiciary and make a despotism." While it is not true that only a lawyer, and he was such, would see the overthrow of the judiciary as the prelude to tyranny, Richardson had made a telling point. The bureau was an alternative to the regular courts. In fact, it could effectually take the place of courts when freedmen brought complaints against whites. He believed in freedom—"freedom for the white race."[59] The regular courts of law had and would continue to protect that freedom (as they had in his native Kentucky and his adopted home of Illinois). Who knew what the Radicals' bureau would do?

This contingent of the Congress could never reconcile itself to any project that might redistribute the property of whites to blacks, even southern whites' property, though a national majority might favor some measure of it. Although Richardson admitted that his cohort had little chance of preventing passage of the bill, he could take some solace in the fact that November elections might restore his party, in the person of George B. McClellan to the presidency.[60] If they delayed sufficiently, they could end the danger with a veto in 1865, as they had done in 1859 with Buchanan's veto of the land grant college bill.

On June 14, 1864, the senators resumed their exchange. Grimes, who had ultimately supported the Morrill Act and the Department of Agriculture, operated in the same manner on the Freedmen's Bureau. He got Sumner to agree to limit the number of assistant commissioners to four per state and reduce their salaries to fifteen hundred dollars a year.[61] These friendly amendments indicate the tight reign that moderate Republican congressmen felt appropriate for any piece of the administrative apparatus. But it was not the last of the compromises they made.

In another go-around the lawyers monopolized the floor. Thomas A. Hendricks (D-Ind.) expressed his disagreement with the placement of the new bureau. The Department of Interior had received the land office, the care of public lands, and should be the repository of an agency that dealt primarily with land. Zachary Taylor's attorney general, Reverdy Johnson (D-Md.), who defended slavery but not secession, wanted to know why a wartime agency had landed in a civil department instead of the War Department. The proper "control" should rest with a wartime officer. Sumner countered that the confiscated lands rested with Treasury, hence so should the agents managing them. Grimes interposed that the functions to be carried out more closely approximated those tasks under the attorney general. The bureau, he argued, should be entrusted to that office's care.[62]

One could say that this reads like quibbling and could assign personal and partisan motives to it. Salmon Chase, far more radical than Lincoln, was secretary of the Treasury. Giving him the power to appoint the commissioners might aid the Radical cause (and Chase's own hopes for the presidency). Giving the bureau to the War Department put the appointments in the hands of Lincoln and might have thus pleased men such as Grimes, who was a backer of Lincoln. But the key point is not who got what but, rather, the inability of the Senate to decide this single small point. The large issue of supervision nearly broke apart on the shoals of the appointment power.

Who, then, should run the Freedmen's Bureau? The United States government did not recruit its employees from professionally educated graduates of government universities, as France or the German principalities did.[63] Oftentimes the only qualification for office was a connection to the party in power. Any enculturation in the task took place as a result of on the job experience in what one scholar has labeled the "clerical state."[64] But these officials would not operate out of a Washington, D.C., office. They would be field agents with only their own sense of duty to aid them. The discussion of the bureau's placement thus became a surrogate for an inquiry into the desirability of a professionally trained bureaucracy. Supporters of the bill could not entertain the new bureau's true problem of finding trained, expert personnel because that would defeat their balancing act of creating a supervisory agency on the one hand and upholding the still potent antibureaucracy ethos on the other.

That ethos ate away at the project. Willard Saulsbury Sr., a Delaware lawyer, claimed that the grant of power was "arbitrary, without any limitation, without any rules or regulations to govern these masters and drivers in the exercise of their most extraordinary authority." He preferred a limited, strictly defined, and traditionally executed instrument. Furthermore, Saulsbury characterized these would-be trustees as "a swarm of irresponsible officers at extravagant salaries." West Virginia's Unionist senator, Waitman T. Willey, repeated this description of "these irresponsible Commissioners," "this overseer general and these deputy drivers" with their "extravagant salaries."[65]

More compromises followed. On June 27 Sumner acquiesced to Grimes and others' concerns about the vagueness of some of the language. The confiscated land could only belong to "disloyal persons"; the agents could only advise their charges, not compel them in any way; and the salary of the commissioner went from four thousand to three thousand dollars, the last amendment over Sumner's objection. Sumner felt a higher salary was necessary to "secure in this office a first-class man, a person who by character, by education, and by sympathy would be the best fitted possible for the responsible duties we are about to impose on him."[66]

The language echoed Horace Greeley's "good men," and not by accident. Character mattered more than expertise. The bill's supporters did not discuss the lack of any qualifications specified for the personnel in the legislation itself. Personal probity, moral rectitude, and general ability constituted the sole requisites for office (though in fact party loyalty and, in particular, loyalty to the president played a substantial role in the selections). Sponsorship and supervision did not displace the older reliance on probity and character. The second state incorporated these values from older republicanism.

Undeterred and unmollified, opponents of the bill fixed on the enforcement powers of the new agency. Missouri's Unionist Benjamin G. Brown, a lawyer, newspaper publisher, and regimental commander in the Union army, initiated the assault with his comment that "there is no necessity for giving these Treasury agents any more power." Charles R. Buckalew, a Democratic lawyer who had served in the diplomatic corps, offered to amend the bill to subject the confiscations to preemptive court rulings. Again, the alternative to bureaucratic supervision was recourse to the regular courts. Hendricks followed with a proposition to allocate the responsibility of determining "loyalty" away from the bureau to the courts. "These assistant commissioners," he reasoned, "have no machinery or opportunity of determining" said loyalty. It was the old trick. Deny to the commissioners the wherewithal to make factual determinations then decry their inability to do so. "Whether land ought to be confiscated is a question that ought to be tried by the courts, and not in this irresponsible mode." Lazarus W. Powell (D-Ky.) supported this notion, asserting: "They [the agents] are not the proper tribunal to try the question of loyalty. That matter must be submitted to the courts."[67]

Sumner answered that the Bureau was an administrative alternative to courts in a South whose courts he would not trust. He protested that "there must be discretion lodged somewhere," admitting, "The discretion is as well guarded as it can be, and it is a discretion which it seems to me is essential to carry out the purpose of the bill."[68] It is not quite right to say that the opponents of the bureau were opposed to the core creed of the second state so much as they preferred the familiar apparatus of local courts. The lawyers did not fear administration so long as it was imposed by lawyers, in courts.

Thus, behind the new group of amendments lay the presumption that the bureau had to be more legal in its operation. All of these lawyers conceived of legal process in the following manner: a prosecution would follow upon a bad act and indication of the requisite intent; the proceeding would then move to a court, where there would be a contest over the facts; a determination would follow with the opportunity for an appeal. Administrative actions without this process were arbitrary at best, tyrannical at worst. American democracy required not only elections but court-based determinations. Sumner's trust in the discretion of his "first rate" men did not violate these strictures, but neither did he satisfy them. Because he could not articulate an administrative alternative to the lawyer-in-court-centered approach, Sumner's system inevitably fell under suspicion.

Surely, these thrusts and counters had been practiced before—why repeat them? Both sides could have predicted the outcome, so why rehearse the pros and cons? Part of the reason lay in the audience outside the capitol. Members were ensuring that their constituents knew where their representatives stood. But another reason was less cynical. Congressmen were truly groping toward an understanding of what each new proposal meant—how it fit, or could be made to fit, into older sets of ideas about the state. And the lawyers, turning debates over policy into more familiar channels of property and crime, led the way. On June 27 the subject of land confiscation then took a more serious turn, when Lyman Trumbull sought to repeal a provision in the Confiscation Act of 1862 which limited the seizure of land to the life of the disloyal owner. The exchanges on this proposal took up a substantial part of the discussions that followed.[69] The lawyers, like Trumbull, seemed eager to apply their expertise directly to a familiar kind of question, moving tangential issues to center stage. Did the no "bill of attainder" clause of the Constitution limit punishment to the life of the offender?[70] Pennsylvania Republican Edgar Cowan insisted that "no lawyer in this country" could disagree with his reading of the fundamental law. He underestimated the congressional bar. Harlan wanted to criminalize fiscal malfeasance with a penalty of up to ten thousand dollars in fines and/or up to ten years imprisonment. James R. Doolittle (R-Wis.) proposed to make the assistant commissioners subject to military tribunals wherever the federal court system was not operating. Hendricks objected to the enlistment in the army of what he called the likely "public plunderers" of the bureau.[71]

Why did the senators need a corruption clause in an organic enactment when there were general federal laws against embezzlement? Once again, lawyers sweated the details. Doolittle could draw upon many years of familiarity with the underside of human nature, first as a county district attorney in New York State and later as a judge of the first judicial circuit of Wisconsin. Following the repeal of the Missouri Compromise, he switched from his original affiliation with the Democratic Party. These safeguards, he thought, constituted a check on bureaucrats while allowing sufficient independent authority to carry out the task.

Hendricks and Garrett Davis opposed any militarization of civilian officials on the grounds that it violated legal precedents. Civilian officials of the federal government had civil rights under the Constitution. Davis, a lawyer since 1823, resorted to courtroom reasoning when confronting matters of state. The majority bowed to the necessity of providing some court supervision of the commissioners and accepted Doolittle's language.[72]

A series of amendments followed this minor contretemps. The senators seemed eager to edit every phrase in the bill according to their own interests and ideologies. Everything from the lands to be leased, the length of the leases, the exact meaning of the words giving authority over the freedmen, the encouragement of immigration to the North, and the nature of the mission received consideration.[73] It might seem like micromanagement, but in fact the senators were asserting that they could confer supervisory authority on an agency if and only if that agency was constrained by the enabling legislation. The more closely they tailored the act, the less room there would be for discretion and independent judgment on the part of the commissioners. In so doing, the senators were acting less like legislators and more like bureaucrats themselves, turning the Senate into an administrative agency issuing its own rules. Legislation is general and prospective. Precise delineations of rules within agencies were usually the work of their administrators and agents.[74] In the second state framework these functions had to close in on one another because the senators were unwilling to abandon older republican ideals.

Grimes came the closest to voicing a genuine concern over the whole of the project when he questioned Sumner's amendment placing the appointments of the personnel with the secretary of the Treasury rather than the president and, hence, obviating the need for the consent of the Senate. "I never will consent to place in the hands of any Government officer the overwhelming power that is being placed in the hands of this public officer by the proposition of the Senator from Massachusetts," Grimes declared. He went on to describe his criteria for officeholders: "I want to know the character of these men. . . . I want to know whether they are humane men, whether they are Christian men, whether they are honest men and will do their duty to the men, women, and children who are committed to their charge."[75] Both he and Sumner, despite their conflict here, agreed on the critical importance of the Senate ensuring the caliber of the staff of government agencies.

Hendricks tried to turn back the tide one last time: "Here is to be a government within a Government . . . within the government and independent of the

States, and almost independent of the ordinary machinery of the Federal Government, there shall be a government established for the control of the inhabitants of a particular class." By *ordinary machinery* he meant the courts. The oath that the bill relied on to prevent malfeasance "will be found practically to accomplish nothing."[76] A clever trap indeed: advocates of the bureau could not create an independent regulatory institution dedicated to the efficient exercise of its function—that would violate the common faith in democratic government on both sides of the aisle. Therefore, the would-be advocate of additions to the national government had to staff them according to the patronage system. But this would inevitably lead, sometimes with justice, to charges of corruption. The "spoils system" had certainly survived Andrew Jackson's time. The Republicans had adapted well to their political climate.[77]

Zachariah Chandler (R-Mich.), an avid abolitionist and former dry goods merchant, ignored this clever trap. For him necessity demanded the new agency, period. "A negro, Mr. President is better than a traitor," Chandler told the Senate. "I would let a loyal negro vote. I would let him testify; I would let him fight; I would let him do any other good thing, and I would exclude a secession traitor." The war itself had pushed this conclusion on the Republicans. Adding supervision to national state functions constituted a pragmatic effort to meet the exigencies of the day: to deprive the rebellion of labor for its war effort, emancipate the slaves; to punish the slaveocracy for the blood and treasure spilled, confiscate their lands; to cement the victory, give land to veterans and freedmen; to prevent future rebellions, secure a national polity with a currency, railroads, and a northern system of free labor in the South; to limit the influence of the white South in the House due to the addition of formerly "other persons" who had been counted as three-fifths, give those males the vote. The Senate voted twenty-one to nine in favor of the retitled Bureau of Freedmen.[78] The bill returned, amended, to the House.

A Fateful Compromise

On December 20, 1864, after Lincoln's reelection and the Republicans' retention of their majorities in both chambers, the lame-duck House considered the Senate's version of the bureau. Democratic hopes were dashed; the sponsorship and supervision of the slaves' transition to citizenship was much more likely. In a conference committee of both houses, without substantive debate, Eliot received the consent of a sizable majority of his fellow Republicans to think big.[79] On February 2, 1865, he reported that the conference committee had proposed a "Department of Freedmen and Abandoned Lands."[80] Eliot and Sumner had resolved their disagreement over the placement of the agency by giving it its own home and, in the process, thought they had validated the second state's most ambitious project.

Because the commissioner would report directly to the president, the job possessed a degree of prestige that "would give to the department a more desirable character than any bureau could have." The commissioner himself, Eliot predicted, was more likely to fulfill the requisites for the job, namely "great ability, and of experience and character." Nothing new in that: character was sufficient to ensure republican administration. The other sections of the act, he maintained, resembled that of the recently created Department of Agriculture. Therefore, on its face the proposed department represented something new in government structure. But in this first explicit reference to the Department of Agriculture as a model for further government expansion lay the groundwork for further sponsorship and supervision. The legislation made the personnel of the bureau part of the military, subjecting them to the military courts in a region in which the federal judiciary no longer functioned. Eliot expected no additional expense because the leases of confiscated land would ultimately pay for the operating budget. Herein the second state spoke in the essentially conservative precepts of its predecessor: a low-cost, limited organization staffed by people of good character who would carry out a sharply circumscribed, supervisory task with ambitious goals. The measure survived a motion to table it, eighty-three to sixty-seven, with thirty-two not voting.[81]

Yet Eliot could not hide the novelty entirely. On February 9 he admitted, "We are stepping upon untried ground." He urged the House "to do something": "There are difficulties and I cannot undertake to say that this bill is perfect; but I think it will be found to be sufficient for the purposes it seeks to accomplish."[82] All proposals from Congress suffered from the defect of too many chiefs. A singular, complex, and flawless vision exceeded the reach of human effort, much less the murky, negotiated, and contested congressional process.

Despite Eliot's protestations that the activity was bounded by its very nature, the department's function still engendered a spirited resistance from radical Republicans such as James F. Wilson from Iowa and Robert C. Schenck from Ohio. Both were lawyers, not surprisingly. Wilson disliked provisions that "give the control of these persons into the hands of any officer of the Government." He recommended a section that would "let them have the responsibility upon themselves of disposing of their own services in such a way as they may deem proper, receiving compensation therefor."[83] The freedmen should be treated as any other American. They should be able to sue in court for what was legally theirs.

Schenck's objections, and his insight, went further. An independent department suggested a large, permanent effort, when all in Congress desired the opposite. "Now, it would seem proper that there should not be a great system built up, under a new Department, of indefinite duration, to be added to the various other Departments of the Government," he argued, because "this new Department would have relation only to this subject of freedmen, provision for whom is, from the very nature of things, a temporary and fleeting necessity." The general aid provisions affected needy whites as well as blacks. At the same time, the Congress should be wary of creating a state of dependency. "There is always danger that we may keep them [the freedmen] too long in a state of pupilage."[84]

Even Republicans wanted the government to tread lightly. They feared the encroaching leviathan not because, like the Democrats, they anticipated an unstoppable police state but because an authoritative, pervasive service provider threatened the self-reliance ideals of a free labor nation. "The Government therefore, I say, has been compelled, from the very necessities of the case, to sanction this relief, and yet it is irregular and without law, but has been done under the prompting of the higher law and the necessities of humanity," he explained, regarding the army's current operations. "Now, I propose to legalize the system," he said.[85] The legalization came from assigning the task, through legislation, to a bureau under a bill that he, as chairman of the Committee on Military Affairs, planned to introduce.

Eliot made a last-ditch effort to advance the idea of a department before the impending vote. He emphasized its temporary existence. "It will last but for a season," he predicted. The freestanding department setup would eliminate the inevitable conflict between Treasury and War if it were lodged within either. The compromises necessary to secure support had produced a very attenuated though expansive mission. With Holman's call for the yeas and nays, the conference report passed sixty-four to sixty-two, with fifty-six not voting. Despite his reservations, Wilson voted with Eliot, while Schenck defected to the opposition.[86]

On February 13 Sumner introduced the same conference report to the Senate. He justified it with the same arguments Eliot presented to the House. An agency that possessed both the lands and the supervisors independent of either Treasury or War would serve best. Their "new trust, so grave and onerous," relied on the qualities of the personnel. "The man for this humane service should be humane by nature, and should sympathize especially with that race which has so long been neglected and outraged. They must be versed, if I may so express myself, in the humanities of the question."[87] The committee had changed the name from a "bureau" to a "department" and given the agency independent standing, but its policy of doing much with little remained the same.

The following day Garrett Davis began the opposition's critique of the compromise. He regretted especially the place of military tribunals in it, labeling them "absorbing and domineering."[88] There was a clear referent at hand. When the Kentucky legislature invited the Union army, it found that military tribunals came with the soldiers.[89] While he did not go further and accuse the Republicans of attempting to rule by bayonet, the implication waited in the wings. The contest between those who wanted to protect liberties through stronger government policing and those who wanted to protect liberties through limits on government suffused every exchange in the Senate.

On February 21 Sumner replied to the critics. He lamented shameful delay tactics. Apprehensions were misfounded. After all, the department was in service to, not in command of, the freedmen. "The power of the Government must be to them a shield." The legislation proposed a limited mission with ample safeguards. "Are we not all under the general superintendence of the police, to which we may appeal for protection in case of need?" he argued. Anxiety about abuse of power might arise, "but the Presiding Officer can do nothing except according to law, and the Commissioner is bound by the same inevitable limitations." Public officials did not act beyond their expressed duties. They sought only to do their duty. Sumner and his allies did not intend some vast conspiracy. "Look at other clauses, and they will all be found equally innocent."[90] Trust in our integrity, Sumner seemed to say. He sought to no avail to reassure those who were nervous about the venture into a new realm, the second state.

For the next few days Sumner sat impotently while senators continued to register their disapproval of "a" department. Perhaps the most worrisome opinion came from the Republican senator from Maine, Lot M. Morrill (no relation to Justin S. Morrill), who gave the conference report a lukewarm endorsement. He described the difference between the Senate's bill and the conference effort: "One perhaps is a little more extended in its details, one perhaps is a little more permanent in its organization." What was more "there is no difference between the law as it now stands and the law as it will be if the bill now proposed by this committee be passed," he added.[91] One cannot tell from the whole of this Yankee lawyer's remarks which bill is which. We can guess that he considered the departmental form to be the more permanent-looking one. The hold of a label on the senators' imaginations seems strong. While the organization itself possessed no more employees or budget or putative mission than it had as a bureau, the independent status conferred a standing, at least in the minds of its proponents and detractors, which would impact its effectiveness, a boon to some, a threat to others.

Sumner's ultimate attempt to sway the moderate fence-sitters did not raise any new propositions or insights. His remarks were impassioned but not particularly persuasive. When Reverdy Johnson notified the Senate of the availability of a more innocuous alternative, Schenck's House bill for a War Department bureau, he sealed the would-be department's fate. The final tally of twenty-four opposed to fourteen in favor, with twelve not voting, led to the formation of another conference committee to resolve the differences between the two houses. Moderate Republicans Lyman Trumbull, Grimes, Hale, and Howe joined Democrats and Unionists against the department. Sumner was not on the new conference committee, ensuring the moderates would have their way even on seeming superficialities.[92]

A Bureau at Last

The second conference committee report reached the Senate on February 28. It dumped the department concept in favor of a bureau in the War Department. Because the commissioner, clerks, and assistant commissioners would be part of the military, those sections of the bill dealing with enforcement and discipline became superfluous. Once again, the bureau had no budget other than the salaries of the officials coming from the expected revenue from the leases on confiscated lands.[93]

On March 3 two senators, Powell from Kentucky and Jacob M. Howard (R-Mich.), voiced substantive objections. They rehashed the familiar distaste for military government and a new system of peonage. Powell asked the rhetorical questions that by then had the ring of cliché: "Do you wish a bureau for every purpose? Do you intend that every interest of the people of the country shall be managed by bureaus in your War Office and your other Departments? . . . This is a step far in that direction." But no one could refute Sumner's initial point that government was the only recourse—at least no one who truly wanted to help the freedmen. The Senate by votes of sixteen to twelve, sixteen to twelve, and twenty to ten refused to adjourn. The next day, without a tally, the Senate agreed to the conference report. With a vote of eighty-nine to thirty-five, with fifty-eight not voting, the House sustained the chair's acceptance of the substitute that the conference committee offered. Subsequently, seventy-seven voted to accept the bill, fifty two to reject, and fifty-three did not vote.[94] The Bureau of Freedmen, Refugees, and Abandoned Lands went to President Lincoln for his signature.

After Lincoln's assassination and his successor, Andrew Johnson, demonstrated his hostility to the new bureau, Senator Lyman Trumbull's efforts to extend the life of and reform the Freedmen's Bureau demonstrate that some minimal commitment to supervision was inherent in Radical Reconstruction's temporary expansion of the national state. The debate on the extension and, then, merely the renewal of the Freedmen's Bureau added little to the arguments already proffered in the enactment discussion.

Nothing in the brief and troubled history of the bureau tutored its sponsors in the need to give it more independence or to train its personnel better. Without these elements supervision did not achieve its objective and perhaps, though this is the verdict of hindsight, could not. An attempt to make the bureau's supervisory role more effective foundered. Eliot in the House and Lyman Trumbull (R-Ill.) in the Senate proposed to extend the powers of the agency. They sought to add assistant commissioners, a budget separate from the War Department, and reconciliation of the bureau's mandate with the advent of the Thirteenth Amendment—in effect to make supervision more effective.[95] Democratic opponents continued to offer the usual reasons for objecting: states' rights, no constitutional power to act, and the bureau's inevitable descent into corruption and patronage.[96]

Cowan hinted at a common ground that Democrats were willing to share with Republican proponents of the second state when he said, "This is *a Government of law;* and if there is anything in the world which contradistinguishes it from all other Governments upon the earth, it is that it is a Government by law and a government of law." This meant that "whoever undertakes to assert a power or exercise an authority under it, is bound to put his finger upon the law which authorizes it."[97] Although Cowan believed that only his party's position rested on these propositions, in fact Trumbull and the Republicans also acted upon them. No less than the Democrats, the Republicans resisted authoritarian institutions and grounded their proposals in the realm of the law. The problem was to find a form of administrative apparatus which was rooted in the rule of law rather than political patronage.

After the Senate and House approved the revision of the bureau with solid majorities, President Johnson vetoed it.[98] On February 20, 1866, Trumbull's Senate failed to override by only two votes.[99] Beginning May 23, the Congress considered extending the life of the embattled bureau once again. This time Eliot and Trumbull produced an even more limited version of the bureau's function. Again, the discussion did not raise any new ideas nor address the Freedmen's Bureau's central hollowness.[100] The House approved it, and, on June 26, so did the Senate.[101] When President Johnson vetoed this version, both the House and Senate voted to override.[102] As the debates demonstrate, even within the most radical Congress following the Republicans' massive victory of 1866, many members did not fully trust executive agencies with substantial powers, independent personnel, and a centralized orientation.[103] Those who did had to pull in their horns to appease those who did not. Limited to a caretaker role, the Freedmen's Bureau carried out its few functions until its expiration on June 30, 1872.[104]

THERE WERE LAWYERS on both sides of the Freedmen's Bureau controversy. They dominated the debate in an even more forceful manner than they had the Morrill Act and Department of Agriculture debates. Some supported and some opposed the bureau. Above all, they agreed on the need for legal forms and formulas in the creation and operation of the bureau. They did not doom it—circumstance did that—but the limitation of their vision of law's power to supervise what it sponsored in an ongoing fashion, and their commitment to an older, court-based idea of the function of law, laid the seeds for the bureau's stunted growth. At the same time, Sumner's trustees, Grimes and Doolittle's concerns about court jurisdiction, and Richard Schenck's attempt to "legalize," derived from their professional backgrounds, gave them the comfort they needed to endorse a new bureaucracy with sweeping functions.

The debates on the Freedmen's Bureau hinted and events would prove, therefore, that Congress could provide supervisory mechanisms if it wished to. They had completed their experiment in second state thinking. Now they would have to apply that thinking on a more permanent basis with the full participation of a partially reconstructed South.

CHAPTER FOUR

The "Two Great Pillars" of the State

The Supervision and Standardization of Education
and Law Enforcement, 1865–1876

The Civil War and Reconstruction burdened Congress with many unwelcome tasks, including the elaboration of administrative agencies, the employment of thousands of clerks and agents, and the collection and disbursement of billions of dollars. Most of the congressmen who served on the key committees monitoring these measures refused to admit they involved permanent changes in the revered structure or basis of government. As we have seen, this was true of the Freedmen's Bureau, as potentially far-reaching as its programs might have been. But how would the institutional manifestations of second state thinking fare when the justification of wartime exigency was over?

The effort to aid the newly freed slaves through direct action was not the end of Reconstruction legislation, nor was it the last word on the reimagining of the national state. A new generation entered Congress in the years after the war and began to make its mark on the course of the nation. Although the link between overtly Reconstruction agencies such as the Freedmen's Bureau and what followed may seem tenuous, in fact many of the people involved with the Freedmen's Bureau advocated a common school system for the South, believed that successor agencies such as a U.S. Department of Education should carry on the work begun under the Freedmen's Bureau,[1] and supported a more organized system for federal law enforcement. These objects of federal administrative oversight took on greater importance to members of Congress in the first years of the 1870s as the Congress considered the "twin pillars" of the state: education and law enforcement.[2] These measures also implicated an important addition to the second state tasks of sponsorship and supervision of those sponsorship activities—an emphasis on standardization.

THE PUSH FOR a federal department of education coincided with the educators' demands for an expanded federal role in elementary and secondary schools. Strong intellectual continuities ran through the dialogue, a counterpoint of first and second state themes. School reform advocates sought efficiency, a high standard, or at least standardization of teacher training and curricula, and uniformity. At times indistinguishable from the aid to higher education lobby that supported the Morrill Act of 1862, the nationalist common school movement possessed a similar heritage. Early plans all fell afoul of the usual factors: fiscal conservatism, fear of central power, and the desire to protect local prerogatives.[3]

In the years immediately preceding the Civil War, a second movement for federal involvement in education arose, centered on the common schools (that is primary and secondary education). Men such as Horace Mann, Cyrus Pierce, Calvin E. Stowe (O. O. Howard's instructor at Bowdoin), and Henry Barnard spread the gospel of systematic education institutions at the state level first, then they and their successors turned their eyes to the federal government. This effort was largely confined to the areas heavily populated by New England and its transplants in the North, making it appear to be one more manifestation of the cultural imperialism of New Englanders. It did not arise in the South.[4] Most of the members of Congress who expressed their support for the educational obligations of central government shared the same cultural backgrounds, religious households, college and work experience, as the educators. They became part of the communications network that spread ideas both native and from overseas, particularly with reference to the school system in the kingdom of Prussia.[5]

Limited proposals for school reform had gotten a hearing before the onset of war. The most popular came from the fertile mind of Connecticut's Henry Barnard. Born in 1811 in Hartford, the son of a well-to-do merchant family, he received a privileged education in two academies. He made his reputation as the Horace Mann of Connecticut, favoring educational systems that were supported, supervised, and professionalized by the state. His tour of northern and western Europe in the 1840s followed much the same course as his predecessors. He came back with similar notions, adopting the Prussian normal school for professional instructors and state-supervised system for use in the United States. Although his record as an administrator of school systems in Connecticut, Rhode Island, and the new university in Wisconsin was decidedly mixed, if not incompetent, he made his most significant contribution as a networker. Through his many correspondents he promoted their common ideas, shared knowledge, and maintained morale. The formal incorporation of this network set root in his dominating passion, the *American Journal of Education*.[6]

As the bloody conflict unfolded between April 1861 and April 1865, many Republicans believed that it constituted a struggle not just between free and slave but also between two different approaches to education. In simple terms the common school ideals of the North were battling the elite academies and common illiteracy of the South. In order to unify the nation, many in the Republican North wanted to remake the South, and school systems constituted an essential element in this reconstruction of the Union.[7] But how could they do it?

Three proposals vied for the spotlight. Each bowed to republican values and Republican political aims, shared concerns about education in the South, but called for a more nationally uniform system or systems of primary and secondary education and promoted a larger federal role. Charles Brooks promoted his idea in favor of a cabinet-level department with extensive supervisory powers. It would encourage, if not force, a virulently Anglo-Saxon education on the illiterate masses of immigrants, former slaves, and children of the nation. Although in tune with the former Know-Nothing, or American, Party recruits to the Republican Party as well as the systematizers among mainstream educational reformers, this plan had little appeal for anyone else.[8]

The second proposal, Barnard's, envisioned a broad federal role in promoting professional, centralized, school systems without a considered attention to specifics—whether it would be large or small, its location in the executive branch, its powers and its personnel. Like Brooks, Barnard mounted a personal lobbying effort to advance his proposal. The farthest it got was into the hands of a hostile Thaddeus Stevens and his House Ways and Means Committee in 1864.[9]

The most popular concept came from a subsection of the National Education Association, the National Teachers Association. Taking their cue from the successful formation of the Department of Agriculture, these reformers favored an organization that would sponsor educational development but not administer it. The plan came from an Ohio superintendent of schools, Edward Emerson White, whose speeches and writings bespoke a concentrated form of republican, antibureaucracy ethic. He also emphasized American exceptionalism. The United States stood apart from corrupt, bureaucratic, and monarchic Europe. It was the shining beacon of liberty whose institutions could not and should not be altered. Rather than give the national government a powerful, controlling influence over schools, White favored having a group that would simply collect and disseminate data.[10]

White's plan would promote the efforts of state officials to borrow the ideas of others and shame them into improving their own systems to compete with those of other states. This agency could also spur congressional action by providing annual reports on the state of American education. The proposal neatly skirted the concerns of local schoolmen, who feared federal interference but still catered to reformers' desires for a federal role. In this way the national government could standardize the provision of education cheaply, unobtrusively, and without a substantial apparatus. The most important part of White's plan was that it had a ready sponsor in Congress, the newly elected James A. Garfield.

White's push gained considerable impetus with the annual meeting in February 1866 of the newly formed National Association of School Superintendents in Washington, D.C. White reiterated his plan in a well-attended speech before the conference. One evening, after conversing with Garfield, he secluded himself in Garfield's library with pen, paper, and a copy of the organic act of the Department of Agriculture. A short time later he emerged with a statute for a Department of Education. The legislation Garfield introduced from his special committee on education was the Department of Agriculture's organic act "with 'Education' substituted for 'Agriculture' at the appropriate places."[11]

Garfield's Department

On June 5, 1866, between the House's passage of the second bill renewing the Freedmen's Bureau and the Senate's favorable vote on that measure, Garfield introduced House Bill 276.[12] With his substantial, bear-like appearance and stentorian voice, honed through years of preaching the Gospels to the Disciples' Christian movement in Ohio, everyone anywhere in the chamber knew what he wanted.[13] The department's purpose was to collect and disseminate information on educational practices in the various states and, "otherwise, promote the cause of education." Through these functions the commissioner, not a secretary, would foster the "establishment and maintenance of efficient school systems."[14] With the assistance of five clerks, this commissioner would also be required to submit an annual report on the department's activities. Despite the language's simplicity and the humble mission—essentially just a clearinghouse for information—the implicit logic behind the plan and the open-ended "otherwise promote" clause marked Garfield's bill as a second state effort. It went beyond the Morrill Act, the Department of Agriculture, and the Freedmen's Bureau, despite the apparent similarity, indeed the correspondence, in language. For the events of 1860 to 1866 proved that agencies created with limited aims in facially restricted language could expand their purview when the times demanded action.

White and Garfield based their plans on the concept that systematization and professionalization produced uniformly better pedagogical results. They appeased local communities with limited means, the minimal expense, and high expectations, as in the Freedmen's Bureau. Not surprisingly, Garfield (like Wade) was a Yankee in ancestry, a lawyer, and from the Great Western Reserve in Ohio. He represented the new generation of politicians who wanted to add to the national government. Having come of age in the 1850s during the battles over slavery, he came into the Congress a celebrated major general from the Army of the Cumberland who had seen battle in Kentucky and Tennessee.[15] His willingness to experiment with standardization fits the notion that the Civil War constituted a watershed in Americans' thinking about the state.[16]

If the Democrats and conservative Republicans had missed Garfield's meaning, Ignatius Donnelly drove the point home in an extensive speech on the bill. The Minnesota Republican told the House that the close of the Civil War marked the end of the nation's "middle ages."[17] The discredited South had to be integrated into the rest of the Union. The critical gap was the difference between the literate and the illiterate, those fit for citizenship and those not fit regardless of race (a reference to the numbers of poor unlettered whites in the South who had supposedly followed the lead of secessionist elites). The nation had to catch up to "France, Prussia, Austria, and Russia" in the privileging of education. Only then could "the freest, the bravest, and the most energetic" country "become the most enlightened people upon the face of the earth; the foremost instruments in whatever good God may yet design to work out upon the globe."[18] Although Donnelly could not claim Yankee ancestry—he was the son of Irish immigrants to Philadelphia—he, too, understood the importance of education in self-improvement. Nationalism in the form of enthusiasm for public schooling did not have to be of New England origin to give a purpose to the Civil War.[19]

Donnelly buttressed his arguments with figures on illiteracy, a not so subtle hint that the gathering of data was the right way to win a case. The data showed the vast gulf between the northern states' expenditures on schools and that of the southern states. The combination of the two lowered the national average below that of Mexico, a disturbing comparison for all congressmen who had disparaged Mexico's fighting qualities a mere two decades earlier.[20] Giving a sop to opponents of the project, he stated that the proposed department would not have any power to compel local or state governments to do anything. Its powers were those of example and persuasion—like the Department of Agriculture. He closed by arguing that "this is a foundation upon which time and our enormous national growth will build the noblest of structures. The hope of Agassiz may here be realized," alluding to the philosopher Louis Agassiz, "or even that grander dream of Bacon, 'that university with unlimited power to do good, and with the whole world paying tribute to it.'"[21]

Although Donnelly's style and physical appearance created a sharp contrast with Garfield's—the Minnesotan was diminutive and pudgy while Garfield's heavily muscled frame reached almost six feet—they shared childhoods marred by poverty and the early deaths of their fathers. While Garfield eventually gained a bachelor's degree from Williams College in Massachusetts and Donnelly only completed Central High School in Philadelphia, they both loved reading and peppered their speeches with references and classical allusions. Their colleagues often found them pedantic but respected their accomplishments. Both men struggled at this time with financial crises. They were an unusual pair, to be sure, and their paths would diverge, Donnelly to antimonopolism (and a decade after Garfield's death, to the Populist revolt) and Garfield to sound money conservatism.[22] At this point, however, they had come to the same conclusion: federal involvement in education was a necessity.

Donnelly would have gone farther than Garfield. Although he mentioned the limits of the plan, he hoped to force the South to provide education regardless of color through a National Bureau of Education. Although the House backed his resolution 113 to 32 in early 1866, the Congress took no further action on his plan.[23] Donnelly had to play a secondary role to Garfield and the special committee's more limited proposal. Even with this substitution, its title aroused serious objections. Samuel J. Randall (D-Pa.), a lawyer and future speaker of the

House, put forward an amendment that would place the entity in the Interior Department and call it a bureau.[24] It was an echo of the Department of Agriculture debate about which Randall would have much more to say.

On June 8 Samuel W. Moulton (R-Ill.), lawyer, school teacher, and member of the Illinois Board of Education, addressed the bill. Behind it lay this central ethic: "What is the true, genuine spirit of our institutions? Upon what are they founded?" He answered these two questions as follows: "The *two great pillars* of our American Republic, upon which it rests, are universal liberty and universal education." The Civil War and the Civil Rights Act had provided the "machinery" for the first. The second would come from the new department which would "harmonize," eradicate errors, and provide vitality.[25] The former and future Democrat, born and educated in common schools in Massachusetts, had himself harmonized the disparate positions of the two parties in this formulation. The federal government's intrusion into elementary education would not constitute a threat to liberty but would be its guarantor through limited means consistent with the genius of American institutions. The post–Civil War state was merely an extension of the pre–Civil War state, working for the same purposes.

Moulton insisted that Congress had the authority to establish such an agency just as it could promote agriculture through a Department of Agriculture and supervise the public lands through a Department of the Interior. The provision for an education for each child so that he may "discharge all the duties that may devolve upon him as an American citizen" was just as necessary as safeguarding commerce or promoting industry. Moreover, he continued, "this is as much a natural right as the right to breathe the air and to be provided with food and clothing." Moulton tried to strike a balance between the pressing need for education in the South and the proposal's sharply delineated functions. If he did not, he left the measure open to the charge that it did too little to be justified or too much to be allowed. He pleaded with the House to respect the educators' expertise in this matter. "Let us have a common center. Let us have a uniform and harmonious system of education," he implored.[26] While he wanted to negate the fears of authoritarian government, he could not help partaking of the systematizers' ideology. Control reduced errors, improved efficiency, and raised performance.

Maine Republican Frederick A. Pike's comments proved that his party was far from unified on the subject of supervision. Pike, a lawyer too, leveled two objections to the bill. First, the expenses of the department, which included the costs of publishing the data collected, the salaries of the officers, and the housing of the department (most likely in the form of rent, for the capital had little space for new offices) would be substantial. And this was at a time when the government should be paring down the huge war debt. Second, the legislation constituted an interference with localities, such as those in Maine, which did not need its services. "At another time it [the scheme] will be more fully developed. The school-houses of the country will go under the control of the General Government. Churches, I suppose, are to follow next," he predicted. "So, taking the railroads, telegraphs, school-houses and churches it would seem Congress would leave little to us but our local taxation and our local pauperism. If they would take them too I do not know as I would object," he said only half in jest.[27]

Randall seized opportunity to promote his amendment, reducing the department to a bureau within the Interior Department. Earnest, upright, of good family, and born to politics (his father was a prominent Whig), he hated expenditures and big government. His most telling point came from a letter he quoted by "a distinguished gentleman connected with education," a Mr. Frederick A. Packard. Packard referred to France, Holland, and Prussia when he wrote: "We must never forget that with them the people depend on the Government, while with us the Government depends on the people. All our ministers of state and of religion combined cannot open a church nor close a grog-shop against the will of the people."[28]

George S. Boutwell, a Republican former governor of Massachusetts and a lawyer, reminded his colleagues of this when he made his pitch for the legislation. He noted that only relatively minor sums were involved, an investment in the population that would pay for itself in increased entrepreneurship, inventiveness, and industrial accomplishments. He maintained that "the industrial power and productive force of the people of this country are exactly in proportion to the extent of their education."[29] This appeal was practical and conservative.

Garfield took the floor to sway the House on his bill's behalf. He made a comparison with Europe which rejected European influence. "In the Old World," he argued, "under the despotism of Europe, the masses of ignorant men, mere inert masses, are moved upon and controlled by the intelligent and cultivated aristocracy." Garfield characterized the United States as a sharp contrast. "But in this Republic, where the Government rests upon the will of the people, every man has an active power for good or evil, and the great question is, will he think rightly or wrongly," will he choose "industry, liberty, and patriotism" or "anarchy and ruin," an allusion to the choices of the northerner and southerner, respectively. "We must pour upon them all the light of our public schools. We must make them intelligent, industrious, patriotic citizens or they will drag us and our children down to their level."[30]

Garfield had few compunctions about compelling the people of the South to accept the ways of an idealized North. His means marked the incremental advance of the state. Service required data, and data had to be collected. The collection and dissemination of the data would "shame out of their delinquency all the delinquent States of this country." Forced to close his remarks prematurely by the expiration of his time, Garfield closed with quotes from Thaddeus Stevens's speech in defense of the Pennsylvania common school system before the Pennsylvania state legislature. Stevens, himself, could not be present due to ill health.[31] The old arguments against a national plan for education lacked their former strength, for during the war the federal government had experimented with sponsorship, service, and a modicum of supervision.

With Garfield's assent to an amendment cutting the number of clerks to three, the House rejected Randall's substitute sixty-seven to fifty-three, with sixty-three not voting. To Garfield's dismay the House then proceeded to reject the bill itself sixty-one to fifty-nine, with sixty-three not voting. It was largely a vote along party lines. On June 19, during discussion of an appropriations bill, Garfield arranged to have the vote reconsidered. It survived a motion to table by a vote of seventy-six to thirty-seven. After two more votes and Garfield's own promise to get the Senate to make the department a bureau, the House passed the measure by a vote of eighty to forty-four, with fifty-eight not voting.[32] Garfield averted defeat outright, but the debate demonstrated that fiscal conservatism mattered as much as increasing government powers in determining the outcome of the discussion.

A Department by Any Other Name

On February 26, 1867, the Senate considered House Bill 276, sponsored by Lyman Trumbull. "Sir, if we had a head to this branch of affairs, those lands [grants for education] would not have been squandered as they have been in many of the new States." Further, Trumbull argued, "oftentimes from a want of system one of the first things the first settlers who have gone into a township have done has been to sell the sixteenth section for a trifling sum."[33] By collecting information, the department could help Congress enforce its programs.

Trumbull's use of the concept of "system" suggests that he shared his colleagues' in the House faith in formal structures' ability to administer programs. It is important to note that a system, as he and others understood it, did not require large organizations, or bureaucracies, only a regularized, rule-laden process. But by implication more facts gave greater discretion to administrators, if they in fact had discretion at the outset.

Sumner and Dixon (R-Conn.) took the opportunity to assault the South. It was the inverse of the Democrats' attack on the bill by belittling New England. Dixon placed the burden of successful reconstruction squarely on the establishment of common schools in the South. His point was well intentioned, though it betrayed a regional prejudice. "The New England system of common school education must reach the whole mass of our people," he declared, "or this country, perhaps we may say, cannot be sustained." The rest of the country should resemble New England. Sumner seconded this idea and regretted that the United States would not have a cabinet office for education like France had. He and Doolittle both urged swift action. "The question is simply on a name; and I hope we shall not take up time with regard to it."[34]

Trumbull's assertion that the department would play a role in the disposal of public lands for education did not go unnoticed. Daniel S. Norton, a native Ohioan and lawyer, now a Unionist from Minnesota, expressed his qualified support for the bill, but he put his audience on alert that, "if I thought it had the scope that the Senator from Illinois seems to intimate it might have, or that it would lead to legislation which would effect that, I should certainly oppose it." Others such as Garrett Davis were not so ambivalent. Davis, who had opposed the Freedmen's Bureau, did not approve of "this thing of Congress drawing into the vortex of the power of the national Government so many subjects and interests that, according to my judgment, belong peculiarly to the States." The department seemed "more of a device to create officers and patronage and to make drafts on the Treasury than anything else."[35] Like other proposals for new institutions in this time of spoils, every new agency was a prospective job for a loyalist of the party in power. Davis and other Democrats had partisan reasons to object to any addition to the state because the Republican hold on the presidency was likely to resume in 1868 as long as Reconstruction maximized Republican votes.

Richard Yates, like Davis, a Kentucky lawyer but, unlike him, now a Republican from Illinois, reacted strongly against the "tenor" of the statements from Davis and Norton. "I think we have had lessons enough in the past to know and understand that for all time to come we are a nation, not States merely, but a nation, with the powers and attributes of sovereignty as a nation."[36] Yates did not take this spirit of nationalism, however, as the basis to advance a powerful, authoritative, administrative apparatus.

Grimes characterized the proposed department best as a "great central depot of information and influence," going farther than Yates and the other proponents. He asserted that "control" should be inferred as an additional function. With Grimes pressing Trumbull on how coercive the department would be in its collection of "statistics," the debate concluded for that day.[37] Grimes had touched a central issue in second state discussions. *Control* implied *power*. On February 28 the Senate resumed consideration of the measure and, in a tally, rejected the Democrats' amendment. It passed the bill, without a division, unamended.[38]

From Department to Bureau, Again

Concerns that the Department of Education would exercise too much influence were allayed by the incompetence of its first commissioner, Henry Barnard.[39] Republicans supported Barnard's appointment, the educational community was pleased, and the supporters of the new department were not opposed to a New Englander taking the most prestigious educational post in the land. Not one of these groups could say the same after a year. Barnard continued writing and editing the *American Journal of Education*. His annual report was a reprint of several prior editions of the *Journal*. Barnard's prolonged absences from D.C. gave his staff an opportunity for mischief. The president insisted that Barnard take Edward Neill as his chief clerk. Johnson had inherited Neill from Lincoln and found him of like mind in his approach to federal power. Neill took advantage of Barnard's lapses and many absences from D.C. to persuade members of Congress that he, Neill, was better suited to be commissioner. After a time Barnard returned and secured Neill's removal, but not before the damage had been done. Although Barnard would be cleared of charges of fiscal impropriety, his agency would suffer for his perceived failings.[40]

By 1868 nationalistic plans for education had withered.[41] The Department of Education's dismal performance under Barnard had not helped, although in some ways the criticisms of Henry Barnard were unfair. He did not have the authority or the funding to undertake the vast gathering of data required. National problems could not be solved without professional, authoritarian, centralized administrations working from a large pool of information.

On February 28, 1868, Congress decided to demote the Department of Education to a Bureau of Education within the Department of the Interior. Donnelly opened the exchange of views with an amendment to an appropriations bill that would have continued funding for the new department. He restated the reconstructive purpose of the establishing legislation and apologized for the problems, saying that "it has not been fairly tested; it has not had a fair trial; it is proposed to slaughter it before it has had any opportunity to demonstrate its capacity for usefulness." John V.S.L. Pruyn declared his support for Donnelly's amendment and added a defense of Barnard, "one of the best men, if not the best man, who could be found for that office."[42]

Donnelly's amendment brought the department's opponents into the open. Thaddeus Stevens was probably the one trying to kill the department without a general vote.[43] Wasting away from a variety of ailments, he was absent from the chamber when Elihu B. Washburne (R-Ill.), chair of the newly created Committee on Appropriations and widely known as the "Watchdog of the Treasury," railed against this demand on the public fisc.[44] He reported that Stevens "regretted [his vote in favor of the creation of the Department of Education] more than almost any vote that he ever gave."[45] While solid Republicans such as Stevens fought to the hilt against Andrew Johnson and others for the suffrage and civil rights of African Americans, their radicalism did not automatically extend to every federal effort to support these goals.

Washburne, speaking now for himself, decried the environment that had led to the establishment of the department as "the mood for establishing almost everything and making appropriations for almost every purpose." He added that comparisons to other nations were inappropriate because they did not have state systems of education.[46] That this logic was perfectly circular—we cannot have it because we do not have it—seems to have escaped him.

Washburne's colleague from Illinois and chairman of the Committee on Labor and Education, Jehu Baker, did not agree. His brief remarks echoed Moulton's of a year before: "Mr. Chairman, it is clear to my mind that to some extent and in some sense we should have in the Republic a system of national education. . . . It is one of the two great means of unitizing the Republic. Education and intercommunication are the two great means of making us one nation."[47] The lawyer and scholar from Lebanon, Illinois, wanted the opportunities that education provided him to be available to others.

So long as the focus of the debate was education, the department had support. When the focus changed, or was shifted to the aggrandizement of the central state, that support waned. Once again, it was all lawyers on both sides. Fernando Wood (D-N.Y.), whose ferocious partisanship marked him even in this era of ferocious partisanship, led the charge. "We have already established a department called the Freedman's Bureau," he sputtered. "The practical operation of that bureau is to support hundreds of thousands of lazy, idle negroes at the expense of the Government, and the object of this Department of Education is to educate those negroes."[48] For the Democrats in this debate the Freedmen's Bureau's operation served as a stalking horse. By playing the Democratic race card, Wood could turn the achievements of the bureau into their opposite—the Freedmen's Bureau imposed the lazy Negro on the South and saddled the Republican Party on the nation. It and its progeny employed the federal government for "illegal and improper political purposes."[49] In hands like his, the Freedmen's Bureau had become an emblem of improper administrative discretion which could be applied to any even remotely similar program.

Garfield returned to the fray to plead for his bill. There followed a dispute over the manner in which the Department of Education had received the House's approval, with Pike, Washburne, and James G. Blaine, the future Republican presidential candidate from Maine, on one side and Garfield, Charles Upson (R-Mich.), and Henry Dawes (R-Mass.) on the other. Donnelly finally resolved the disagreement by quoting from the *Globe*. The contretemps concluded without a distinct outcome but strongly indicated that Barnard's mismanagement had encouraged critics of the Department of Education.[50]

On February 24, 1869, in the course of consideration of another appropriations bill, the Department of Education again became a topic for discussion. Once again, in 1870, a member of the Committee on Appropriations, Glenni W. Scofield (R-Pa.), sought to reduce the department's budget and eliminate the department.[51] Scofield was a former district attorney and a judge of the Eighteenth Judicial District of Pennsylvania. Benjamin F. Whittemore (R-S.C.) intervened to prevent both actions. Whittemore, unlike Scofield and most of his colleagues in all of these debates, was not a lawyer but a minister. It is not surprising that a Republican from South Carolina would favor any kind of federal aid to education in the South. Scofield's motives are unclear.

John F. Farnsworth (R-Ill.), like Garfield and Whittemore, had served in the Union army. He was also a lawyer and, despite his avid support for other elements of radical Reconstruction, he saw no great need for federal involvement in education. "What earthly use to the Government is this Department of Education?" he queried. "And why not, if you have a department of education, have a department of religion, or a department or [of] blacksmithing, or of shoe-making? Why multiply these departments?"[52] Of what value was the Department of Education to the United States government? Without fanfare Farnsworth had reversed the polarities of the discussion. Now the government's interest itself was the object of concern against which the contribution of its agencies and departments had to be measured. Would they make government more effective? Seen in this light, asking, "Why multiply these departments?" did not repeat the old Democratic slippery slope objection. Instead, it introduced a simple calculus for measuring the value of administrative novelties.

Using his own internal cost-benefit analysis to come to the conclusion that the result did not justify the expense, Farnsworth continued, "The Department of Agriculture is about as far as it seems to me we ought to go in this experimental business of creating departments."[53] War experience had not produced a unified opinion on the second state. Farnsworth's innovative contribution to the debate went unremarked at the time, but it demonstrates how subtle shifts in attitude toward new agencies took place within the traditional framework of ideas.

The younger members, lawyers and Union officers, did not object to sponsorship and supervision, but some wanted more congressional supervision of its own creations. John F. Benjamin (R-Mo.) proposed eliminating all but the commissioner's salary from the appropriation. He entered the war already a lawyer and rose from private to brigadier general. He challenged the House members to "tell where the office was located, or what it had been doing, or what had been the result of its labors." An extraordinarily gifted patent attorney, state law reformer, and civil service reformer, Thomas Allen Jenckes (R-R.I.), picked up this gauntlet, reminding the House of the purposes of the department: "By this appropriation we do not propose to educate the people, but we undertake to create an exchange where ideas can be passed back and forth through this national office, and where the commissioner of the different States can obtain information concerning European systems of education and anything that would aid in the progress of education."[54]

Farnsworth replied, "But a gentleman stuck up here in the third or fourth story of some building in Washington, surrounded by a dozen clerks writing essays or compiling learned statistics to be sent to the constituents of my friend from South Carolina, who never were inside a school-house, and who will not be able to read them for a year or two, and who will not be able to understand them for five years—of what earthly use is such information as that?" The congressman could not comprehend the advantage to education professionals of a professional report tailored to their needs. Practical use was still his yardstick and the common schools before professionalization his model. Scofield's amendment reducing the budget succeeded, but his amendment to abolish the department by 1870 failed.[55] Its opponents had to settle for demotion.

The new bureau fell into the Interior Department, the "Department of the Great Miscellany."[56] But this was not the end of the controversy over the federal role in primary and secondary education. From 1869 to 1870 many radical Republicans wanted the Freedmen's Bureau educational functions transferred to the Bureau of Education, now under the leadership of President Ulysses S. Grant's appointee, John Eaton. Eaton had left the Freedmen's Bureau for a short stint as superintendent of schools in Tennessee. Although it would not be a successor to the Freedmen's Bureau as such, under his leadership the Bureau of Education would play a critical role in fostering the second state approach in future debates.

Good Legal Housekeeping

The stillbirth of efforts to create standardized, centrally administered education policy did not reflect the sum total of Reconstruction additions to the U.S. state. As the Freedmen's Bureau and the Department of Education met their respective fates, Congress chartered a new organ, the Department of Justice. Although its advocates did not depict it in this fashion, it provided the kind of standardized, uniform, centrally directed supervision which the earlier planners had proposed. If all its congressional supporters did not justify it as a vital tool in the enforcement of federal civil rights but as little more than a long-needed house-cleaning measure, within it nevertheless were the seeds of a very different federal bureaucracy than had previously existed. It was the very model of the second state philosophy.

Before 1870 the attorney general possessed very little power and a tiny staff. U.S. attorneys operated under their own recognizance, dependent, like the U.S. marshals, on local authorities to carry out their functions. Like the marshals, they received pay in the form of fees for each function they performed. Appointments to these positions constituted part of the substantial patronage network. In short, federal law enforcement mimicked national-state relations, weighted toward local power.[57]

This situation became more unwieldy after the 1840s, when the legal activi-

ties of the various branches received permanent staffing in the form of department solicitors. These staff attorneys handled the legal work of their respective
office, further dividing the efforts of law enforcement among the various organizations in the administration. This state of affairs presented a formidable obstacle to congressional oversight. Furthermore, many congressmen saw the situation as inefficient. In the aftermath of Civil War spending, the resulting debt,
and the subsequent drive to cut taxes, then expenditures, Republicans and Democrats could agree on a restructuring of the legal services in the executive to promote solvency, proper management, and clear lines of authority.[58]

Senator Lyman Trumbull's persistence, among others, eventually persuaded
his colleagues to consider two measures, one from William Lawrence (R-Ohio)
and another from Jenckes. The Joint Committee on Retrenchment reported a
modified version of Jenckes's bill on February 25, 1870. But the measure constituted far more than a simple reorganization of the solicitors serving the U.S.
executive agencies. It propounded a tremendous centralization of authority in
the attorney general (in his absence the solicitor general). What was once a loose
confederation of offices was to be a hierarchical bureaucracy with considerable
strategic force.[59]

One would expect considerable debate on the implications of such an enormous shift of power to an agency of the national government. Instead, debate
was perfunctory. On April 26, 1870, Jenckes presented the committee's "bill to
establish a department of justice."[60] His presentation merely summarized the
nineteen sections. The measure moved all of the solicitors and their officers into
a department under the attorney general and his new deputy, the solicitor general. In addition, the attorney general received exclusive authority to offer the
legal opinions of the United States government. The U.S. marshals and U.S. attorneys now fell under his direct supervision, with the explicit power to "make
all necessary rules and regulations for the government of said department of justice, and for the management and distribution of its business." The legislation
prohibited the use of outside counsel. The Department of Justice would provide
in-house lawyering for the federal government unless the attorney general
demonstrated a special need.[61] One scholar described the cumulative effect of
this proposal as a "definite action to establish that which the founders had
feared—a centralized agency to administer a growing body of federal law."[62] It
supervised and standardized federal law enforcement.

Jenckes had seen how second state programs engendered fierce opposition.
Therefore, he framed the measure as a reform without any kind of a Recon-

struction tint. It was not a new department "but simply [a move] to transfer to an existing Department some things properly belonging to it, but which are now scattered through other Departments." The new Department of Justice would harmonize the legal opinions of the United States government. For lawyers consistency and uniformity in law are greatly desired and this measure would provide both. The law offices in the Treasury, Interior, War, and Naval departments existed independently of the attorney general. The new department would "make one symmetrical whole of the law department of this Government." The second hoped-for outcome constituted the considerable savings that would result from not engaging outside counsel. From the onset of the Civil War, Jenckes reported an outlay amounting to several hundred thousand dollars paid to private attorneys to conduct litigation on the U.S. government's behalf, no longer necessary with in-house counsel.[63]

Both the savings and the "unity of decision, a unity of jurisprudence," would follow from this consolidation of law offices under a single head.[64] It was the same language and argument that Donnelly, Banks, and others had used to support the need for the Department of Education. The idea that one person could manage an organization better than many stood in stark contrast to the older conventions of collective management, but by now the arguments for centralization and consolidation were familiar to Congress and, couched in inoffensive terms, seemed unobjectionable.

That Jenckes could not only get away with using this type of argumentation but incurred little to no questioning suggests several important conclusions. It is possible, of course, that the measure was seen as a belated addition to the "organic acts" of 1789, in which the First Congress created the departments of War, State, and Treasury to support the secretaries of war, state, and treasury. The attorney general was the only cabinet-level officer without a department. This explanation, however, fails to account for the timing of the new department's birth.

Congress might have been, again somewhat belatedly, taking control of some of the functions of the presidency. The budget for the new department and its senior officials would all require Senate confirmation. This may in fact be true—Congress had proven that it wanted to manage Reconstruction closely, and many of the functions of the new department would directly concern Reconstruction. Indeed, this move by Congress, coupled with the timing of the new department's creation, suggests that the role of the attorney general and the scope of federal law enforcement itself had changed dramatically during and after the Civil War. Exigency once again dictated a step toward a larger national state.

If the goal took the form of a reduction of expenditure and/or eliminating confusion, the first state impulse would be confounded. Supposedly, politically neutral reform did not inspire a response because it did not raise fears of the leviathan. Second, if the outward effect of the proposal did not seem to favor a section or party, then it would receive bipartisan support. Third, the Civil War, whether in its psychological effect or the emergence of a truly national, industrialized economy, convinced some legislators that government operations should conform to contemporary managerial innovations in industry and commerce. At the center of these developments were the concepts of efficiency and control.[65] Jenckes proposed that, in operation, a single head actually aided congressional oversight of the federal government because, "if any error is committed we shall know who is chargeable with it. We have then the assurance, if he be the proper person, that the office will be administered economically."[66]

William Lawrence provided another line of defense of the new department: "It devolves all legal duties on the proper law officers of the Government, and will thus secure efficiency in legal services, economy in the expenditures therefor, and prevent the danger of favoritism and the lavish expenditure of money." Efficiency was an irrefutable argument, although Lawrence could not prove it would result. Instead, the term had gained a kind of automatic credence. To substantiate his points, he gave concrete examples, including seven separate outlays over the course of eight years to one attorney named William M. Evarts, totaling $47,500.[67] The implicit accusation amounted to an indictment of Andrew Johnson and the Lincoln administrations for funneling money to political favorites for legal services. Evarts's fees were for negotiating settlements for Union shipping losses to Confederate gunboats built in Britain and Johnson's impeachment trial. Although the fees were consistent with his reputation as one of the foremost trial attorneys in the United States, they were immense. After the successful conclusion of these services, Evarts also received a brief term as Johnson's attorney general.[68]

With a law degree from Cincinnati Law School and nearly thirty years experience as a lawyer in private practice, a prosecutor, a judge, and a law journal editor, with a brief stint as a colonel in the Civil War, Lawrence knew how to frame a successful argument. Like his lawyer colleagues, his speech resembled a legal brief. For all intents and purposes it succeeded. Even though unreconstructed Democrats such as "Sunset" Cox questioned him briefly, they ultimately expressed their support for the measure. The only serious challenge emerged when Horace Maynard, a committed Unionist from east Tennessee, disputed a part of

Jenckes and Lawrence's argument that a single department would harmonize the government's jurisprudence. The Amherst graduate and lawyer correctly pointed out that the heads of the departments were authorized to make their own decisions regarding their legal obligations. They were under no obligation to follow the advice of the attorney general or even to consult him. "If they have to interpret the law and execute it accordingly, how are we to prevent it?" he asked.[69]

Again, one might inquire why the measure had found such favor. True, economy and efficiency were shields against the conventional assault tactic of limited government adherents, but the Department of Justice had something more going for it. It was a lawyers' bill, and it viewed the operation of government in lawyerly terms. It would provide the kind of professional expert advice and service that lawyers understood. The Department of Justice would be the government's law firm. No practitioner could deny the legitimacy of this sort of organization.

When the bill's consideration resumed on April 28, Jenckes and Lawrence accepted criticisms from Garfield and Logan on the army's judge advocate general and the navy's judge advocate general place in the legislation. Jenckes then answered Scofield's about whether or not cabinet officers were bound by the opinions of the attorney general with a definite no. Scofield responded that "the bill only takes care, then, that these officers shall be well informed on legal questions; and if afterward they choose to go wrong they are responsible." Garfield added, "The decisions of the law officers are to be recorded in a single office."[70]

The compromise between those who favored a more effective national state with the new functions and those who were suspicious of the state can be discerned in the silent interstices of the debate. Congressmen could aggrandize the administrative apparatus of the federal government if they could cloak their proposals in the language of the old republican synthesis: government growth to secure liberty and democratic government. The Department of Justice, a centralized administration of a growing body of federal law, thus became an easier to monitor and cheaper alternative to more decentralized and private market arrangements. It was a masterful, lawyerly, sleight of hand.

The House voted overwhelmingly without tellers to record the names to send the bill to the Senate. It reached the Senate on May 4, 1870. Unusually, the Senate's consideration of the measure did not last nearly as long as that of the House. Only five senators spoke more than a few sentences, and they all endorsed it. The opposition hardly participated at all and, then, only to voice unexplained qualms. William T. Hamilton, lawyer and unreconstructed Maryland Democrat, said only, "The name strikes me very sensitively," before he withdrew his objection to having the bill read. His political opposite, Charles D. Drake, lawyer and radical Missouri Republican, protested a quick passage of the measure because he believed it was "of too great importance to be passed under the present order of business."[71] The bill's proponents also did not add much to the discussion which had not already been offered in the House.

Trumbull admitted he was unable to give an opinion on "its details," but he had "looked over it somewhat" and recommended that the Senate consider the bill. New Hampshire Republican James W. Patterson served as its chief sponsor and presenter. In his relatively brief remarks he promised that the department would save the outside expenses and produce "harmony in the legal business of the Government." With only mild questioning from Thomas F. Bayard Sr., lawyer, peace advocate Democrat, and son of James A. Bayard, Patterson easily brought the bill to a second and third reading and, then, passage by acclamation on the second day of consideration, June 16.[72] As passed, the Department of Justice would play a considerable role in Reconstruction, belying its nondescript origins.[73]

The debates on the Department, later Bureau, of Education and the Department of Justice seemed to mark the limits of second state thinking. One could go this far but no farther. While that might be true in implementation, it turned out not true in the elaboration of the core ideals of the second state. Congress was still feeling its way toward an approach to governance. Future proposals would clarify the issues further.

Subvention or Subversion? George F. Hoar and His Bill

At the end of the debates over the Department of Justice, a first-year congressman returned to the subject of educational reform in the South.[74] In June 1870 George F. Hoar of Massachusetts introduced a measure that would have appropriated monies from the general revenue to the support of common schools in the South. Hoar sat on the House Committee on Education and Labor, generally a backwater for legislation, but his proposal was not just a rehash of older ideas of sponsorship and service in education. Hoar added to his bill a means of supervising the use of federal funding: federal officials appointed for the purpose.[75]

The idea of having direct federal subsidies for education predated the war. Financially strapped teachers and schools and public education advocates were always on the lookout for additional revenue. Joining them in the aftermath of the Civil War, the Peabody Fund as well as northerners who toured, wrote, and publicized the educational needs of the freedmen and women of the South lobbied for federal help.[76] Radical measures for sponsoring schools as part of Reconstruction proved disappointing, but, beginning in 1870, the reformers found a new champion in John Eaton Jr.

Born on December 5, 1829, the eldest son of a farmer in Sutton, New Hampshire, Eaton was a career bureaucrat. After graduating from Dartmouth College, in 1854, he found work as a school teacher in Toledo, Ohio. There he became superintendent of schools in 1856. Later he enrolled and received a degree from the Andover Theological Seminary, and, as a newly ordained minister, Eaton volunteered to be the chaplain of the Twenty-seventh Ohioans upon the outbreak of hostilities in 1861.[77] He headed the army's provision of aid to runaway slaves, the "contraband." Eventually, Eaton became superintendent of the freedmen's department, which had as one of its functions the provision of schooling.[78] After brief service in the Freedman's Bureau, Eaton became a newspaper owner and operator in 1866 in Memphis, Tennessee, where he continued his fight for the radical Republican cause. When the legislature created a public school system, Eaton readily accepted the appointment as its first, and last, superintendent in 1869. Eaton did not have to wait long for another task. Grant appointed him the second commissioner of the Bureau of Education in 1870.[79]

Eaton's tenure as commissioner of education has been alternately criticized and heralded as the triumph of diminished, mediocre bureaucracy.[80] When he took office on March 16, 1870, he inherited an agency teetering on the brink of elimination. His bureau's resources consisted of a six thousand dollar a year salary for the commissioner, two clerks, and the dwindling support of the common school movement. Eaton set the tone for an entirely different course for his agency in a speech before the National Teachers Association in August 1870. He promised to work for federal involvement consistent with the states' preeminent role in primary and secondary education.[81] The Bureau of Education would promote schooling. He proceeded to lobby congressmen to convince them of the usefulness of his bureau, encouraging lobbying efforts, conferences, and associations through unsolicited mass mailings of the output of his agency and public speeches; he coaxed, cajoled, and exchanged favors in order to receive

nationwide information that was essential to his lobbying efforts.[82] In this political pragmatism lay his success as well as the limitation of his strategy. With
his reports in their pockets, like-minded politicians could see how supervision,
administration, and federal support for education came together.

As a rule, congressmen were not political theorists. In fact, it was just the opposite: they preferred practice (and interest) to theory. When they generalized
or waxed eloquent in debate, they tended to import the commonplaces of the
day, from which they pragmatically selected ideas fitting their position. The
emerging second state concept thus came in bits and pieces, sometimes pulled
together nicely, sometimes awkwardly juxtaposed. But in Hoar the concept of
the second state found its first consistent and self-conscious voice.

Hoar was born on August 29, 1826, to a well-connected and distinguished
family in Concord, Massachusetts. His ancestry went back to the early years of
the Bay colony on both sides. Through extensive genealogies Hoar was related
to Roger Sherman, signer of the Declaration of Independence, as well as the
prestigious Shermans of the Civil War and post–Civil War years. The Hoar family could also boast its share of luminaries, including Hoar's older brother Ebenezer Rockwood Hoar, who briefly served as attorney general under Grant. One
could say that he embodied New England's history and traditions literally as well
as figuratively.

Hoar was also that rarity among the members of Congress—an intellectual.
His childhood consisted of a strong mix of play, genteel associations (family
friends included Ralph Waldo Emerson and Henry David Thoreau), Unitarian
worship, and formal schooling. His education swiftly proceeded from academy
to Harvard College when he was sixteen and to Harvard Law School in 1849.
He was an extraordinarily busy attorney in Worcester, eventually becoming a
member of Emory Washburn's distinguished Massachusetts law partnership in
1853. He also married that year and remarried one year after his wife's death in
1861.[83]

During these years of private practice Hoar was politically active, associating
with the political interests consistent with his state patriotism. His political beliefs combined his conception of national patriotism, the principles of Unitarian
tolerance, the Hamiltonian program for the sponsorship of industry, and opposition to the slaveholding South. As a member of the Free-Soil Party in Massachusetts, he easily won a series of state offices beginning in 1852, including state
representative and state senator by 1857. He retired briefly from state politics to
attend to his law practice during the war but accepted nomination for and won

a seat in Congress in 1868. His networking as a lawyer gave him a substantial number of backers throughout the state which enabled him to run for office without the formal assistance of a political machine.[84]

Hoar refused to pander to his constituents and preferred to take an independent course that he could defend later. He favored women's suffrage, fair labor laws, an open door policy on immigration, religious tolerance, and temperance. He opposed nativism, though he conceded that its policies were a prophylactic against infiltration by "foreign ideologies."[85] His identification of the Republican Party with his beliefs and the Democrats with the treason of the Civil War created in him a peculiar mixture of righteousness, egalitarianism, elitism, and obstinacy. All of this was on display in his support for federal involvement in education in June 1870.

Hoar knew that his predecessors had fought for federal support for common schools in Congress and lost. Could he turn the tide? He had a quick tongue in debate, an erudite breadth of references, and a fiercely principled morality that came down like a hammer blow on his opponents. His oration on June 6, 1870, most likely carefully prepared and memorized beforehand, demonstrates that Hoar fully understood the idea of a second state and, perhaps more important, was willing to articulate its premises.[86]

His argument resembled a legal brief not because Hoar's training had prepared him for law alone, for his education had been broad and his interests wide, but because Hoar likely knew that any moderates he needed for a majority wanted to act within constitutional strictures. He based the authority to carry out his massive undertaking for federal support for primary and secondary education on four clauses in the Constitution, all but one of which were staples of the Civil War and Reconstruction debates. Federal common school authority rested squarely on the power to guarantee a republican form of government to each state; the power to appropriate for the general welfare; the implied powers, or "necessary and proper," clause; and the citizenship clause of the Fourteenth Amendment. While the "necessary and proper" and general welfare clauses' justificatory implications are self-evident, Hoar's use of the guarantee clause, his primary focus, exemplifies his position best. Put simply, the only way the federal government could truly ensure republican government was to provide a universal, common school education for all when the states did not.

Hoar insisted that the Civil War led to a single nation governed "only by an irresistible central power prohibited from doing wrong and constrained to do right in those things which are essential to republican liberty." He noted the changes in the economy from animal power to steam and electricity meant those nations that once dominated the world, such as England and France, would be undone by those such as Prussia that were committed to universal education. He implored his colleagues, "Let not America incur the disgrace of lagging behind all civilized nations in that popular education of which she set the first example."[87]

Hoar's view echoed an *Atlantic Monthly* article from 1871 entitled "The New Departure of the Republican Party," written by Massachusetts Republican Henry Wilson. In tune with the older Yankee Protestant veneration of public schools, Wilson argued the task was similar to the one Prussia had undertaken in Germany.[88] Like other supporters of a more active role for the national government, Hoar looked abroad for inspiration. In case his listeners had any doubt about whether he wanted a Prussian system for the United States, he placed the Prussian ruling class in the same category of tyrants as the leaders of the southern rebellion. "Unless this national education is practicable, unless it is to be accomplished," he warned, "the tyrant, the despot, the monarch, the noble, the slaveholder are right." The choice, Hoar declared, was stark. "There is no middle ground between men educated and men enslaved." That concession to the received wisdom of American exceptionalism done, Hoar expressly made his bill a Reconstruction measure: "The blood, the treasure, the life which have been poured out like water will be wasted."[89]

Hoar, being new to the game of words in Congress, did not know how hard his predecessors had had to work to gain approval for the Morrill Act and the new departments. Under Speaker James G. Blaine of Maine, who had made his opposition to agencies such as the Bureau of Education known, and Democrats such as "Sunset" Cox, now a representative from New York, H.R. 1326 slumbered until January 28, 1871, in the lame-duck session of the expiring Forty-first Congress.[90]

Although fully in the orbit of the second state, Hoar's ideas could not escape the gravitational force of the old sectionalism. He believed that reconstruction of the South could only take place once northern institutions were successfully transplanted to the South.[91] The Hoar bill's title, an exaggeration at best, hinted at its possible impact—"a bill to establish a national system of education." Its actual provisions were far more modest, but they nevertheless reflected a commitment to supervision and standards. When the president certified that a state did not have a school system available to all, regardless of color, he could authorize the secretary of the Interior to appoint a state school superintendent and district supervisors who would appoint inferior, supervisory personnel. The money for construction of school buildings and salaries would come from a Treasury Department–administered property tax in proportion to the state's population. A state could avoid the imposition of a federally administered school system if it acted within one year of the president's certification. Until the state's enactment of satisfactory legislation, the superintendents would be empowered to choose everything from school design to the textbooks.[92] Southern Republicans could not fail to recognize the benefits of the bill for their constituents, and southern Democrats could not fail to recognize that its coercive powers aimed directly at their interests.

It was supervision, sponsorship, and standardization with teeth—and therefore a threat to state autonomy in some minds. Hoar's bill encountered just such criticism from northern Democrats John T. Bird of New Jersey, Thompson W. McNeely of Illinois, and Michael C. Kerr of Indiana and one southern Democrat, Anthony A. C. Rogers of Arkansas. All except Rogers, a businessman of limited education, were lawyers. In their view the "monstrous" plan constituted an unconstitutional, unnecessary, insidious plot to centralize government in Washington, D.C. It would either provide patronage positions to help the Republican Party dominate the country or further a New England conspiracy to enrich the manufacturing and financial interests of New England.[93]

Hoar's supporters were all Republicans, but, before one concludes that party affiliation influenced their views, one should consider that their estimation of the role and purpose of government determined their party affiliation. Edward Degener of Texas, Samuel M. Arnell of Tennessee, William T. Clark of Texas, Washington Townsend of Pennsylvania, James C. McGrew of West Virginia, and William F. Prosser of Tennessee, appearing in that order, shared a commitment to the Republican Party's second state approach. Some of the southern representatives were natives who had opposed secession. Others had moved south for advancement. Some were lawyers. Others were businessmen or professional politicians. They all endorsed Hoar's proposition that universal education was necessary to the maintenance of a free republic. They all viewed the federal authority to act as plain as any other power, such as the ability to establish the Department of Agriculture.[94]

But the legislation's fate rested with moderate Republicans, such as Ohio's Lawrence, who favored federal involvement but faced political realities of anti-integration constituents and their own antibureaucracy views. Unfortunately for House Bill 1326, Lawrence himself, while endorsing the measure's constitutionality with ample citations, opposed the legislation. Lawrence objected to the bill's provision for the seizure of private land for tax and building purposes without a proceeding in court. Like McNeely, Lawrence quoted several founders and cases to buttress his propositions.[95] Once again, a good lawyer could convincingly argue a point in many ways.

Lawrence proposed several operating principles of the second state approach. First, the government should always act in accordance with accepted rules of legal practice. Second, "discretionary powers are always dangerous; but Congress, as the body which speaks the legislative will of the people, should determine their legislative wants."[96] Congress should not delegate matters of policy to an executive officer. This view of the limitations of delegation anticipated the United States Supreme Court's view of the matter when regulatory agencies such as the Interstate Commerce Commission began hitting its docket.[97] Third, "all past experience proves that each State can better judge of its local wants and supply them more efficiently and economically than the national Government."[98] The national government should only act in the case of a state's failure to do so.

The public responded predominantly in the negative. While the chairman of the Republican Party, the National Labor Union, and some educators endorsed the measure, the National Educational Association, E. E. White, the National Association of School Superintendents, and representatives of the Catholic Church registered strong objections.[99] They all feared that a national system would limit local autonomy, permanently relegating them to inferior status. A national, authoritarian educational bureaucracy might well squelch local initiative in favor of uniformity. Experimentation, variation, and the influence of particular local political elites would suffer. This was the fundamental flaw in the second state reasoning on education. To advance their cause they had to provide for enforcement. Besides the fact that the very act of federal funding enlarged the power of the federal government, thus enhancing the national state, enforcement once applied to one region could affect other regions, stirring national opposition.

Unable to secure a place on the agenda of the House, the Hoar bill lay unceremoniously on the House floor toward the close of the session on February 17, 1871.[100] Hoar's bill could not command support from congressional leadership necessary to reach a vote, but the concept embodied in it did not die. Education remained an important policy issue. Its successor, the Perce bill, rectified the Hoar bill's supposed flaws. Legrand W. Perce, a Republican from Mississippi, represented in his person the tenuous nature of the Republican Party's immediate postwar position.[101] He was born June 19, 1836, in New York and graduated from Wesleyan College and Albany Law School, practicing law until fighting broke out. He served in a Michigan regiment, in which he was recognized for gallant service. At the conclusion of hostilities he had risen to the rank of full colonel. Taking advantage of his presence in Natchez, Mississippi, he set up a law practice, becoming registrar in bankruptcy for the southwestern part of the state in 1867. His natural affiliation with the Republican Party suited him well when the Congress instituted its plans for Reconstruction in 1867.[102]

Perce lost the first election for Mississippi's new congressional delegation in 1868 to a Confederate general named William T. Martin, but the voters had voted down the "black and tan" constitution under which the election was held, so a new election followed. This time around, Perce and the Republicans gained a substantial victory. Upon his arrival in D.C., he quickly became associated with Hoar and other like-minded Republicans who favored educational measures.[103] It was in this vein that Perce offered his version of the federal aid to education program.

First, the Perce bill abandoned the federal supervisors. The measure recast its purpose as mere aid to schools—sponsorship—rather than an attempt to establish a national school system. Federal circuit courts were to exercise exclusive and outright jurisdiction over enforcement of the bill's provisions. In what was known as a "right of action," private citizens could sue state and local governments over the use of these monies for education, the misuse of which became a felony. Only the state's acceptance of federal funds triggered enforcement.

Second, instead of garnering funds from general appropriations, the legislation created a national fund supported from public land sales following the precedents set by the Northwest Ordinance and the Morrill Act of 1862. Third, the support would follow from the state's proportion of illiterates. This element arose from an earlier plan for federal funding of public schools which did not make it out of committee. This provision ensured that most of the monies would go to the undereducated South, in particular the newly freed African Americans.[104]

Despite all of these concessions, the Perce bill met substantial hostility. Not the least of the reasons was that, in the Reconstruction Congress, Democrats were no longer a weak minority. Unlike the period immediately after the war, when objecting to Reconstruction was associated with recalcitrant Confederates, it was politically safe to criticize Radical Reconstruction. They attacked all legislation that gave the Republican-appointed federal judiciary any role in local affairs. One must bear in mind that the Civil Rights acts of 1866 and 1871 had put the federal courts center stage in the enforcement of Radical Reconstruction. The division between the parties still centered on their differing interpretation of the range of proper federal action and, thus, the developmental course of the U.S. state.[105] Despite the severe disagreement, as one scholar noted, "both the supporters and opponents of the bill seemed sincere in their desire to avoid anything resembling a national system of education."[106] The Democrats joined in this view through the most outspoken critic of federal aid up to that time, Charles W. Eliot of Harvard University. He denounced any federal measure as injurious to the American system.[107]

In a close tally the House voted to remove the mixed schools guarantee, weakening the measure's ties to Radical Republicanism even further. Only the last minute defection of several conservative Democrats saved it from destruction, due to the now reluctant Radical Republicans.[108] Despite its concessions to all sides, the Perce bill barely passed the House, 117 to 98, with 24 abstentions. Perhaps the most significant attempt, outside of the courts, to expand the administrative apparatus of the national government in the years 1870 to 1880 the Perce bill died in the Senate. Justin S. Morrill, friend of civil rights, the New England system, and integrated schools, who had invariably opposed the slave power, and a loyal Republican who believed in education's formative powers, squelched the measure that served his agenda more than any other. His opposition lay in his strong commitment to the essence of the Land Grant College Act of 1862 which bore his name. Morrill felt that the Perce bill's draw on the public land sales would endanger funds for colleges. To protect his achievement, he buried the new measure in committee as per his prerogative as a U.S. senator.[109]

While Morrill continued his lustrous career in the Senate and, in 1876, Hoar joined him, Legrand W. Perce lost his fight for the Republican nomination to J. R. Lynch, a former slave, now a lawyer and prominent Republican Party politician. Perce left for Chicago, where he became an attorney and real estate investor. He died in 1911.[110] The fight for federal support for education continued with the Burnside bill, the Goode bill, and finally, most significantly, sitting across the 1880s like the Colossus of Rhodes astride the harbor, the Blair bill.

ALTHOUGH MOST HISTORIANS look to the "Compromise of 1877" or the final defeat of the Elections bill in early 1891 as the end of an era of thinking about the U.S. state, one can look to the Republicans' proposals for new institutions as early as 1860. Their legal concepts—Moulton's securing of liberty through education, Yates's evocation of national sovereignty, Jenckes and Lawrence's call for harmony in the law, and Hoar's constitutional arguments—undergirded their goals as well as that of their opponents. Only their common understanding of court-based trusteeships led to a consensus view. This phenomenon would repeat in the years to follow in the vital areas of education, civil service reform, labor strife, railroad regulation, and court reform. But in these areas standardization became an accepted part of the second state mentality, inaugurating a fruitful period of congressional thinking about the scale and scope of the national government.

CHAPTER FIVE

"To Change the Nature of the Government"

Standardizing Schooling and the Civil Service, 1876–1883

As Reconstruction politics expelled its last gasp with the Compromise of 1877, politicians, opinion shapers, and activists such as Carl Schurz became disaffected from the so-called bayonet politics of civil rights, voting rights, and race relations. Their pivotal constituency, the increasingly professional middle class in the North, shied away from the commitments necessary to bring forth a more unified, race-blind, and egalitarian society. But a new set of problems forced U.S. congressmen to revisit the increasing scale and scope of the national government. The second state thought pattern framed the debates as legislators sought solutions to the problems presented by the changing economy and reform replaced reconstruction on the nation's agenda.[1]

Their efforts culminated in the Pendleton (Civil Service Reform) Act of 1883. In retrospect, when viewed alongside the decade long debate on the Blair bill, one can see that these pieces of legislation looked ahead to the foundation for the third state, a fully developed regulatory state. The civil service and federal funding of education, like that proposed in the Blair bill, stem from the concept of "standardization," a key ingredient of the second state. Standardization is a function of government in which government agencies are intended to promote the harmony of industrial, commercial, and educational practices nationwide. As such, it is a step beyond the sponsorship and supervisory roles readily accepted in earlier discussions on items such as the Morrill Act; the Department of Agriculture; the Department, later Bureau, of Education; and the Department of Justice. While direct supervisory proposals such as the Freedmen's Bureau's original form and the Hoar bill had attracted attention, they had failed to gather broad-based support from the prevailing set of ideas in Congress. Contemporaries may not have seen this, but all of the proposals debated in the early 1880s were long in gestation.

A closer inspection of key moments in the debates on these two controversial pieces of legislation shows that the post-Reconstruction strategy for expanding the state was foreshadowed in the second state language of men such as George F. Hoar, Thomas Allen Jenckes, and William Lawrence. The encoded phraseology of efficiency, economy, and responsiveness had emerged triumphant from the latter. Relying on it and confining themselves to it, often preferring silence to a fuller explanation of their objectives, those who wanted new institutions gained their objective—what one opponent lamented would be "to change the nature of the government."

Aid to Common Schools

On June 13, 1882, Senator Henry W. Blair introduced S. 151, to give aid out of the general treasury for state common schools based on the number of illiterates in that state. Until 1890 the Blair bill, as it became known, prompted a series of remarkable debates, now largely forgotten, on the proper relationship between the national and state governments, the meaning of the Civil War and Reconstruction, education in the United States, religion in American life, civil rights, and the appropriate bureaucracies for the republic. But in its day the debate spilled out of the capital and onto the pages of newspapers, pamphlets, and magazines.[2] All this occurred despite the fact that Blair had not even proposed a substantial addition to the administrative apparatus of the U.S. government.[3]

Although the Blair bill generated substantial debate in the Congress in 1884, 1886, 1887, and 1890 as well as 1882–83, only the analysis of the 1882–83 installment—which set the framework for all that followed—forms a part of this work. Contemporary legislation on the civil service, the labor question, regulation of the railroads, and court reform picked up and transformed bits of the Blair bill's oratory, but these pieces of legislation succeeded, while the Blair bill did not.

The originator of this bill to provide a ten-year allotment to common schools was the chairman of the Committee on Education and Labor, New Hampshire Republican Henry W. Blair. Like Morrill, Blair did not have the opportunity to attend college. He was fatherless at two and orphaned at twelve. He managed to attend common schools and private academies only briefly. His work on the farm ended in 1856 at the age of twenty-two, when he studied law in the office of William Leverett of Plymouth. Admitted to practice in 1859, he became solicitor for Grafton County in 1860. After several rejections on the grounds of physical infirmity, he managed to join the fight against the Confederacy, rising to the rank of lieutenant colonel. After several terms in the state legislature from 1866 to 1869, he served three terms in Congress from 1875 to 1879, when he became a U.S. senator. In the intervening years he built one of the most successful law practices in the state. He was a conservative on the tariff and the currency who opposed Chinese immigration and promoted Civil War pensions, but he was also a firm supporter of prohibition, women's suffrage, African-American civil and political rights, and labor.[4]

Like Hoar, Blair did not disguise his purposes, his orientation, or his view of American history in his lengthy introduction to his proposal on June 13, 1882. His presentation hit all of the hot-button issues of post–Civil War nineteenth-century American politics. "There is no truth better established or more generally admitted than that the republican form of government cannot exist unless the people are competent to govern themselves," he claimed.[5] Like Morrill, Hoar, and others before him, Blair proposed the New England common school system as the bedrock of American government. But he did not rely on his audience's acceptance of this principle. He went on to explain why Congress could constitutionally appropriate tens of millions of dollars over ten years.

For him, the key to constitutionality was an expansive view of the state: "In its most enlarged sense it signifies a self-sufficient body of persons united together in one community for the defense of their rights and to do right and justice to foreigners. In this sense the state means the whole people united into one body politic, and the state and the people of the state are equivalent expressions."[6] To back up his definition Blair cited John Bouvier's 1856 law dictionary.[7] He argued that all states by definition had the power to defend themselves. Ignorance was a threat to the survival of the republic. Therefore, the U.S. government, "a state," could defend itself by funding education. In his use of *the state* as a term of art, Blair was the first of U.S. congressmen to rely on that concept.[8] In doing so, the granite state's unusual senator had made the leap from mere custodianship to sponsorship, supervision, *and* standardization. Although sponsorship was nothing new, funding an enterprise out of the general revenues was. Like the Morrill Act of 1862, Blair's bill also stemmed from a desire to sponsor not a locally generated activity but a model form of activity that the locality could not take on.

A casual observer might conclude that Blair was overreaching. The Democracy of the South was hardly likely to favor legislation that empowered the national government over such a vital concern as elementary education. But Blair had anticipated these fears (not a difficult feat considering that they had been repeated so persistently by opponents of the second state). Using data that John Eaton at the Bureau of Education had assembled at his request, he laid out the schooling figures for each state, several European nations, and how each jurisdiction compared to the other.[9] The second state mentality was all about the use of executive branch agencies to gather information for legislators' use. Despite some skepticism about how statistics could be manipulated, there was a growing, widely held belief in the explanatory power of numbers.[10]

Blair also couched his arguments to eviscerate a states' rights critique through his characterization of how the money was to be supervised. Taking great pains to distinguish his thinking from those who would subject the states to forfeiture or suspension of the payments in cases of misuse, he proposed instead to have no strings attached and only one superintendent per state. What was more, the federal superintendent was to be "a citizen of, identified with, and interested for the people of State for which he is appointed."[11] Once again, a would-be creator of a new agency had shied away from the most obvious way to ensure the proper enactment of a national policy of education, a national bureau, and proposed a lighter, familiar, old-style apparatus. Presumably, enforcement would be the threat of federal prosecution for misprision—the misuse of federal funds. It is unlikely, however, that the former county prosecutor was unaware of the potency of this enforcement mechanism.

Blair's opening address was not perfect; it revealed a series of telling prejudices, missteps, and flaws, the first his use of the word *reconstruction* while arguing that the guarantee clause allowed for preemptive action.[12] A wiser wordsmith would have avoided anything that might have conjured up memories of that period. While today we know that Reconstruction was not a *Birth of a Na-*

tion or *Gone with the Wind* horror story but a much more complicated tale of southern white violent resistance to half-baked attempts to establish race-blind politics in the South, the southern Democrats embraced the myths as a drowning man clings to a lifeline.

If the Redeemers in his audience had missed that first reference, more followed. In his praise of learning, Blair gave a version of U.S. history which left no doubts about his sectional affiliation: "But for ignorance there would have been no slave. But for ignorance among the nominally free there would have been no rebellion." If describing support for the Confederacy as ignorance were not enough, he drew the link to present politics in the very next sentence: "The contest we now wage is with that still unconquered ignorance of both white man and black man in all parts of the country which hurried us by remorseless fate to fields of death for four long years."[13] Blair's argument that a national program in support of education would seal the Union victory would have played better in the Reconstruction Congress. Former Confederates, many of whom now occupied seats in the Senate, were unlikely to be receptive to such rhetoric.

Perhaps his greatest error was in depicting education as a continuation of the Civil War by other means. Only through the funding of public schools, especially in the "rebel states," could the nation achieve final victory. "The country was held together by the strong and bloody embrace of war, but that which the nation might and did do to retain the integrity of its territory and of its laws by the expenditure of brute force will all be lost." If he was attempting to rekindle the martial spirit of "the bloody shirt" in the service of education, he was not going to make friends. Whether from insouciance or genuine commitment, Blair did not counter the suggestion that he was reviving the ill will of the war: "This work belongs to the nation. It is a part of the war. We have the Southern people as patriotic allies now. We are one; so shall we be forever."[14] It was a risky gambit tying his proposal to an overtly national purpose in an era in which states' rights Democrats had resurrected their party's fortunes.

On January 9, 1883, in the second session of the Forty-seventh Congress, the Senate resumed consideration of S. 151 and its accompanying legislation, S. 936, for "the establishment of a permanent fund, the interest whereof shall be appropriated to that object [support of common schools, universities] from year to year as it shall accrue."[15] Morrill had made an arrangement with Blair so that S. 936, an expanded version of his bill of 1862, could come up for an immediate vote.

Unfortunately for their plans, John Logan (R-Ill.) objected because the funding arrangement of S. 936 was based on illiteracy rates. As he put it, "A bill can not pass with that provision in it, without debate. I say it can not for the reason that I do not think our people propose to pay the taxes for the schooling of others when they get none of the benefit themselves." His reading of the more literate state populations found that they had no objection to federal funding of schools as long as they received their per capita share. Blair's reliance on the North's desire to win the other Civil War—paying for southern schools—had foundered on the rocks of individual state interests. With its arrangement in shambles the Senate moved into executive session and adjourned before any vote or further discussion could occur.[16]

The "Blair Bill" in the House

On January 15, 1883, the House of Representatives considered its own version of the Blair bill, H.R. 6158. Its sponsor, John C. Sherwin (R-Ill.), from the Committee on Education and Labor, needed the House to suspend its rules so that the body could consider his bill. With a vote of 117 to 11 the House seconded the resolution and began its debate on aiding elementary education in the form of the common schools.[17] Unlike Blair's bill, which provided money on a sliding scale from year to year, Sherwin's bill gave ten million dollars a year for five years. Second, Blair's bill involved the appointment of federal superintendents to look after the expenditure. Sherwin's left it entirely to the state commissioners of common schools. Third, while Blair conspicuously refused to penalize a state for noncompliance, Sherwin's measure suspended payment to a state if it did not report its school data to the national commissioner of education.[18] In spite of these differences, the two authors defended their respective versions in much the same way.

Just as in the Senate, Sherwin encountered opposition from northern representatives who resisted a proposal that would redistribute wealth from their areas to others. In particular, the Democratic representatives such as Roswell P. Flower feared the effect a popular expenditure out of general revenues would have on their efforts to reduce the tariff.[19] But the terms of the debate included, and the participants conceded, that sponsorship, supervision, and standards were legitimate concerns of the nation-state.

The most significant voice of opposition that day, William M. Springer (D-Ill.), knew something of education. He had attended common schools in Indiana before his family had moved to Illinois, where he attended Illinois College in Jacksonville, before clashing with the faculty on his support for Stephen Douglas's Kansas-Nebraska Act. He returned to Indiana for a college degree from the University of Indiana at Bloomington, but his career as a lawyer ultimately led him back to Illinois, where he became involved in state politics. A trip to Europe from 1868 to 1870 did not mean that the traveler became a cosmopolitan, and so it was with Springer. He repeatedly asserted that the bill had no value for his state and had no appeal for its residents.[20]

Springer's defense of an individual state's right to its own wealth did not go unquestioned. Judson C. Clements (D-Ga.), William H. Calkins (R-Ind.), and Albert S. Willis (D-Ky.) disputed the argument that Indiana and Illinois had not gotten any help for their respective common school systems. They forced Springer to admit that both states had received federal land grants in support of their common schools. In so doing, they pointed to the larger issue at stake in a debate over tariffs, redistribution, and schooling. The conception of American government lay at the heart of the matter. The three congressmen, all lawyers, voiced the creed of the second state approach: sponsoring (with some supervision) the welfare of the republic through the funding of beneficial programs that would standardize the activity. Willis argued pointedly, "Only two days ago we voted out of the Treasury eighty-five millions to pay the wounded and disabled citizen soldiers of our country. High as our obligation to them, it is not higher than what we owe to that other and more numerous class of our disabled citizens whose lives are cursed by the blighting effects of vice and ignorance."[21] Backed by statistics, concerned with follow-up, and desirous of enlarging state activity for the sake of a public good, the second state congressmen had taken in their stride the steps from mere dissemination of information to sponsorship to national supervision and standardization. No longer did opponents dismiss the tasks as undoable. They had to rely on principle.

The otherwise curious alliance between a former Confederate officer, Clements, and the former Union cavalryman, Calkins, was only one example of the coming together of people and second state ideas in this proposal. Although the Democracy would revert to its former no-federal-aid-please-we're-Democrats stance when it suited, its number could not only join with Calkins but also with John R. Lynch (R-Miss.), a former slave, in speaking out on behalf of a national funding program. Lynch put it most clearly: "This in my judgment is a very important measure, but one not connected with politics; one for which I think that every member of the House, without regard to political lines or to the section of the country from which he comes, can vote willingly and readily, for it is a measure of justice alone." The more prosperous states "can afford to expend a little of it [their money] in the South for so noble a purpose as that contemplated in this bill."[22] One hundred twenty-nine to twenty, the House adopted the resolution and committed itself to further debate on Sherwin's bill.

On February 24, 1883, Sherwin gave an extensive speech on H.R. 6158. On his mind was the Fifteenth Amendment, denying to states the official power to disenfranchise African Americans. Like Blair, Sherwin emphasized the "urgent need" for this legislation. Special circumstances could override precedent, he argued; the common schools were essential. One of government's purposes was to educate for the "plain reason that religion, morality, and knowledge are necessary to the common good and to the happiness of mankind." Unlike Blair, Sherwin put the blame on the Republican leadership during the war and Reconstruction and associated the high rates of illiteracy in the South with "a race of people different in educational acquirements, to teach whom it was, under that old system of which I speak, held to be a crime." The contrast between the Republican and the Democrat became readily apparent. "The nation not only made them free but it became necessary, it was supposed in the wisdom of the statesmen of that time, not only to make them free, but to make them citizens, and consequently the ballot was bestowed upon them."[23] With elections coming, racialism had made its place in the second state. No longer grounds to attack the second state, racial prejudice had found ways to incorporate second state doctrines of governance.

Sherwin's bill thus did not reflect the old school of the Democracy. He took pains to point out that, even though states had free reign in their administration of the money, the bill demanded that "there shall be no discrimination in its expenditure in regard to color, and . . . that none of it shall be used to support sectarian or religious schools."[24] Because he did not mention it outright, a listener could only assume the last phrase meant the parochial school system northern Catholics had set up as a counter to the Protestant-dominated public schools.

Sherwin's terminology is worth a second look. Describing the apparatus that would carry out the large expenditure, he invoked the language of his day: "It utilizes the machinery that already exists; it uses the engines that are already constructed in the different States for the purpose of expending this money."[25] The railway age was in full swing, and the country was industrializing at a staggering pace. Government officials might be the honest, moral men of the first state ideal, but the organizations in which they worked were now the "machines" and "engines" of government.

Just as Blair used Eaton's Bureau of Education to great advantage, Sherwin raided his committee's hearings and U.S. Census data from 1880 to buttress his case at length. The data showed that the southern states were spending as much per capita as they could afford. Their difficulty stemmed from the paucity of their wealth compared to the North. He also noted the special needs of a section that had segregated its schools. "We may say that it ought not to be so; that those who brought about this state of things ought to suffer for it. But the fact exists; and this is a national question, not a state question," because in a national election "if the ballot is not intelligent, if it is not honest, if it is not republican," then all states were affected.[26] Once humanity had bitten into the fruit of knowledge, it must accept the responsibilities of exile from the Garden of Eden. Once the nation had committed to universal suffrage of populations unprepared for the ballot, the nation had to act. The war had not created the agencies called for in the second state, but its aftermath had.

Under continued prodding, Sherwin expanded on his remarks. More statistics tied the problem of illiteracy to emancipation and enfranchisement. He did not accuse African Americans of abusing freedom or causing trouble in voting. He attributed this peacefulness to their loyalty toward their liberators: "The black man, I believe, has continued true to the Government. I believe generally he has performed his political duties in a praiseworthy manner; certainly much beyond what we had any right to expect from his condition of ignorance. But one great reason for this is because of his attachment to a party that gave him his freedom."[27] The warning was clear. Once the southern states had arranged for the destruction of the Republican Party in the South or the current generation gave way to the next, the nation would confront a horror. One might be tempted to point out that the great mass of illiterate southern whites had posed an even greater danger, in terms of their support for the war, but that would be missing the main point: the South was now reconciled to being part of the Union. Their support for national measures followed, at least for some.

Again like any other proponent of another bureau, Sherwin drew on foreign examples as needed, for inspiration or to frighten. Germany, Denmark, the Netherlands, Sweden, England, and France had school systems. English expenditures exceeded the South's.[28] But he could only draw on the outside world in a limited way. As with many other like-minded proposals, foreign systems of educations were not a model. Information on other nations could only serve a general purpose.

By now, at the tail end of the session, time was short. At the beginning of his presentation he had said that he did not plan to get a vote on his bill that day. When Mills reminded him of it, John H. Reagan (D-Tex.) noted, "The vote had better be taken to-day or it never will be taken." Clements and Joseph Wheeler (D-Ala.) could not be muzzled. Clements wanted to get on the record that the money would be "wholly free from Federal supervision or interference." The South had a special burden to bear because of the special condition of the "colored people." Clements also made an argument that a nonlawyer might have missed. The "Federal Government" was bound by "justice and equity." The Virginia and Georgia cessions to the Congress under the Articles of Confederation had created a "trust" of those lands to be distributed for "the equal benefit of all the states."[29] A trust was a solemn legal obligation whose administration was supervised by the courts. He invoked it to reason by analogy to a new kind of expenditure. The national government acted as a trustee of the people's money and was obligated to use it in their general interest, under rules of equity which all lawyers understood.

Wheeler's defense of the bill was just as erudite as Clement's. The West Point graduate and former lieutenant general of cavalry for the Confederacy quoted from philosophers ancient and modern, the Northwest Ordinance of 1786, the founding fathers, and the Bible, among other sources, in support of a cause, he believed, which served the greater good of the denizens of northern Alabama. Religion, politics, merit, and history all came together to demand temporary funding for the public schools. He, too, offered tabulations of data, emphasizing the second state link between detailed information gathering and policy preferences.[30]

Wheeler's outright contention that it was Christian faith that distinguished education in the United States from that of other historical societies deserves specific mention. In contrast with the hidden meanings in Blair's propositions, Wheeler stated his religiosity plainly: "In this age of enlightenment we are daily more and more convinced that no education is worth having which does not crystallize around the principles of Christian virtue, and that the heart must not lie fallow while the mind is subjected to cultivation."[31] The first-term congressman was most likely making a campaign speech that he could then frank to his constituents, but his overall purposes are the relevant matter here. It is common knowledge that members of Congress on both sides of the aisle frequently had strong religious reasons for much of their legislation.[32]

George M. Robeson (R-N.J.), former prosecutor, brigadier general, attorney general of New Jersey, and secretary of the navy in the Grant administration, pressed his motion to adjourn. Because it was a privileged motion, it took precedence over Sherwin's motion to call the previous question, which would have led to a vote on the bill. Whether it was the lateness of the hour or because they did not want to have to commit themselves to a vote on the bill, the House voted eighty-two to eighty to adjourn, effectively killing the bill.[33] Sherwin's proposal failed by a narrow margin. It turned out that this was the only time the House of Representatives would debate a form of the Blair bill. The Senate would periodically revisit Blair's initiative, but it never passed. It was a bill too far ahead of its time—not so reform of the civil service.

Cleaning House: Civil Service Reform

Civil service (federal job) appointments were part of the executive patronage. Early in the nineteenth century everyone understood they were the gift of the president and his party. For six weeks or so after a new president took office, he or his friends received applicants and petitions for jobs. To the victor belonged the spoils of office. The civil service reform movement in Congress originated prior to the Civil War. Proposals for reform were either enacted on an extraordinarily limited basis or immediately pigeonholed in congressional committee.[34] This made perfect sense within the contemporary political system because no one in Congress wanted a professional bureaucracy insulated from the demands of the congressmen or their constituents. Instead, reform notions were tied to older partisan methods. Thus, Senator Sumner had introduced a bill remarkably similar to the Pendleton Act (not coincidentally, as it was inspired by the same sources in Britain and France) in 1864 but withdrew it from consideration because it failed to embarrass the Lincoln reelection effort, its likely purpose. The civil service reform movement received a second impetus from critics of Andrew Johnson's cynically effective use of appointments to derail Reconstruction, in particular the Freedmen's Bureau. Johnson's attempt to undermine the Republican Party through political appointments spurred Representative Jenckes from Rhode Island to make several proposals for a merit-based reform of the system for federal employment.[35]

Civil service reformers rejected the Radicals' patronage appointments in the North and South but did not replace them with anything like the Continental notions of expert, standing bureaucracies. The reformers wanted a civil service that was above politics but not above democracy—something of a contradiction in terms but wholly comprehensible within the political context of that era. Reformers such as E. L. Godkin of the *Nation,* George W. Curtis, Henry Adams, Charles Francis Adams Jr., and Carl Schurz wanted changes to the American plan. Curtis's lobby originated in Boston under the slightly deceptive title of the Social Science Association, with Henry Villard, an activist who had emigrated from Germany, as its leading spokesman.[36]

To be successful in their efforts, they had to convince a majority of Congress that some reform was necessary. If they had hoped Ulysses S. Grant's elevation to the presidency would further their cause, they met early disappointment.[37] Scandal close to home and a horde of office seekers besieging him induced Grant to call for reform in 1870. The next year Senator Lyman Trumbull added a rider on an appropriations bill giving President Grant the power to frame guidelines for selecting federal personnel. To general surprise, Grant created a commission to fulfill this duty and enforce its results.[38]

Given that presidents were often overwhelmed by federal job seekers to the point of exhaustion, Grant's action was less altruistic than self-serving.[39] A hostile Congress—congressmen also depended on patronage for their own political machines—strangled the commission's funding in 1873. A weary Grant, battered by the internecine warfare within his party and within the ranks of the reformers, acquiesced in the commission's demise.[40]

Civil service reformers found an ally, however, in the new politics of professionalism. By the end of the 1870s an emerging if still inchoate coalition of white-collar workers, college-educated teachers and other professionals, the well-to-do, and a handful of intellectual activists joined hands against the corruption of machine politics. In standard fashion among manufacturers, lawyers, doctors, educators, and social scientists, the civil service reformers formed an organization, the National Civil Service Reform League, with the New York City organization at its head. Their program was consistent with the compromises of second state ideas: to inject the American participatory ethic into the federal administrative apparatus.[41]

In 1881 Charles Guiteau, a disappointed office seeker, assassinated newly elected President James Garfield. In response there was a popular outcry for coherent, fair, and efficient civil service reform.[42] Riding on this surge of publicity and in the face of mounting corruption scandals in the Post Office Department, among others, Senator George H. Pendleton (D-Ohio) reintroduced a bill for civil service reform.[43] On January 16, 1883, President Chester A. Arthur signed the amended Pendleton Act into law.[44]

Although supposedly modeled on the much praised British civil service system, the Civil Service Act of 1883 constituted a uniquely second state system. The president could classify posts as civil service positions by executive order. The act did not specify any timetable or number of positions. The president received a carte blanche, and the success of civil service reform depended greatly on his views and political needs. Once a position became part of the permanent civil service, the proposed Civil Service Commission would administer a uniform exam, make the rules regarding appropriate cause for dismissal, and oversee the execution of its decisions. As with the future Interstate Commerce Commission, the president had to appoint a bipartisan commission subject to the approval of the Senate.[45]

On December 12, 1882, Pendleton reintroduced his bill to the Senate.[46] The proceedings were preserved in the Congressional Record, a Government Printing Office publication that had replaced the privately printed Globe in 1872. This change itself represented the shift in the federal government from the pre–Civil War small, state-dependent, self limiting shape to a government that could rely on its own resources.

In the second session of the Forty-seventh Congress which Pendleton addressed, the Republicans had a majority in the House, 147 to 135. The Senate was evenly divided, 37 to 37, with one senator unaffiliated with either party.[47] One might have predicted a fierce and fairly evenly divided debate, with Republicans bickering among themselves about the exact nature of a civil service for a national state and Democrats firmly in opposition to any addition to the administrative power of the federal government. The actual debate was far more complex and demonstrated how far opinion on administration had advanced since the 1870s. Members of both parties had objections to the civil service as it was and, at the same time, were unsure how to alter it. The elections of 1882 had gone against the Republicans, most notably in New York, where a civil service reform–minded Grover Cleveland ousted the Republican machine's candidate. The lame-duck session that met in December was ripe for action of some kind, but much depended on Pendleton's framing of his proposal's merits.

A lawyer who had attended Heidelberg University in Germany, Pendleton was another of the second state generation in the Congress. He was tied by family and tradition to the revolutionary history of the country. Pendleton himself existed at odds with Democratic Party politics. His successful state legislative and congressional career stemmed from an identification with his hometown of Cincinnati's middle course in antebellum politics. Not either wholly slave or free, neither a classic northern industrial city nor a southern town, neither New

England surrogate nor southern clone, Cincinnati straddled two worlds. He tried to serve both sides of this split political persona with a program of rectitude, limited government, and public mindedness. Now in his second stint as a national politician (his first took him to congressional leadership and a few votes short of the vice presidential nomination in 1864), he had seen national politics from the top. Pendleton thus had a unique perspective from which to advance civil service reform.

He placed the blame for the current state of affairs squarely on the Republicans, just as others in his party supported educational reform by blaming the Republicans. His rhetoric combined romantic fustian and old-fashioned jeremiad. The Jeffersonian ideals of the early republic had supposedly given way to a "spoils system" that was "inefficient, expensive, and extravagant, and that is in many instances corrupt." (Pendleton's history was poor—Jefferson was a spoilsman, and Jackson brought the Jeffersonian system of political reward to its peak efficiency long before the Republican Party was born.) What was more, the Republicans had turned public offices into a political machine in order to rig at least two presidential elections. The system "demoralizes everybody who is engaged in it." Pendleton implored the Senate to sponsor a civil service of "purity, economy, efficiency," to ensure the survival of republican government.[48] His belief that the enlargement of the government led naturally to a threat to "free institutions" "republicanism," and "republican government" partook of the first state's rhetorical style.[49]

In his rhetoric, redolent of the images of pre–Civil War America, Pendleton seemed to be a holdover from the pre–Civil War generation of politicians, and his perspective on how to shape American government was merely proof that first state ideas were alive and well. But the war and Reconstruction had not been forgotten, and Pendleton was not a throwback. Postwar lawyers in Congress had learned a thing or two.[50]

Pendleton's rhetoric aimed not at the Republicans, but at his fellow Democrats, who might fear that a newly instituted civil service meritocracy would steal the spoils they expected to gain in the next presidential election. He promised that the system should be "free for all, open to all, which shall secure the very best talent and the very best capacity attainable for the civil offices of the Government." Unlike Sumner and his like-minded successors, however, Pendleton pointed to the consistency of the proposal with the proper "democratic theory of the Federal Constitution and Government; that its powers are all granted; that the subjects on which it can act are very limited; that it should refrain from enlarging its jurisdiction; . . . that it should scrupulously avoid 'undue administration.'"[51] According to this presentation, reform need not be nationalizing.

Despite his argument, Pendleton's bill inaugurated a shift from pure political patronage to a government with tenured bureaucrats, professionals in particular fields of government operation that required specialized knowledge.[52] The legislation that would bear his name helped create a more powerful state because it separated the servants of power from the governed, a key step to true administrative autonomy and a logical consequence of sponsorship and supervision.

The Republican response to Pendleton's partisan-sounding introduction of his measure demonstrated the complex transformation that had taken place in the debate since the onset of the Civil War. William B. Allison of Iowa, John Sherman of Ohio, and Joseph R. Hawley of Connecticut all agreed on the need for the legislation, though they contested fiercely the Ohio Democrat's characterizations of Republican cupidity and partisanship. All were lawyers and both Allison and Hawley had served in the war, though Allison's Civil War service consisted merely of being the military aide to Iowa's governor. In a refrain other Republicans would echo in the days to come, they defended the Reconstruction era's budgets, appointees, and campaign efforts. Hoar joined them with a prediction that "this scheme . . . will be regarded in the future by the American people almost as the adoption of a new and a better constitution."[53]

Hoar had frankly acknowledged what Pendleton had merely hinted at: the times required and Congress must provide administrative means for the government to protect itself from excesses of partisanship. Pendleton might promote his project as a return to democratic self-government, but Hoar, characteristically, saw to the heart of the measure and spoke candidly of his vision. The bill's beneficiary was not the people but the government itself. Some Democrats conceded that Hoar was right, and they were not happy about it. If they could not derail the bill's momentum, they could slow its passage with obstructions.

The Reaction

The first of the Democrats to speak, Joseph E. Brown from Georgia, rejected the bill's supposed inspiration, the civil service system of Great Britain. "The system that may work well there in a limited monarchy, the policy of which is to maintain an aristocracy, even a landed aristocracy, is not appropriate to a republican form of government like ours," he claimed. Brown rejected Pendleton's embrace of the paradox and suggested that Democrats should wait for their inevitable presidential victory to make any change. Summarizing the philosophy underlying his objections, he stated, "This is a republican government; it is democratic in form, and you have to change the nature of the Government and change human nature also before you will be able to adopt in practice here any utopian theories about civil service."[54]

Despite his pose as a country farmer, Brown's qualifications as a lawyer were almost without equal. He had passed the bar with hardly a blemish and graduated from Yale Law School two years later. In between his local judgeship, four consecutive terms as governor from 1856 to 1865, and membership on Georgia's supreme court during radical Reconstruction, he created a lucrative private practice and invested successfully in railroad and real estate ventures. His return to the Democracy in 1879 after his Reconstruction-induced affiliation with the Republicans marked him and his arguments as the embodiment of practical politics.[55]

That Brown's approach did not persuade all of his fellow Democrats became immediately apparent when James Z. George (D-Miss.) stated, "If political proscription is wrong in the Republican party it will be wrong in the Democratic party." At a later point in the proceedings, George elaborated this disagreement with Brown. The moral impurity of the spoils system presented a danger to both parties. He fervently believed the probity of a Democratic administration could not resist contamination. What was more, "the people mean to have a purified administration."[56] His repeated use of purity evinced the evangelical prism through which he viewed political questions. George, like many of his fellow southern Democrats, attempted to steer a moderate course once they had removed African Americans from the voter rolls. Their Bourbon politics should not be mistaken, however, for Jacksonian Democracy. George, a lawyer who had been chief justice of Mississippi's supreme court, was willing to use national government power to benefit his constituents as he tried to reconcile his pro-development attitudes with his distaste for monopolies, illiteracy, and labor strife.[57]

Despite Pendleton's attempt to frame the reform as an anti-Republican measure to get Democratic votes and George's jeremiad about the baleful influences of greed on both parties, opposition to the bill came mostly from Democrats. This belied the sponsors' portrayal of the bill as a bipartisan reform. Democrats George G. Vest from Missouri, Middleton P. Barrow from Georgia, Wilkinson Call from Florida, John S. Williams from Kentucky, and Francis M. Cockrell from Missouri took turns denouncing the legislation as a Republican trick to prevent the certain to be elected Democratic president from staffing the federal administration.[58] The sectional nature of this counterattack is clear. All had served either in the Confederate government or army, and all but Call were lawyers.

When he was not linking Republican predominance to the influence of the whiskey industry, Vest offered the operating principle of his party toward how to shape the national government in a paraphrase of John Stuart Mill: "local self-government and the right of each individual to govern himself so long as he interferes not with the rights of others." Williams proffered the flip side of this principle when he remarked on the course of American government in recent years. With "an army of office-holders" at his beck and call, "the President of the United States is to-day more powerful than the ruler of any constitutional monarchy in Europe," he declared.[59]

While a number of determined southern Democrats held the floor against swift passage, two Republicans, Warner Miller from New York and Henry L. Dawes from Massachusetts, joined the Democratic defectors, George and Pendleton, to praise the bill. Miller contended, among other things, that the common heritage of Great Britain and the United States made it perfectly appropriate to seek inspiration from that realm. With the exception of universal suffrage and the election of the executive, he asked the Senate, "what great civil rights do we as free American citizens enjoy which we have not taken directly from the English constitution and English law? . . . Our Government was based upon English law. . . . The fact, then, that the system is English should not be any bar to our adopting it."[60] Congress should look past the monarchy to the shared institutions of the two nations. The shared common law tradition had special resonance for lawyers who had studied Blackstone's Commentaries just as easily as Story's or Kent's, though Miller himself owed his living to paper manufacturing and had never practiced or studied law. Perhaps these arguments pervaded the atmosphere so greatly that even manufacturers knew them.

Dawes chose to emphasize the modernizing aspects of the situation. Just as endorsements for the Morrill Act, the Department of Agriculture, and the Department of Education contained references to the need to keep up with changing times, the Yale graduate, lawyer from western Massachusetts, and expert debater and skillful manager of committees reminded the Senate of the reason for the vast increase in personnel.[61] The country was no longer thirteen states confined to the Atlantic seaboard. "It can be administered but little longer in the methods of the past," Dawes reasoned. "It has outgrown those methods adapted for an old system of things never sufficient for them; but it was never dreamt by those who created it that it would be applied to the condition of things now existing in this country," he posited.[62] While those opposed to new functions and institutions saw an insatiable bureaucracy, Dawes and his compatriots saw a developing country that required more and better government to serve the new needs. To what degree aggrandizement of the state and aggrandizement of the perceived need for the state fed upon each other did not enter the discussion.[63]

Thus, the argument dressed itself in familiar code terms: simple need, a set of problems requiring practical solutions, and the civil service reform the least intrusive and most American solution. Advocates of reform did not mention anything more than they had to; they did not expose their arguments to the thrusts of the bill's opponents, nor did they directly reply to its critics. Time moved on, and so must the administrative apparatus of government. Practical men—and lawyers were always practical men—should know this. The second state had its consensus.

A cadre of southern Democrats made one last attempt to alter the bill's impact. Brown and James L. Pugh (D-Ala.) collaborated on an amendment to make selection of classified civil service officers proportionate to state population without regard to examination. This requirement would, according to Brown, "deal justly with all parties, all States, and all sections."[64] Depending on how exactly the commission would interpret this phrase in constructing the tests it would administer, those who had grown up in states with comprehensive school systems would have a substantial advantage in gaining office. Given the South's inadequacy in this area, the national administration, regardless of the president's party, would be filled with northerners who had been schooled in the New England tradition of public education.

Pugh, Brown, John T. Morgan (D-Ala.), and Augustus H. Garland (D-Ark.), all lawyers, addressed the Senate at various times to make their case for Pugh's amendment. They based their arguments for a confederated civil service, one apportioned by state, on the grounds of basic justice and equity. Harking back to the familiar notions of a federal union, their effort praised the original framers and ignored the considerable seismic shift in political weight prevalent since at least the first vote on the Morrill Land Grant College Act in 1858.[65] The fairness-to-each-state proposition resembled the policy behind admissions to West Point and the Naval Academy, though, when Preston B. Plumb (R-Kans.) offered this analogy in support of his substitute for Pugh's suggestion, Brown dismissed the idea as creating a third "privileged class."[66] Most important, however, was the dog that did not bark: even those who wished to amend the legislation acquiesced in the professionalization of the civil service by standard tests. Standardization had become part of the discussion.

The vote on Pugh and Brown's amendment went largely along sectional lines, with a substantial number of absentees. Eighteen voted in favor, including George and Pendleton, with twenty-three opposed, including Bayard, Hoar, Logan, and Justin S. Morrill. There were thirty-five absentees.[67] This particular outcome could validate any one of several possible conclusions. One stands out—a substantial change since the Civil War in Congress members' thinking about the nature of how government should work. At the same time, the vote demonstrated that the sectional divide was still in place, just as it had been with the first vote on the Morrill Land Grant College Act in 1858. The supporters of additional agencies had successfully framed their proposal as a bipartisan reform, which reduced party partisanship. The mood of the country after several decades of corruption and scandal and the assassination of President Garfield forced the Congress to do something.

On December 23 the Senate accommodated the largely Democratic objections by adding proportional selection from each state and territory to the list of criteria that centered on examinations.[68] In this way the Senate finessed the difficulty over whether to have a federal administrative apparatus or a national one based on merit. They would try to have both. The rest of the Senate's time was tied up in Hawley's amendment to prevent the solicitation or giving of money by any member of the civil service for any political purpose and Blair's to prevent the hiring of any one with a reputation for drinking.[69] Suitably discussed and changed to fit the vagaries of those who remained in the chamber, these provisions passed by fifty votes to none, with twenty-five absences, and thirty-five votes to nine, with thirty-two absences, respectively, drinking having more support in the Senate than bribery.[70]

After several more changes that did not affect the substance of the bill, the Senate passed the proposal to "regulate and improve the civil service of the United States" thirty-eight to five, with thirty-three absences. Brown commented that the measure that several of his fellow Democrats voted for, including Garland and Vest, should be retitled "a bill to perpetuate in office the Republicans who now control the patronage of the Government."[71] Despite this bit of raillery, the Senate committed itself to the initiation of a different system of recruitment and promotion for the national administrative apparatus.

Civil Service in the House

On January 4, 1883, the House began its consideration of S. 133. The Republicans had a majority for the first time since 1875, 147 seats to the Democrats' 135. Eleven men represented other parties. The speaker, J. Warren Keifer of Ohio, cooperated closely with his fellow Republicans to manage legislation effectively.[72] Most likely by prearrangement, John A. Kasson (R-Iowa) secured the floor on behalf of the Pendleton bill, as he called it, under a special order and then successfully motioned to have the bill read and ordered the previous question. Under the rules of the House, as Speaker Keifer repeatedly enforced them against the protests of Democratic would-be amendment makers, debate was limited to a half-hour.[73] The Democrats could either vote for or against civil service reform. Given that civil service reform was avowedly their biggest issue of the campaign, the maneuver ensured at least some Democratic support. Under these restricted conditions, only a select few could express their opinions on the matter. None was especially revealing.

The opposition reiterated Brown's remarks. John H. Reagan from Texas and Hilary A. Herbert from Alabama ridiculed the bill as "a mock pretense" and "a pretense—a half-way measure."[74] Both congressmen were southern Democrats steeped in sectional patriotism, bigotry, and limited government. Reagan had been Confederate postmaster general, Herbert a colonel in the Confederate army wounded at the Battle of the Wilderness.[75] They could not help resisting what they saw as a Republican effort to protect federal jobs from a Democratic president to be elected in 1884.

The bill's supporters used their time to assert the minimal justification for any piece of legislation: it was better than nothing. The tactic of saying as little as possible (the chief rhetorical weapon of the antibureaucracy proponent of new bureaucracies) worked like a charm. Kasson even gave brevity a curious twist when he asserted, "The present bill is less bureaucratic than the original."[76] His use of a form of the word bureaucracy likely shows that he meant the changes corrected some of the "evils" of the current system—namely, corrupt rule contrary to the will of the people. With this concept in mind Kasson, like other supporters of additions to the state, could caricature the Pendleton Act as antibureaucracy. Pendleton's paradox had claimed another victim. A Vermont-born lawyer who had practiced in Massachusetts as well as the cities of St. Louis and Des Moines, Kasson had been on enough diplomatic missions in Europe to know the art of being practical as well as the difference between a European bureaucracy and that which prevailed in the United States.[77] His statement served as another reminder of the particular verbal gymnastics at play in the second state.

With the presentations concluded, the House voted not to recommit the bill to committee by 113 to 85, with 91 not voting. The House then approved the Pendleton Act 155 to 47, with 87 not voting.[78] Almost all of the Republicans joined with a smaller number of Democrats, including "Sunset" Cox, to implement an American version of the civil service. Like other enactments to expand the apparatus of the national government, this one also contained the conceptual as well as the institutional compromises necessary to secure working majorities. In subsequent years the price of such compromise would become obvious, as true reform in the appointment process and the operation of the civil service moved forward fitfully.[79]

The Blair Bill Lives, Briefly

On March 18, 1884, Senator Henry W. Blair reintroduced his bill for the temporary support of common schools with the state-by-state allocation based on illiteracy. He did not introduce any new arguments. His valuation of his means did not indicate any change in his approach to government. What he did differently was prove a consensus for his spending plan had grown up around the country. Thus, the letters from reform groups, legislatures, newspapers, and journals of opinion showed the feeling across the country that this vast new enterprise did not yet jar with American conceptions of the proper role of the national government. Once again, the many pages of tables with statistics on local taxes, literacy, spending on schools, and wealth which Blair presented were from the Bureau of Education at his request.[80]

Altogether it was the embodiment of the second state orientation. The use of data, the republican purpose achieved through new means, the sharply limited staffing, the immensity of the project, and the popular agreement that the new conditions required national government action combined with the newly found affluence as a result of the tariff to create a new zeitgeist. It was Blair's particular blind spot that he did not address the more mundane concerns that would play so critical a role in the defeat of his project.

The opponents did not share any particular trait except their profession, law. John Sherman (R-Ohio) spoke against it because he did not trust the southern state authorities with an appropriation that was largely to go to them for their lack of effort.[81] His fellow Republican John James Ingalls of Kansas made the same objection a short time later in no uncertain terms: "If we are to be told that this money is to be expended upon a national theory for the education of the children of this country, . . . and that it can only be expended as the authorities of the States see fit, I have done with the bill."[82] John Logan joined this particular argument's supporters. It seemed that Blair's project was caught in the usual American governance Scylla and Charybdis: those who wanted closer supervision versus those who wanted local control.[83]

Meanwhile, a southern Democrat defended the bill. On March 21 Charles W. Jones (D-Fla.) stated that the Reconstruction amendments to the U.S. Constitution, at least in the Supreme Court's reading in the *Slaughterhouse Cases*, had produced a new kind of "General Government," especially with regard to the emancipated and subsequently enfranchised former slaves: "These people owe their present status to this change in the organic law which made them citizens of the United States, and if there is anything in the reason of the law or in our system of jurisprudence it is that the legislative arm of the Government is always competent to carry out its organic provisions."[84] Just as his Democratic colleagues in the House had remonstrated two years before, Jones agreed with Blair that this was a national issue. The Democracy's unanimity on the constitutionality of federal appropriations was gone—gone south, along with the majority of the funds.

Perhaps not coincidentally, Jones quoted the same poem that his fellow Democrat, James H. Hopkins would recite when Hopkins introduced the bill to create a Bureau of Labor. Jones prefaced the excerpt with this telling endorsement, "After all, in a great country like this the people are the state, and there was as much philosophy as poetry in the utterance of that great namesake of mine on the other side of the water when he said: What constitutes a state?"[85] Blair's proposal had cut across traditional party lines.

When habitually small-state, limited-government men such as Garland could make common cause with those who desired to expand the sponsorship, supervision, and standardizing activities of the federal government, both groups entered into a different way of looking at that national state. Garland's brief on the constitutionality of the bill also showed the importance of proficient legal argument to the debaters as well as their understandable penchant for making such speeches.[86] The issue of supervision entranced them.

The old opposition to this kind of expenditure had not disappeared; it merely was no longer dominant. Samuel B. Maxey's (D-Tex.) remarks were revealing in this regard: "The tendency is to convert this into a parental government, a centralized power, and to strengthen this Government by weakening the States, to strengthen this government by lessening in the people that independence which is the very bulwark and vital force of every State, the *manhood* and individuality of its people."[87] The former Confederate general, county clerk, master in chancery, and district attorney's linking of masculinity and politics was notable if for no other reason than his rhetorical flourish was unusual in congressional debate, at least in the discussion covered thus far, though not unheard of in popular discourse.[88] Moralists, physicians, and philosophers of this time, like their predecessors, made a connection between gender, identity, morality, and political economy.[89]

On March 25 future president, attorney, former Union general, and Republican from Indiana, Benjamin Harrison made the points that would ultimately defeat the Blair bill and, more subtly, summed up the quandary of the second state reasoning: "If it be true, then, that we are not to maintain education in the States; if it be true that we are to discharge our obligations toward the freedmen of the South in this indirect way . . . I submit that we ought to make these appropriations so that they will stimulate, energize, and encourage—not pauperize—the efforts of those States in the direction of a through popular education."[90] Here was the old federalism philosophy in the form of economic and moral degeneracy. Taking federal funds would sap the independence of the states. That this may have been Blair and others' intent seems to have escaped the great Hoosier. Harrison's position displayed the same fear as the older republican, first state idea of a corrupting central power.

His solution was to delegate the matter in its entirety to the localities. "One dollar voted by the people of any school district for the support of common schools is worth $10 given out of the Treasury of the United States. It evinces an interest in education, and guarantees a careful and intelligent supervision." Harrison had placed his faith in local government; the supervisory function could not be entrusted to distant, central authority. Standardization was assumed. Even though the legislation itself placed the matter in the federal courts, and consequently would become an issue for the local U.S. attorney, he nevertheless put greater trust in neighborhood political organs: "Only a local supervision and interest will bring these constituencies that are now so backward in the race of education abreast with the other States."[91] Leave native groups to their own devices. Competition will spur them to greater efforts. Supervision was not just a result of entrusting an issue with a particular group; it had to arise out of interest, a personal investment in the matter. Standards would rise out of competition.

Hoar could no longer hold his tongue. Referring to the provision that required the reporting of statistics in order to receive an appropriation, Hoar declared, "It was that little thing by which Horace Mann revolutionized the education system of New England."[92] Now the cat was out of the bag. The New Englanders had in mind to revamp the educational system of the South not only on the common school model but also according to the more centrally directed, professionalized, teacher-certified system of education the common school reformers in New England instituted in the 1840s and 1850s. They believed in the power of statistics to inform legislatures, spur localities, and standardize the provision of any activity. They wanted all of the second state.

But New Englanders did not oppose frugality. On April 7, 1884, the Senate agreed to Hoar's amendment cutting the initial appropriation and subsequent appropriations, thus reducing the total from $105 million to $77 million. Sherman moved to exclude sectarian common schools from the bill, while Hoar disputed the need to do so. "May I make a suggestion that I think will satisfy everybody?" Blair chimed in. "We need to put this provision in so that the Mormons will not get any of the fund."[93] Religion had a particular impact on these discussions. Former prosecuting attorney Daniel W. Voorhees (D-Ind.), known as the "Tall Sycamore of the Wabash," had included being able to read the Lord's Prayer as one of the objectives of the legislation. Blair, among others, was plainly worried about subsidizing Mormon schools. These remarks indicate the intimate association between Protestant Christianity and public functions such as education. Even what we might term "progressive" thinkers who advocated a positive view of the state's function in this period did not see the conflict between advocating a more expansive national state and their own sectarian views. Sherman had to admit confusion on the issue when Saulsbury questioned him on the recent Ohio court cases that had held, to his understanding, that reading the Bible in common schools was an impermissible violation of the separation of church and state.[94]

As the Senate lumbered toward a vote, another indicator of the importance of legal expertise in congressional debate arose.[95] Morgan offered an amendment that would have taken into account states like his own, Alabama, whose Constitutions mandated that any money received from the federal government go into a fund. John F. Miller (R-Calif.), New York State Law School graduate originally from South Bend, Indiana, asked, "Does the Senator as a lawyer think that that clause would prevent the use of this money for school purposes as described in this act?"[96] This appeal to professional opinion seems a natural one, but it is not.

Reading a constitution and a law side by side to determine their compatibility is not a skill that can only be acquired by reading for the law. Reading for the law is the way to earn permission to practice that skill professionally before a court. That Miller, a lawyer of no little reputation himself, would call upon Morgan's expertise speaks volumes about the special status lawyers held in that forum regardless of their actual proficiency. Morgan had no formal education, and his expertise on Alabama law had come from several years of general practice. His ability to argue, to memorize, and hold forth on various issues earned him his reputation, not his grasp of jurisprudence for which he had little use.[97] In any case Miller spoke as one lawyer to another—another instance of the predominance of the legal profession during this period.

With the time allotted under the special rule for the debate extinguished, the Senate proceeded to pass the Blair bill, thirty-three to eleven.[98] This vote concluded both a complete House and Senate debate on the measure and would go no further. The House never concurred.

BOTH THE BLAIR BILL and the Pendleton Act proposed new mechanisms for dealing with national problems. The Blair bill addressed illiteracy; the Pendleton Act addressed the civil service. Each attempted to standardize, supervise, and sponsor its respective areas with minimal apparatuses, minimal variation from typical practice, and within a certain perspective that may be termed the "second state mentality." While the Blair bill was an obvious attempt at standardization and sponsorship, it was a less obvious attempt at supervision. Its provisions for reporting, treating all children equally regardless of race, and the types of schools eligible were all part of an effort to supervise education. While the Pendleton Act was plainly meant to standardize and supervise the civil service, its sponsorship of the agency was less clear. As the debate progressed, however, the Pendleton Act's debaters could not hide their desire to sponsor a better civil service that would, in the language of an opponent, "change the nature of the government."

Both measures showed the entrenchment of a set of ideas surrounding the creation of new government organs. The gathering of statistics, the sense that new conditions mandated new solutions, the faith in the national government's power to help, and the commitment to solutions that cut across traditional divides were all part of the new second state ethic. This did not mean that the older, more cautious, first state mentality had evaporated. It remained in force. The slavery issue was now a race issue. Sectionalism and federalism had never left the capital. A strongly centralized and authoritative bureaucracy was still feared and avoided. The lawyers, their ways of arguing, their ways of framing issues, still permeated the debates. Blair's use of a law dictionary, Garland's oration on constitutionality, Pendleton and Hoar's belief in a democratic Constitution, and the nonlawyer Miller's reference to the transfer of English common law to the United States spoke volumes on the prevalence of law-oriented issues and legal thinking in the debates. What lingered after the initial debate on the Blair bill subsided and the Pendleton Act took effect was the question of how to reconcile these older notions with the function of supervision over areas that Congress had no intention of directly funding. Growing problems with labor and the railroads would force the Congress to address this question.

CHAPTER SIX

"What Constitutes a State"

Supervising Labor and Commerce, 1883–1886

At roughly the same time that the Senate was considering Blair's bill to aid common schools at length in the spring of 1884, Congress began to debate of the first of two additional proposals that would mark the culmination of second state thinking and, under its aegis, a significant era in the expansion of the national government. After the landmark passage of the Pendleton Civil Service Act, the Congress considered and ultimately created an agency for collecting labor statistics and, still later, concluded its long deliberation on what to do with the railroads. The Interstate Commerce Commission (ICC) which most students of the administrative state regard as the inaugural event of the regulatory state in fact marked only one of the achievements of the second state.

Analysis of the congressional debates on these two agencies, one for labor and one for the railroads, reveals the pivotal concerns, terms, prejudices, and assumptions that surrounded the second state at its high-water mark. Congressmen proclaimed the importance of information gathering, clarified whom the national government served, and fixed those procedures in keeping with second state ideas. Congress conceded the need to erect agencies that functioned in an expert and professional manner.

The Problem with Labor

The labor question had been a pressing concern for some time before the Congress debated any concrete solutions at length. Industrialization, the formation of large corporate enterprises and monopolies, among others, combined with periodic depressions and their accompanying cycle of wage cuts, labor actions, and strike-breaking to place the conflict between wage earners and capitalists in stark terms. The employers' use of federal courts' injunctive relief powers was not sufficient to end worker protest. More and more frequently, federal troops were called up as strikebreakers. Following the Great Railroad Strike of 1877, labor relations in the United States plainly defied the free labor idealism that had held sway over the Republican Party. With Democrats and Republicans fiercely fighting over battleground states and districts, the labor question took on greater prominence—especially once laborers began to flex their political weight, most notably in organizations such as the Knights of Labor.[1]

Although the Knights of Labor through its grand master, Terence Powderly, were the key lobbying force behind the proposal of a labor bureau, the idea that an occupational constituency should receive attention from a government agency was nothing new, thanks to the Department of Agriculture. The idea of a bureau of labor statistics arose out of the common process of individual state practice, experience, and developments, in this case in Massachusetts.[2] Federalism could be a positive force for change as well as a hindrance to administrative expansion. But the debate at the national level took its own course. In debates over a bureau of labor statistics bill, Congress explored key questions of how to supervise matters of interest to labor.

It should come as no surprise that Henry W. Blair took a prominent role. After all, his Committee on Education and Labor had undertaken a massive study of the labor question which lasted a year and a half before the proposed bill of labor statistics reached either floor of Congress. Thanks to Blair's own handling of the committee, it proved to be less of a partisan rallying device than a measured effort to gather testimony from all quarters. The committee's visits to New York City, Manchester, New Hampshire, and Birmingham, Alabama, helped forge a middle-of-the-road coalition in Congress centered on Blair, Pugh, and George. In creating an invaluable treasure trove of testimony from labor, capitalist, and reform-minded luminaries, as well as comparatively unknown ordinary business owners and workers, the committee laid the groundwork for a variety of proposals to deal with the labor question.[3]

The repeated calls for a national bureau of labor statistics entailed a host of interdependent issues, including growing concern about the labor question, the increasing pace of the nationalization of the economy, developments at the state level, and the by now ingrained fascination with the gathering and use of statistics. While other nations simply collected information on their populations, American culture seemed to thrive on it.[4]

The first significant exchange in Congress on an agency for labor took place on March 7, 1884, in the first session of the Forty-eighth Congress. As chair of the Committee on Education and Labor, Blair took center stage. His "bill to establish a bureau of statistics of labor," S. 140, occupied the Senate on two occasions, 7 and 10 March. Even as outspoken and ambitious promoter of the second state as Blair was, he nevertheless couched his arguments for the new institution in the language of limited, neutral, government fact-finding: "It is simply for the collection and dissemination of information in regard to the subject-matter of labor in the same way that we now have a bureau established for the collection and dissemination of information relating to the subject of education."[5] To avoid raising the same objections as had been voiced about his education bill, he explained that the new bureau was a small thing and would do good through very limited means. It was a sunshine approach: expose conditions in a systematic way, and best practices would follow. Massachusetts had followed this course in creating its Bureau of Labor Statistics and its railroad commission.[6]

Blair's cautious approach did not forestall criticism. Morrill was friendly but worried about the expense, perhaps the Senate could merely add to the task to an existing bureau, he suggested—"the Bureau of Education, perhaps, or the Bureau of Agriculture."[7] This seems an odd objection to an expenditure of fifteen thousand dollars a year for three jobs or so in a national government that spent tens of millions and employed tens of thousands. Perhaps it is not so odd. New England was expected to press for frugality. After all, Morrill himself had once been a shopkeeper. The fiscal matter might also have been a proxy for Congress's suspicions about direct government involvement in the labor-capital struggle.

The usual suspects followed Morrill to enter their remarks into the *Record*. Hoar, for example, announced that the republic depended on a well-compensated labor force: "It is impossible to have a republic founded upon universal suffrage unless the great mass of the community can receive as the reward of their labor a sum sufficient to afford them education, leisure, comfort, and to develop a patriotic interest in the country to which they belong."[8] Congress needed the information to legislate on labor's behalf.

Speaking from the Democracy's side of the issue, Wilkinson Call from Florida gave a slightly different set of reasons for supporting a separate agency for labor. "I think we should be careful not to pay too much attention and too much regard to the interests of capital and too little to those of labor." Labor had organized both in the United States and in Europe. They deserved representation in the executive department. The Kentucky-born lawyer had made an important conceptual shift. Instead of speaking out against the enlargement of the national government, the former Confederate adjutant general endorsed a broadening of the bureaucracies to represent a vital constituency. He praised Massachusetts's bureau and called for the system to be "extended throughout the whole of the country." In language analogous to Jefferson's praise of the yeomanry, Call reminded his listeners that "the interests and the rights of labor is the great problem on the proper and wise adjustment of which the future of our own and all other industrial countries depend."[9] Kentucky coal miners were among the most ferocious of labor's advocates.

Caution and capital had their advocates as well. Nelson Aldrich (R-R.I.) and Garland made one of the odder tag teams in the history of the Senate. Although one could argue that their shared experience as career politicians from their respective states gave them common ground, they represented opposite poles in American politics. Whereas Garland had studied how to be a lawyer in a law office, Aldrich had learned parliamentary procedure and debate from his avid participation in the debates held in Providence's lyceum.

Yet the attorney from Arkansas, who had won back his right to practice law in a Supreme Court case, and the grocer from Providence, Rhode Island, made common cause to restrict Blair's bill to a mere extension of the work of the Bureau of Statistics in the Treasury Department. Garland rested his argument on efficiency: "There is one difficulty in many of our laws at this time, that we scatter, if I may use the expression, the work of different Departments, so that they are first in one place and then in another."[10] His solution to the scatterbrained approach to creating new agencies was to consolidate under "one head" all the statistics gathering and reporting of the government. Although this would have made the organizational chart simpler, it would have also nullified the symbolic point of including "something for labor." Perhaps this was the object.

On March 10 Hoar and others objected to the investigatory powers the bureau would have as well as the fact that the head of the bureau could appoint the clerks. It was acceptable for Congress to delegate but not for the inferior agencies it created to be independent. Blair had to admit his bill's key defect as well as its appeal: "Much of the phraseology of this bill is taken from the Massachusetts act establishing a like bureau in that State."[11] He conceded what his critics insisted on—that state governments could do more than the national government would be allowed to do. That older piece of the first state, the concept of the "government of states" referred to in the first debate on the Morrill Act, remained despite the Civil War and its aftermath.

In that brief but revealing passage of arms one can see a key difference between the second state and the federal government in the Progressive Era. Advocates of federal regulation after 1900 did not limit its scope or function because states had similar institutions. The balance in federalism was readjusted to favor the national government. This was not so in the 1880s. The Republican Senate's busy calendar left the initiative to the Democrat-controlled House of Representatives.

The House Agrees on a Bureau of Labor

On April 19, 1884, Representative James H. Hopkins, chairman of the newly renamed House Committee on Education and Labor, introduced H.R. 1340, "a bill to establish and maintain a bureau of statistics." Despite the legislation's title, the prominent lawyer from Washington, Pennsylvania, sought to establish a department.[12] His proposal was almost exactly the same as Blair's, his arguments the equivalent, and his couching of the new department as one that "simply provides for the accumulation of information as an auxiliary to judicious legislation," for they had both drawn on the Massachusetts bureau precedent.[13]

Hopkins tried to cast the agency in neutral terms: "Mr. Chairman, this bill is not in the interest of any particular school of political economists. It will furnish information for all, and just such information as all political scientists desire and demand."[14] He chose a curious way of characterizing the dispute between capital and labor. Instead of a mean-spirited conflict over money, the legislators in this formulation are closer to academics or philosopher-kings. Hopkins had placed congressmen at the top of the legislative process; the bureaus would be of service to the Congress. He quoted a William Jones poem to illustrate the point that a nation was its people, not its land:

What constitutes a state?

    Not high-raised battlement or labored mound,

Thick wall or moated gate;

    Not cities proud with spires and turrets crowned;

Not bays and broad-armed ports,

    Where, laughing at the storm, rich navies ride;

Not starred and spangled courts,

    Where low-browed baseness wafts perfume to pride.

No; men, high-minded men,

    With power as far above dull brutes endowed.

    *   *   *   *   *   *

Men who their duties know,

    But know their rights, and knowing dare maintain.

    *   *   *   *   *   *

These constitute a state.[15]

In using these lines to support his case, Hopkins encapsulated the eclectic, inclusive philosophy of the second state: high-minded men who know their duties would put aside party and section to administer state agencies.

The extension of federal administration into new areas was assumed to be natural and unexceptionable. "All are interested in promoting the welfare, increasing the prosperity, happiness, and contentment of all our people, and in thus perfecting the stability, the beauty, and symmetry of the Republic."[16] Rather than simply providing security or protection, Hopkins wanted an active role for the national government, and he was not afraid to increase the apparatus in order to do so. His omission of several key lines from the poem may be significant in that regard. In particular Jones's original declared,

> dare maintain,
>
> *Prevent the long-aim'd blow,*
>
> *And crush the tyrant while they rend the chain:*
>
> These constitute a State,
>
> *And sov'reign LAW, that State's collected will,*
>
> *O'er thrones and globes elate*
>
> *Sits Empress, crowning good, repressing ill.*[17]

These lines may have been too redolent of the Confederates' rhetoric for Hopkins's purposes. All in all he made as good an attempt as any in trying to reconcile the contradictions between the first state's prevailing attitude toward new agencies and the second state's.

All those who spoke in favor of the bill either on the whole or in part undertook this same labor. They were united in their optimistic appraisal of what well-informed legislation could do, their dismissal of any claims that this overreached or broke with precedent, and their support for the working men of the country. First-term Democrat and lawyer John J. O'Neill from Missouri presented the full case for the department using letters, reports, and his own lament that "we have fallen behind to the extent that in some cases mere unsigned newspaper articles are published in the record, and have an influence on the result of the pending discussion."[18] Besides the fact that his remarks show that congressmen valued what appeared in the *Record*, the ideas behind the words express that confidence in scientific, informed policy making that would become the hallmark of the third state: the trust in experts.

O'Neill only trusted Congress with the information. He was not ready to trust the bureaucrats to act on their own. If Hopkins had read him another line from the ode, O'Neill might have support in it for his view. "Smit by her [the Empress or Sovereign Law] sacred frown / The fiend Discretion like a vapour sinks" was not just the view of opponents of the bill but of its proponents as well.[19] Bureaucracy, rule by bureaucrats, was an evil not just for its lack of humanity but also for its arbitrariness.

Opponents of the bill seized on the bugbears of discretion and the proliferation of bureaus. In the phrasing of Hiram C. Young (D-Tenn.), "One of the complaints against the legislation of the past two decades is that its tendency has been to enlarge the machinery of government, to multiply its different parts, and to render it more unwieldy, less effective, and more expensive in its administration."[20] Like his fellow Democrats O'Neill and Hopkins, he did not object to the additional activity, but he did take issue with its ungovernability. But he was swimming against a tide of the new social sciences.

Those sciences found a spokesman in Martin A. Foran (D-Ohio). Like Young, Foran was a lawyer who had served in the cavalry during the Civil War (though on the opposing side of his Tennessee colleague). "I firmly believe that the laws governing the science of sociology are as fixed as those of astronomy," he intoned. He went on at great length to put his forward-looking philosophy to work for the department. His statement of higher principles was the same as that of his fellows across the aisle: "Man is undoubtedly the true object of legislation, and to produce better men, freer men, men of more advanced thought and civilization, should be the object of every law placed upon the statute-books of the Republic."[21]

To hear the reason for Foran's break with the Democracy's traditional stand against trying to legislate improvement, his audience had to wait only a few minutes. "The centralization of wealth means the centralization of political power, and the centralization of political power marks the decline and possible death of republican institutions in this country."[22] In this way many Democrats made their peace with the second state. Only with the effective use of the national government could they work against the industrializing forces that were undermining their constituents. Only by using legislation could they use the state. And only through the gathering of data could they use legislation effectively.

The Democrats were still divided. David W. Aiken (D-S.C.), James H. Blount (D-Ga.), and Young argued among themselves, as well as with Hopkins, over whether information should be gathered by a department, a bureau, given to an existing bureau, or not done at all.[23] Blount, a lawyer and standard states' rights Democrat, and Aiken were opposed to the activity altogether. Aiken, farmer, head of the South Carolina Grange, and advocate of scientific agriculture, spoke at length on the issue. Young proposed a compromise between their position and Hopkins's. Hopkins had begun deriding his fellow party members as followers of the "ghost of 'State rights,'" and Young may have recognized the danger to party unity.

The Tennessean suggested a bureau. After all, he argued, "If it should work evil, as he [Blount] thinks it would, then it would be easier, very much easier, to abolish a mere bureau than a department of the Government. A department is a fixture. Once you establish it, and whatever its evils may be it is likely to remain."[24] As with the debate on the Department of Agriculture among Republicans some twenty years before, Democrats now confronted the stickiness of labels. The grandeur of a name had very real power among the congressmen participating in the debate. A perception of reality became reality. Whether or not the labor agency was a department or bureau mattered because they believed it did.

Blount had another exchange with a first-term Democrat, Charles Stewart of Texas, another lawyer. Stewart wanted to protect labor against "selfish, exacting, and not infrequently oppressive" capital through the creation of a neutral, fact-gathering agency. He added another reason for its utility: "it will be the means of bringing capital and labor together in more friendly relations than they have been heretofore, of forming a closer alliance." He defended the proposal against

Blount's criticisms with citations to the precedents of agriculture and education: "Your object is to afford information upon that subject to the people of all the States, so that they may all receive benefit from it."[25] The goal was not compulsion of the states but their aid.

The last substantial period of debate on H.R. 1340 centered on the salary of the commissioner, whether the nomination process of the commissioner should specify a role for organized labor, and the wording of the assigned categories to be studied with regards to religious affiliation.[26] After the amendment process ran its course, a bureau emerged with a carefully delineated function. While there was some scuffling regarding a quorum and Hopkins's efforts to avoid the bill being talked to death, the House voted 182 to 19 to create a bureau of labor statistics, with 121 representatives not voting. Underscoring the value of the *Record* as an official, publicly distributed source, O'Neill made sure that Richard P. "Silver Dick" Bland's (D-Mo.) quorum call was properly recorded under Bland's name in the *Record* in order for "the people of your [Bland's] district to understand it." The former school teacher, lawyer, and prospector responded, "And they will understand you, too." With Hopkins's title change from *department* to *bureau*, H.R. 1340 moved to the Senate.[27]

The Senate Reconsiders the Labor Bureau

On May 14, 1884, Blair again reported a bill for the establishment of a bureau of labor statistics. This time he was armed with the House of Representative's approval and a letter from John Nimmo Jr., head of the Bureau of Statistics in the Treasury Department, dated May 1, 1884, in support of the establishment of a separate bureau for labor statistics. Blair presented several other letters from interested parties to emphasize that groups from several states supported the measure.[28] In this way he could demonstrate an emerging consensus around the creation of a new bureau.

In asserting the value of this approach, senators Call and George spoke in favor of the bureau. Both southern Democratic lawyers decried the condition of labor, repeated the need to follow through on so many labor organizations' requests for a bureau, and defended the Committee on Education and Labor's decision to report the House bill without amendment.[29] But this compromise with the demands of the new economy only stirred John T. Morgan's steadfast opposition. He was known for his impassioned performances on the Senate floor. By the end of his years in the Senate, in 1889, he had established a reputation as one of the foremost speech makers of his day. This combination of old-style, court-room lawyering with the commitment to states' rights was on full display as he condemned the proposed bureau as an impertinent intruder into the private af-fairs of states and the peaceful white farmers of the Alabama upcountry, along with their compatriots in other states.[30] He could find no reason why the con-gressmen could not rely on their own knowledge of their constituents' situation.

Morgan reserved his choicest invective, however, for the chair of the com-mittee and the motives that inspired the education bill as well as the Bureau of Labor Statistics: "The Senator from New Hampshire has signalized himself, dis-tinguished himself in this effort to impress his personal views of universal im-provement upon the people of the United States at large."[31] Through the haze of Civil War, Reconstruction, and Redemption, the division between the old-style South and New England was alive and well. Blair stood for the second state's prevailing ethic; Morgan looked back to the first state's ideal that the best government governed least.

If anyone had had any doubts about Morgan's motives, they were dispelled by the questions he asked others. As George spoke once more for H.R. 1340, Morgan asked him which groups would be studied under the label of labor.

Morgan: Does the Senator refer to agricultural laborers at all?
George: So far as I know I have heard no complaint from them.
Morgan: This bill, then, does not apply to them?
George: Yes; it applies to all.
Morgan: It applies to alien laborers also?
George: It applies to all laborers in the United States.
Morgan: And the negro laborers in the South?[32]

The lawyer from Tennessee representing Alabama had led his fellow lawyer into a trap through cross-examination.

If George came out in favor of a national government agency inquiring into the true nature of race relations in the South, he could kiss the North-South al-liance good-bye. The slavery question's impact on the conceptual approach to governing the United States had not gone away; it had only been transformed into a question of race relations. Like any good advocate, George dodged the question: "I say I have not heard the complaint urged by that class that I have heard from others."[33]

On May 19, having finally read the bill in detail, Morgan asserted that there were too many tasks for any one commissioner to fulfill and, arguing in the alternative, that the Senate, the country's laboring men and women, and the national government did not require the information to legislate. Charles H. Van Wyck (R-Neb.) crossed the party aisle to lend his voice to the point, asserting that debate on the Bureau of Labor Statistics took away valuable time from actual legislation on behalf of labor—for example, ending the importation of Italians and Chinese under the contract system.[34] The two attorneys and Civil War veterans could make common cause on this one idea: do not increase the apparatus of government to gather information.

Call and Blair rose to defend the bill. Call referred to the situation in Great Britain and Germany. He also repeated his point that labor organizations themselves had called for the bureau. He dismissed Morgan and Van Wyck's complaints as "captious" and overwrought. The bureau was a limited one for a limited purpose to serve a vital, numerous, and supportive constituency. Blair provided another letter from Nimmo asserting the necessity of a separate bureau to serve that special purpose. Moreover, Blair rebutted the concept that "this man" could not be trusted with all these tasks and the budget of twenty-five thousand dollars per year to accomplish them like "any other officer of the Government."[35] Once again, a congressman's notion of personnel did not extend beyond the republican ideal.

On May 22 the Senate continued its debate on H.R. 1340. A small matter was fostering a major debate. Two new participants registered their objections to the bill. Bayard took issue with Van Wyck's amendment to make the commissioner a member of the laboring classes. This former U.S. district attorney endorsed Blair's view that any good man could hold the position so long as he had the following qualities: "the faculty to group and arrange them [facts] in an orderly and intelligible manner," "whose habits of life and study will enable him to perform it [the job] sensibly and well," and "a statistician." But Bayard's desire to restrict the growth of the federal "machinery" overrode any other sensibility. He still did not see the utility of a new bureau. "If we have the facts," he argued, "the American people can draw their own inferences. They do not want the opinions of statisticians; they do not want the opinions of officers whose duty it is only to obtain the facts."[36]

Ingalls questioned the bureau's purpose.[37] His Kansas constituents were laborers, but they shared nothing with the labor organizations that had called for the bill. What was more, the former judge advocate of the Kansas Volunteers declared the entire notion of a rivalry between capital and labor a project of "transparent demagogues" seeking to set class against class. Inequality was the natural result of a free society, and no redistribution of wealth would ever change that.[38] Whereas Democrats such as Morgan, Bland, and Bayard spoke of states' rights and the individual liberty of whites, Republicans such as Ingalls spoke of the Social Darwinist republic: merit determined success or failure, and rightly so.

As the hour grew late, Blair, George, and Call found their effort to preserve the House bill from amendment facing serious difficulty. The challenge came not only from the detractors but from meddlesome allies. Allison and Sherman pressed Blair to concede to their reading of article 2, section 2, clause 2, of the Constitution: "the Congress may by Law invest the Appointment of such inferior officers, as they think proper, in the President alone, in the Courts of Law, or in the Heads of departments."[39] In their reading of this language this meant that the new agency had to be labeled a "department" and not a "bureau" because the bill gave the commissioner of the bureau the power to appoint the chief clerk. George and Blair tried to convince him that a name was just a name, but the self-made attorney from Lancaster, Ohio, known to many as "the Ohio Icicle," refused to give ground:[40]

> I do not think it is wise for the Congress of the United States to make new bureaus. . . . A bureau is a desk; that is what it means—a desk in a department or in some branch of the Government. That is the literal and proper meaning of the word bureau—a desk or office in a department of the Government. A department of the Government is a branch of the Government, a branch of the executive department of the Government, and it is therefore called in the Constitution a Department separate and distinct from the other departments of the Government, the whole, under the President, making the executive branch of the Government of the United States.[41]

What seemed a simple definition of terms and a lesson in basic civics was actually a legal argument with many hidden assumptions. That the word *bureau* was not in use at the time of the writing of the clause in question and that the branches were called "departments" are beside the main point.

George and Blair's more flexible definitions might have been the more accurate interpretation of the framers' intent, but the senators bowed to their elders in a room filled with lawyers quoting law. At one point even Garland began citing case law, *United States v. Hartwell,* in support of Allison and Sherman's position.[42] The end result was that Blair allowed Sherman, Hoar, and Morrill, among others, to open the floodgates to amendments. It was the Senate at its pedantic best and practical worst.[43]

On May 23 Blair tried again to secure a vote. Garland was still citing case law to support his substitute. This time it was *United States v. Germaine*, and which Garland asserted that it was analogous and applicable to his argument.[44] Blair trumped it with a telegram from Terence V. Powderly, grand master–workman of the Knights of Labor which read, "Three thousand assemblies of Knights of Labor request of Senate to concur in action of House on bureau of labor statistics bill," which he introduced into the *Record*. Blair now pressed for a vote. To speed the process further, he withdrew his own amendments changing the bureau into a department.[45]

With little more substantive debate the Senate proceeded to reject the Garland motion to recommit, twenty-eight to eighteen; his substitute, twenty-six to twenty-four; and accepted Aldrich's substitute in the form of an amendment, thirty-seven to eighteen; which they then passed fifty-five to two. The president pro tempore ruled as being out of order George's remarks about the Democratic House's bill receiving wide support in the House while his, Call, and Voorhees's no vote on the Aldrich substitute were the sole Democratic votes in opposition, but their withdrawal did not expunge them from the *Record*.[46] Everyone had had their say, and it was all in the public record; the Senate, after all, was a body of honorable, if wordy, gentlemen.

The conference committee of senators Aldrich, Bayard, and Blair, and representatives Foran, O'Neill, and James reported back on the establishment of a bureau of labor within the Department of the Interior. The only concession to the Hopkins bill was that the commissioner could make recommendations to the secretary of the interior for chief clerk and the rest of the clerical staff.[47] As such, the bill received President Grover Cleveland's signature, and organized labor received a bureau. The United States Congress had added another agency to the many already in existence.[48]

Both proponents and opponents had borrowed from the second state's catechism. Labor had achieved recognition as a constituency with a voice. All but a few members of Congress accepted Congress's role in the general welfare of labor. Even those few were forced to deal with the new political climate. While the minority still clung to the first state notion of stewardship, the prevailing beliefs centered on the gathering of data, the enactment of policy to address certain groups' needs, and the acceptance of a supervisory role for government—a second state view. Congress was not willing to entrust that supervision to administrative agencies. Even committed aggrandizers such as Blair saw the agencies as handmaidens to Congress. Finally, congressmen continued to express the republican notion that the personnel should be good men of common sense, which meant something akin to the professionals of the time such as lawyers. It was with these concepts in ascendance that Congress turned from the labor question to the problem of the railroads.

To Regulate (by the Courts) or Administrate (by Commission)

As the debate continued on the Blair bill, the civil service issue was absorbed into the stream of ordinary politics, and the Bureau of Labor began its humdrum existence, the long-standing question of what to do with the railroads took center stage. The controversy led to the United States's first comprehensive foray into administrative regulation of the economy. Was it to be a part of the second state, or did it fall outside the set boundaries of sponsorship, supervision, and standardization?

Like other developments in the evolution of the U.S. state, the advent of the regulatory commission derived from colonial precedents and later state-level politics. Boards of oversight, such as the Board of Trade, arose in Britain in the seventeenth century, crossing the Atlantic to the colonies in the form of special courts, commissions, and regulatory bodies. These oversight agencies spread in the years following the American Revolution.[49] The first railroad commission arrived in Connecticut in 1832 with a charge of overseeing charters for railroad companies. The construction boom after the Civil War, in part fueled by army-railroad relations during the war, sparked two new forms of supervisory agencies. Charles Francis Adams Jr. created the "weak," or Massachusetts, model in 1869. The Granger-inspired, "strong" commission first appeared in Illinois in 1873.[50] The weak commission had no regulatory authority. It served as a conduit for information on the assumption that transparency would ensure probity. The strong commission that prevailed in the Midwest received extensive rate-making authority, with enforcement powers against discriminatory pricing, rebates, and collusion.[51]

The considerable impact of the railroads on any given industry or region, their large impersonal organization, and their unusual economics combined with their incredible influence over state, local, and national political bodies through everything from free passes to outright payoffs caused considerable public pressure for some form of control. The Granges—farmers' social, political, and economic organizations—advocated national and state regulation throughout the 1870s and early 1880s, while a group of gentlemen reformers including Charles Francis Adams Jr., Arthur T. Hadley, and Simon Sterne favored a loose supervision of what they viewed as a natural monopoly. Adams in particular opposed nationalization as a measure inconsistent with the United States's institutions and traditions.[52]

Judging from the proposals that Congress considered, Adams would have found considerable support there for his sentiments. Certainly, this was not Congress's first foray into the railroad question. It and the federal courts had been intimately involved with the railroads since the 1850s.[53] Although the exact derivation of what became the Interstate Commerce Act of 1887 establishing the Interstate Commerce Commission is controversial, its direct predecessors involved the independent oil refiners and producers in western Pennsylvania and shippers in New York. Faced with the continued attempts of John D. Rockefeller's oil trust to gain overall control of the railroad industry, the independents' lobbying organization pressed for federal regulation of interstate commerce in 1872 and again in 1876.

At that time Representative James H. Watson of Pennsylvania was unable to convince the influential member of the Interstate Commerce Committee, John H. Reagan, that action would be constitutional. When the Supreme Court ruled that it was, in 1877, Reagan, a fervent opponent of anything resembling a monopoly in transportation, took up the cause. He brought his bill to the Congress twice, in 1878 and 1885. Reagan's proposal forbade pooling, rate discrimination based on distance, and collusion among railroad companies while requiring the publishing of a schedule of rates. Enforcement was to come through private suits in court.[54]

In what was either an effort to make the measure unpalatable to the white South or a genuine concern with equal rights, the Republicans supported an amendment from James O'Hara, an African-American representative from North Carolina. The amendment required all railroads to provide equal accommodations regardless of race. Reading this provision as consistent with segregation, Reagan kept his largely southern and western majority intact and sent the bill to the Senate.[55] In this fashion the Democrats, long the opponents of federal government enlargement, reconciled themselves to the new state of affairs. They had effectively made a deal in order to protect themselves from the private economies' giants, the railroads. As long as the national government tolerated the "Jim Crow" South, white southerners could compromise their big government antipathy. National Democratic leaders were looking to capture that murky middle of the U.S. electorate vital to winning the swing states of the Gilded Age. A "reform" such as regulating the railroads fit this strategy perfectly.[56]

The Senate, however, preferred another approach, that of Shelby M. Cullom, a Republican from Illinois, who proposed a commission with rate-setting and enforcement powers. While the popularly elected House favored outright prohibition of rate gouging, a substantial group of senators wanted a degree of flexibility in rate setting and enforcement. A recent negative characterization of this position ascribes to it a desire to weaken the prohibitions on pooling, cooperation, and the like in favor of the railroads. A more charitable view recognizes that there may have been a genuine concern about the health of the railroad industry, an industry that was vital to the nation's well-being.[57] After the Forty-eighth Congress expired, Cullom conducted hearings on railroad practices to inform the Senate on this extraordinarily complex subject. On April 14 the Senate, with the information gathered at the hearings at their fingertips, once again took up the issue of railroad regulation.

Although the Senate devoted most of its time to the long- and short-haul provisions of the bill, on occasion the senators turned to the commission. It would be the first of its kind at the national level, and Cullom was well aware of the danger involved. The former governor, an accomplished lawyer and former radical Republican congressman, introduced the committee's proposal, S. 1532, from a wealth of experience few legislators could match. As speaker of the Illinois legislature, he had presided over the creation of the Illinois Railroad and Warehouse Commission in 1873.[58] S. 1532's commission resembled this earlier effort in many ways.

The commission would have the power to investigate allegations, publicize rates, and make general rules when confronted with a possible violation of the rate discrimination provision. The commission's findings would constitute prima facie evidence in the courts, the actual enforcers of the commission's findings. Cullom asserted, "The method of procedure marked out for the commission is intended to provide for the speedy adjustment of all such complaints." He based this judgment not on the British model but on American precedents. The "existence of such a tribunal" would ease the adjustment of complaints through its very presence, the influence on popular opinion, and its evidence before the court should the matter progress that far.[59] Cullom's five-member commission plan avoided an extensive bureaucracy and existed in harmony with a lawyer's model of court-centered administration of public policy. It also bore a characteristic of American law which went back to the federal Constitution itself: it was based on state-level experience with law, an example of the "corresponding powers" doctrine of borrowing.[60]

All who spoke in favor of the bill portrayed the commission in these limited, derivative terms. Thomas W. Palmer (R-Mich.), noted orator, farmer, and businessman, seconded Cullom's presentation. "This commission will be regarded as the people's attorneys," he stated, as such, it "should be composed of men at least the equals in legal acumen and practical force of those whose unjust schemes they are expected to thwart and whose unprecedented powers they are designed to direct."[61] Even a nonlawyer such as Palmer espoused the belief that the legal profession supplied the appropriate managers of government operations. Neither businessmen nor academics nor engineers were expected to fill what most senators regarded as a court-like institution, a tribunal. The administrative state was to be a lawyer-run state. Even nonlawyers could see this by now.

The only substantial controversy surrounding the creation of this new piece of the administrative apparatus centered the commission's leeway on how to interpret the long- and short-haul section, the fourth of over twenty items in the bill. Opponents lined up to disapprove of the commission's authority to determine what was a "just and reasonable" rate; what constituted discrimination; and whether the arrangements between railroads amounted to a criminal collusion. John C. Spooner (R-Wis.), lawyer extraordinaire for his state's railroad and lumber interests, spoke for all when he expressed the misgivings to which his lawyer's life had contributed: "I would not give the competitive benefits which we have in the country to-day and the interest of commerce over into the keeping of any board unless it was made up of angels."[62] He and his fellow objectors preferred to spell out the matter so the commission would have next to no discretionary authority, with a corresponding diminishment in the chance for corruption.

Other senators, including Cullom, Arthur P. Gorman, Maryland's Democratic "boss," Allison, Blair, Brown, and William J. Sewell, an Irish immigrant and decorated Union veteran who represented New Jersey's railroad interests, felt that iron-clad rules made bad law. It was far better to trust a commission to interpret the situation, gather facts, and make generally applicable rules to fit the circumstances. The railroads were too vital, the matter too complex, and the Congress's time too limited for anything else.[63] They might have added, but significantly did not, that the same problems their colleagues attributed to any future commission went doubly so for the United States Congress. Leland Stanford, one of the "Big Four" founders of the Central Pacific, then Southern Pacific, Railroad and now a Republican from California, was only the most obvious senator with ties to the railroad industry.

If the Congress could not be trusted with such an authority, neither could its designates under the more rigorous purview of the courts. George F. Edmunds (R-Vt.) summed up the limited means the majority had in mind: "If we can lay down a rule and we are to lay it down at all, we ought to lay down that rule as positively as we may, so as to relieve the commission from the responsibility and the danger . . . of their soon being the charms on the watch-chain of the railroad president."[64] Edmunds was prescient. In time Congress would create and the federal government would staff a myriad of regulatory agencies with a variety of discretionary powers, and business interests would immediately set about capturing the agencies.[65]

Morgan, a voice for states' rights throughout these debates, initiated a last-minute exchange on May 12. He proposed an amendment that would clarify the commissioners' status and constrain their operations. It read in full, "The commissioners appointed under this act shall be considered and regarded as being executive officers and shall not exercise either legislative or judicial powers." Orville Platt (R-Conn.) objected on the grounds that the legislation was specific enough "to avoid the exercise of judicial powers by these commissioners." Edmunds expressed concern about the baleful precedent set over an exertion of congressional will covering executive discretion. Morgan replied that the bill conferred an array of powers on the commissioners. "Perhaps" he mused, "they are even more than that [legislative officers]; they are autocrats." In any event, he declared, "we ought to know what they are."[66]

Although the Senate summarily rejected his amendment, Morgan made a noteworthy point.[67] The commission possessed functions that could be described as containing the characteristics of all three branches of the U.S. government. The exchange indicates that, while the senators were cognizant of the "uniqueness" of the legislation, they did not think it represented a challenge to the old order.[68] Cullom, Henry M. Teller (R-Colo.), a lawyer and former president of the Colorado Central Railroad, and Eli Saulsbury (D-Del.), another lawyer and a Unionist Democrat, reminded their colleagues that this was "an initiatory measure," "an experiment," and "a venture."[69] The Senate should not demand perfection. On May 12 their colleagues agreed and by a vote of forty-seven to four, with twenty-five absent, approved the modified Cullom bill. Brown and Morgan were two of the four dissenters.[70] The bill now moved to the Democratic House, whose Interstate Commerce Committee chair, John H. Reagan, would finally have his say.

The Railroad Problem Returns to the Lower House

Republican opposition to Reagan's bill and the press of other matters prevented Reagan from introducing his committee's output until July 21, at the tail end of the session. To allow for a vote before the close of the term, the House agreed to limit debate to one hour and five minutes for each side. Others could get their views out by posting their remarks in the *Record*. Reagan introduced his own bill in the form of an amendment to S. 1532, the Cullom bill, which struck out all but the enacting clause and placed the Reagan bill's provisions in its stead. The differences between the two pieces of legislation were the same as in the year before.[71]

In a way the two houses' disagreement over interstate commerce regulation reflected the conflict between Democrat and Republican supporters of national government action at this point. The Democrats had moved to a position that favored federal government action in the economy but did not want to add to the administrative apparatus. The Republicans were more reluctant to intervene in the economy but were amenable to the creation of government agencies if any action needed to be taken. Reagan made the contrast quite plain. He ridiculed the Senate version as temporizing with the evil or worse, compared to the House's plain, prohibitions. The commission was a way that the railroads could defeat strict enforcement. What was more, he argued, "this system belongs in fact to despotic governments; not to free republics." Reagan posited that, unlike the federal judges who received the sole power to enforce the House bill, the commissioners were specialists, easy targets for capture by the railroad companies.[72] The strange politics of railroad regulation had turned a former Confederate into a defender of the integrity of federal judges.

Other Democrats joined Reagan in his denunciation of the pusillanimous commission plan. Andrew J. Caldwell and Charles T. O'Ferrall, a Confederate veteran and graduate of Washington College after the war, both hailed from southern states, Tennessee and Virginia, respectively. As lawyers, they disparaged the commission as a tribunal created to come between the people and the courts for the benefit of monopolistic railroad interests. It was impossible for even an honest commission to cope with the workload and make proper judgments, given that it would be dependent on the railroads for information. The whole idea redounded to the advantage of their supposed targets.[73]

Their opponents were all Republicans, another indication that the disagreement over the ICC had become a party matter in the House. Charles O'Neill from Pennsylvania, Robert R. Hitt from Illinois, William P. Hepburn from Iowa, and Jonathan H. Rowell from Illinois, all lawyers except for Hitt, who as a stenographer had recorded the Lincoln-Douglas debates and many a congressional investigation, endorsed the commission approach as the best possible course. They adopted the same arguments that Cullom and his supporters used in the Senate. The commission would smooth out differences, apply its specialized expertise, and safeguard the competing intents of the law, both to protect shippers against injustice and to ensure the continued functioning of a vital piece of the American economy. Judges, in their view, were no less corruptible than any commissioner.[74]

Despite these statements and Hepburn's prediction of the Senate's likely rejection of a commission measure, the House proceeded to pass Reagan's substitute by a vote of 192 to 41, with 89 not voting.[75] Predictably, the Senate fulfilled Hepburn's expectation and did not concur.[76] Both houses appointed members to a conference committee to resolve the differences—Cullom heading the Senate delegation, Reagan the House contingent. A compromise bill would have to wait until the next session.

A Compromise, Again: The Conference Committee's ICC

When the conference committee finally acted, its effort produced legislation that closely resembled the Senate version, with a section added to outlaw pooling. The vagueness of the commission's powers remained, as did its uneasy place within a court-based system of review and enforcement. Reagan had bowed to the inevitable commission in order to get a piece of legislation passed.

The Senate began its consideration of the conference report on December 15, 1886.[77] The vast majority of the senators' extensive remarks once again focused on the long- and short-haul provision and the anti-pooling section. Curiously, Hoar spoke against the bill that he had voted for in May. He lambasted the commission's discretion as exceeding that of "a Persian satrap or Roman proconsul." With a salary of seventy-five hundred dollars each, he asked, how could they resist the temptations of their office? Brown joined him in this negative appraisal of the commission's "Czar"-like arbitrary power. Morgan called it a "little Star-chamber."[78]

Sherman disagreed with these assessments. He asserted that the problem was not too much authority in the commission but the lack of it: "This limits their power only to particular cases as they arise and which have to await their decision."[79] The future sponsor of the nation's first antitrust act pointed out the commission's key weakness in addition to its salient feature. The commission did not make policy like a legislature. It made policy like a court, or, in the congressmen's parlance of the time, a tribunal. Filled with lawyers, some of whom had practiced railroad law, the Congress could not help but envision lawyers as the Interstate Commerce Commission's personnel. Indeed, it was the embodiment of the lawyer's ideal American system of governance.

The Senate voted to concur with the conference report on January 14, 1887. Forty-three voted in favor, and fifteen voted against, with seventeen absent. True to their words, Hoar and Brown joined Platt, Morrill, and Evarts, who believed the bill had gone too far against the railroads.[80] Certainly, it had gone beyond the expansion that Hoar and Morrill had sponsored, though the supporters of the new bill used much the same language as Morrill and Hoar had deployed. The words remained the same, but the administrative apparatus was different.

The House took up the report the very next day but without Reagan, who was in Texas to begin his successful bid to become a senator.[81] The manager of the conference report in Reagan's absence, Charles F. Crisp (D-Ga.), the future speaker of the House, faced a difficult task. His mentor, Reagan, and the Democratic majority that followed him were on record against the commission plan and fervently in favor of placing the whole matter solely in the courts. But Crisp, a former state judge and solicitor general of the southwestern judicial circuit, possessed the skills necessary to make the case. He simply argued that this was substantially the same bill that the House had confirmed for the past three sessions.

Regarding the commission's flaws, Crisp asserted, "I should be ashamed to come before the country and state that I did not believe it was in the power of the President of the United States, with the concurrence of the Senate, to select men wise and upright and honest enough to carry out this law."[82] Echoes of Sumner's proposal for staffing the Freedmen's Bureau, Greeley's ideal Reconstruction, and Schurz's explanation of American exceptionalism: lawyers were men of character and probity par excellence. One had only to ask the lawyers. In this context Crisp's words might be misread as politically and legally non-committal. Instead, they were a recitation of the new, final portion of the second state catechism.

Despite the Democratic concessions to the commission, O'Neill reversed his position on the bill. Like Hoar's reception of the conference report in the Senate, O'Neill could not bring himself to support a measure that seemed to fall too heavily on the side of rigid prohibitions of pooling and rate discrimination. O'Neill and Crisp sparred over the resemblance between the conference report's compromise and the Cullom bill. O'Neill clarified his view on Crisp's urging and denied that this was the Cullom bill, conceding, "I only wish it were." The new structure of the commission, with detailed procedures for how to conduct its hearings, "makes it almost a court," he lamented.[83]

The Pennsylvania Republican had seen something of the future of regulatory agencies in this first attempt at federal legislation, and he did not like what he saw. The fierce antibureaucracy ethic latent even within the mildest and most self-effacing efforts at increasing the scale and scope of the American state would sometimes bubble to the surface, as it did in O'Neill's remarks. Lawyers knew courts, believed in their suitability, and replicated their form and personnel in their enactments. But the flip side of the lawyers' notion of a necessary administrative state was a fear that it could resemble a court too closely for its own good.

Thus, proposals such as the conference report's notion of a commission received mixed reviews from the lawyers in Congress. James B. Weaver, a Greenbacker from Iowa; Samuel Dibble (D-S.C.); and William C. Oates (D-Ala.), "the one-armed hero from Henry County" who had played a prominent part at the battle of Gettysburg, among others, bucked the Democratic leadership to speak against a commission. All were lawyers and Civil War veterans. Weaver, the future Populist Party nominee for president in 1892, believed the commission would be either impotent or, "unless the commissioners are stronger than human nature has generally been found to be when tempted, they will have the strongest possible temptation to make their decisions such as to gain the greatest amount of political power." Dibble declared that the discretion given the commission in section 4 to be an unconstitutional delegation of "legislative power." Oates observed critically, "The history of legislation and the course of administration of this Government prove that whenever an office is created it is never abolished, but rather that those who are appointed to execute it are increased in number if any change whatever be made."[84] With the exception of the Freedmen's Bureau and the Department of Education, Oates was telling the story of the course of the U.S. federal government. Although one might quarrel with the implied negativity of this tale, the almost natural tendency of any large institution toward aggrandizement of its administrative apparatus is incontrovertible.

On January 21, 1887, the House approved the conference report by a vote of 219 to 41, with 58 not voting.[85] The federal government's first independent regulatory agency was barely worthy of the name. The legislation that had arrived for Cleveland's signature on February 4, 1887, outlawed pools, set up a commission, but then contradicted itself with a section 4 that seemed liable to cartelization. By the 1890s, when the Supreme Court ruled that Congress could have granted, but did not, regulatory powers to the ICC, the new agency became suspended in legal limbo between a regulatory regime it could not provide and an investigatory function it could not perform.[86] Conceived of in limited terms, not meant to contradict American notions of governance as nationalization would have, the ICC lingered in this condition until the Roosevelt administration Congress gave teeth to the agency.[87] Only then—in the full flowering of the third state—did the full potential of this exercise in expanding the reach of the national government emerge.

At the end of the 1880s, however, it was perfectly natural that congressmen would conceive of the second state in terms of lawyers' practices, approaches, and moral sensibilities. After all, the Interstate Commerce Commission was to perform a legal function that would be subject to court review. It would have to gather information, make legal judgments about whether violations had occurred, and avoid the perceived evils of bureaucracy. There was also the unavoidable fact that most congressmen were lawyers and therefore tended to project versions of themselves into their vision of future agencies.

TAKEN TOGETHER, the Bureau of Labor and the Interstate Commerce Act debates demonstrate many of the same perspectives, approaches, concepts, and political jockeying for position exhibited in other debates on proposals to expand the national government. In particular, members of Congress repeated the arguments typical of second state exchanges. Even advocates of a larger national state had no outward intention of delegating their authority to bureaucracies. Almost no one wanted to import wholesale the institutions that they saw in other nations. Even though many were engaged in a transatlantic dialogue about policy, political institutions, and social concerns, they adapted their ideas to native conceptions of appropriate legal arrangements. Influences came from state developments, legal constructions such as the trust, and new ideas in business, philosophy, the sciences, and religion. Blair, Bayard, and Crisp's descriptions of the officers of the national government might have fallen out of a legal treatise on professional ethics. Cullom's tribunal and Palmer's "people's attorneys" made it plain to all that lawyers as well as laws provided the key concepts that allowed them to endorse these expansions of the U.S. state.

Yet the Congress had not completed its elaboration of this second state compromise. In three more debates—on elevating the Bureau of Labor to a department, the federal judiciary's circuit courts, and a second Morrill Act—the dialogue reached its culmination. In the process it laid the groundwork for supplanting the second state mind-set with the third state approach.

CHAPTER SEVEN

"A System Entirely Satisfactory to the Country"

Standardizing Labor and the Courts, 1886–1891

After having substantially altered the civil service, debated the Blair bill, provided the first independent regulatory commission in the U.S. government, and created a new agency in the form of a Bureau of Labor, the Congress had begun an important decade in its consideration of how to give concrete form to the ideas of the second state. Rather than being a decade of thwarted goals, inactivity under the label of laissez-faire, and stagnant thinking, the 1880s saw a time of evolution and growth in the U.S. administrative state. The trend continued as the decade came to a close.

The national forum still rang with the clash of raised voices regarding the critical functions of the American state in regulating the rails when the Congress elected to return to the matter of labor's continuing difficulties, respond to the pressure to reform the federal courts, and elaborate on Morrill's plan for agricultural and mechanic arts colleges. Each of these initiatives had its own particular demands, but the discussions that surrounded their ultimately successful enactment shared some common characteristics. All three contained the emergent consensus on how to approach governance: information gathering and dissemination, limited means, generalist personnel, and a consistency with American legal norms. In all three discussions one profession dominated—the law. All three repeated a discourse on the need to avoid bureaucracy while dealing with issues that required immediate national help. In each of the debates the Congress strived to find "a system entirely satisfactory to the country." The first item was the enhancement of the Bureau of Labor into a department, completing a process and concluding a conversation that had begun several years earlier.

A Department of Labor at Last

On March 21, 1888, the House took up H.R. 8560, a bill to establish a department of labor.[1] As the chair of the Committee on Education and Labor, John J. O'Neill was in charge of the debate. There was almost universal support for the measure. Most of the members' remarks came under the five-minute rule in which a representative could only speak for five minutes on a particular amendment. Some representatives managed to speak on the topic, getting their views into the *Record* in the process, by moving to eliminate a word and, then, after finishing, withdrawing the amendment. The more substantive amendments took two forms: those that reflected concerns about bureaucracies and those that were directly tied to economic policy issues such as the tariff and the currency, the two overriding political questions of the era.

The bureau, under Carroll Wright, was well regarded. Both William C. P. Breckinridge (D-Ky.), a lawyer whose reputation as an orator had few equals, and "Sunset" Cox spoke highly of Wright and his activities. Wright had understood his job. Bringing in reports that could be used by both parties, the Bureau of Labor had perfected what the Department of Agriculture and Eaton's Bureau of Education had initiated: the gathering, sorting, and release of nationwide data. Even with his open admiration for Wright and the reports, Holman (D-Ind.) could not help but lament the growth of these functions, expenses, and continuing requests: "We are departing rapidly from the old landmarks."[2] The second state was the consensus view of the national government.

In a series of exchanges over the proposed increase in personnel which would accompany the bureau's change in status, the representatives explored another facet of the second state mind-set. Whether the issue was one of having two watchmen or two messengers, whether the clerk should be the acting commissioner or there should be a new deputy commissioner, and whether the commissioner should set the travel allowances or the House should leave that to a subsequent appropriation, the matter was worthy of their attention.[3] They sweated the details. That the committee had not perfected the bill so as to be consistent with prior practice is one point. That the congressmen had the time to debate these points, much less care about them, is another. When a measure received this level of scrutiny, one conclusion dwarfs the others: representatives wanted to keep a tight reign on the government.

O'Neill's remark that Wright himself had helped draft the legislation said a great deal about the intimate associations in Washington, D.C.[4] Moreover, bringing the administrators back into the conversation closed the distance between the agency and Congress while raising the status of the bureaucrats. Representatives might not trust agencies with autonomy in general but now relied on them to help prepare laws that would increase the scale and scope of the administration.

Much of the rest of the discussion that day dealt with the desire to add tariff and currency investigations to the new department. The liveliest argument ensued over the indebtedness of Iowa farmers and just what the specific valuation of their land was. Like every other discussion in the halls of Congress, the debate over whether to create another department involved local concerns as well as broad principles. On April 18, 1888, without further debate and a dissenting vote, the House made eight more amendments to the bill and sent it to the Senate.[5] This cursory discussion was unlikely to be repeated in the upper house.

On May 15, 1888, Henry W. Blair, once again chair of the Committee on Education and Labor, took up a bill to expand the national government. Once again, he remarked that he did not expect much debate and hoped for a vote that evening.[6] Once again, he was wrong. If he had thought that this bill was different because it had passed the House unanimously, he did not know the Senate as well as he should have. The senators proceeded to pick the bill apart, ensuring the need for a conference committee and a delay in its enactment.

Reagan objected to the upgrade of the bureau. His lengthy oration was filled with fierce metaphors and fighting words. He even cast aspersions on the manhood of those who had proposed this legislation: "If the founding fathers and founders of the Republic could have been called back to life and could have witnessed much that has been said in the discussions in Congress on these questions for the last few years, they could hardly have failed to blush for shame on account of the degeneracy and want of manhood of their descendants in dealing with these questions."[7] He railed against "class legislation" and attributed the bill to "the money power." His alternative was the already proposed "department of industries," which would combine a bureau of labor with the Bureau of Statistics.[8] Evidently, despite his rhetoric, Reagan was just as committed to the second state ideas as his opponents. Taking very little time to dispense with Reagan's substitute, the Senate moved on to consider the bill at length.[9]

After the Senate passed its version, the conference report adopted it and recommended that the House concur in the Senate's changes. Because the changes were "formal in their character, being simply a change in the phraseology of the bill," the report urged acceptance. The House did so, resulting in the elevation of the Bureau of Labor into a department on June 18, 1888.[10] Including the Department of Education, Congress had fabricated four new departments since 1862. While this was not a massive change in the size of the national government, it constituted as great an accretion as in the previous hundred years in less than half the time. Viewed together with the Pendleton Act, the creation of the Interstate Commerce Commission, and the consideration of the Blair bill, the Congress had laid the intellectual precedents for the administrative state. But this significant decade of discussions about the shape of the U.S. national government had not concluded.

A Government of Courts

The story thus far supports the thesis that portions of the intellectual foundation for the administrative state were conceptualized, if not realized, before the advent of Progressivism and certainly before the turn of the century.[11] In the congressmen's minds this was no longer the state of "courts and parties" and had not been for years.[12] Instead, a nuanced transformation in words and legislative acts had led them to place their trust in the formulations of second state thinking. The lawyers led the effort, convinced and confident that lawyerly habits of mind, respect for the legal process, and personal training could cope with the problem of creating a larger state without creating a distant and dangerous bureaucracy. In the end the courts, manned by other lawyers, were always there in case an unexpected problem developed. This was the second state mentality.

Properly conceived, therefore, courts were part of the conception of the national government apparatus of the United States as much as any executive branch agency.[13] It is thus difficult to understand why courts have been separated from the conventional description of the growth of the administrative state. True, students of the growth of the U.S. national state divide into those who study the courts, and their attendant issues such as jurisdiction, and those who study Congress and the executive branch. A few legal historians have crossed the divide, but the two fields remain separate subspecialties.[14] At the very least with the shape of the lower court system, the two areas of concern—Congress's approach to designing agencies and its approach to the shape of the federal judiciary—overlap to the point of being indistinguishable. Members of Congress spent a great deal of time since the founding of the republic disputing and refashioning the shape, jurisdiction, appointments to, and role of the federal judicial apparatus.[15] But the debates over the structure of the federal courts from 1870 to 1891 took a new turn in the context of second state thinking.

In the aftermath of the Civil War congressional relations with the federal courts, particularly the Supreme Court, played a substantial role in the administration of the conquered South, in particular the enforcement of the Civil Rights acts. In fact, federal judges were the fulcrum of the civil rights program.[16] The open reference to federal courts in the Perce bill, among others, indicates this important aspect of Reconstruction planning. As noted in chapter 3, on the Freedmen's Bureau, this program came out of a compromise between moderates such as Lyman Trumbull and radicals such as Charles Sumner. Both camps believed that federal courts to be an essential bulwark against the former slaveocracy and wanted the freedmen to have open recourse to them. In addition to the Thirteenth, Fourteenth, and Fifteenth amendments, the Civil Rights acts, the temporary Reconstruction Acts, the Habeas Corpus Act of 1867, and the Freedmen's Bureau, Republicans vastly expanded the removal power of state cases into federal courts, thus enlarging the jurisdiction of federal courts, most prominently with the Jurisdiction and Removal Act of 1875.[17]

Scholars disagree over whether the vast surge of cases these policies fostered served corporations seeking a more favorable venue for the lawsuits they incurred.[18] Yet the vast surge did exist and proved a crushing burden to the federal judiciary, especially to the highest court, the United States Supreme Court.[19] Its justices still had to ride circuit, journeying from state to state sitting en banc with other federal judges to hear appeals that in ever greater numbers came before the highest court for review. The caseload had become so enormous that justices pleaded with the Congress directly for relief. Many U.S. attorneys general recommended an overhaul, but the Congress was deeply divided, not surprisingly, on several different grounds.[20] Out of this morass of conflict came two proposals. The first, the Davis bill, would have created a secondary layer of courts that would winnow down the number of cases before they reached the Supreme Court. These courts would be located in a single place and exercise authority over a set geographic region. The second proposal came from Representative David B. Culberson (Tex.) and would have limited corporate access to the federal courts.[21]

Under the Judiciary Act of 1789 district courts and circuit courts were both trial courts, with slightly different substantive jurisdictions and personnel. The only appellate courts in the system were the circuit courts and the United States Supreme Court. The Federalists had tried to create an intermediate level of appeals courts in the Judiciary Act of 1801, but it was repealed in 1802 by the Jeffersonians, who were rightly suspicious of the all—Federalist composition of the new tribunals.[22] This new round of debates about the overloaded federal courts promised to be just as divisive as those a century earlier.

The same questions regarding the proper role of the national government, party politics, Reconstruction's legacy, approaches to the practice of law, and the impact of economic and technological changes on U.S. government which impinged on education, labor, and the rails were embedded within the dispute about the federal courts. The congressmen had a great deal to resolve if they were to enact legislation in this tumultuous atmosphere. They did have one advantage in their favor. They had already forged a consensus around the ideas of the second state.

Under the heading "United States Courts," the House of Representatives in the spring of 1890 took another look at the overburdened federal judiciary. Speaking for the Judiciary Committee and the Committee on the Rules, Joseph G. Cannon (R-Ill.) introduced the measure that would form the basis of the discussion.[23] But there was now a joker in the deck—the "House Rules." By April 15, 1890, the House had shed the looser procedures of the previous decades for a more structured existence with standing committees governing the course of legislation. The newly elected speaker, Thomas B. Reed (R-Maine), had just started his rise to dominance over the rules with the dismantling of the "vanishing quorum" tactic in February.[24]

Cannon had studied at Cincinnati Law School, served as a state's attorney in Illinois from 1861 to 1868, and begun his congressional service in 1873, rising to become chair of the powerful Appropriations Committee in the Fifty-first Congress. Given that members of the House depended on his favor to get pet bills funded, his proposal could not be ignored.[25] But it could be opposed.

Southern Democrats denounced Reed's order limiting discussion. The prime contributors to this not-so-loyal opposition, John G. Carlisle (D-Ky.) and William C. Oates (D-Ala.) constituted the rear guard of antibureaucracy advocacy. Carlisle had been speaker of the House until the current Congress, when the Democrats lost their majority. He was a lawyer with several years in private practice then a long stint in the Kentucky legislature. Throughout his career he had vigorously resisted increases in expenditure because they would have jeopardized his concerted effort to roll back the tariff.

Oates rightly asserted that the bill "revolutionizes our judicial system."[26] The bill's alteration of the circuit courts reduced the power of the district courts, making the process of appellate judicial determination, at least in terms of actual location, less local and more hierarchical, with more clerks, more judges, and more expense to follow.[27] Besides implicating the importance of place, Oates's objections reflected an entire political, social, and cultural conception of how the world should work. The power should reside with the familiar, the accessible, and the near. That this method of allocating responsibility should lend itself to the Democratic domination of the South should come as no surprise. The two fit together so seamlessly that it is futile to discern which produced which.[28]

Richard P. Bland (D-Mo.) joined Oates in expressing these concerns, while David B. Culberson (D-Tex.) and John H. Rogers (D-Ark.) spoke for the bill, with Breckinridge plying them with pointed questions. It was a conversation similar to one in chambers, among sitting justices, akin to a conference on a case. All five men had practiced law before entering politics. The rest of Congress listened. Rogers stressed the need for "reform" in order to relieve the caseload, while Bland preferred to give jurisdiction to the state courts to alleviate the backlog.[29] Rogers introduced the phrase "administration of the law in our courts" to the debate, articulating a telling insight into the courts' function within U.S. government.

Courts, in his use of this phrase, are the organs in which law is processed. Like some form of political alchemy, ingredients enter, law is applied, and justice is served. In another part of his remarks Rogers referred to the "administration of justice" in the courts.[30] *Administration* has its basic meaning here: "to carry forth or dole out responsibilities, resources" or "to tend." What is more, a greater perception that the courts are the administrators of political goods lurks behind these phrases.

Rogers went on to list the values he saw in the measure, including practicality, increased speed, and, "so that the whole system may conform to the requirements of Government," efficiency in the future development of the country. These "requirements" were actually tautological, for they did not describe the proposal so much as they idealized the operation of the courts. That this list sounded aspirational rather than practical does not diminish its importance. It was as near a statement of the goals of government as the supporters of a larger national state would make. Values may not seem to have any substantial effect in actual, immediate circumstance, but they do determine the resultant structure of institutions. Rogers's equation of growth in activity, here the burgeoning dockets of the courts, with development of the government itself bespeaks of a fundamental belief that more is better.[31]

Breckinridge countered Rogers's assertion that creating appeals courts was a nonpartisan reform. "Is that not a very great, if not a radical, modification of our present judicial system?" While the use of the word *radical* may be without hidden meaning, its implications were surely prejudicial and intended to cast aspersions on the bill. There were plenty of radicals in the 1880s including labor radicals who had clashed with police throughout the country. It recalled as well the Radical Republicans of Reconstruction, now fallen into disfavor. Breckinridge asserted that he was only trying to get a thorough debate under way on a complex issue, but the tactic could also bog the measure down in order to kill it.[32]

Cannon fired back: "This bill is the consensus of opinion on the part of the bar throughout the United States, and everybody knows that it is equivalent to a denial of justice to refuse to enact legislation of this character."[33] The opinion of a professional cadre, the federal bar, which might have its own agenda had become an authority that must be accommodated. Cannon suggested that the legislation had to be neutral, for it merely corrected a problem. Reform, after all, does not redistribute, tax, or command; it simply improves. This was the same tactic that the defenders of the Pendleton Act had employed so effectively.

On Cannon's motion the House voted on the circumscribed timetable for deliberation: 118 yeas, 101 nays, and 108 not voting.[34] This was representative government, American style; one-third did not even participate, most likely engaging in the practice of the "dying quorum." Although Cannon spoke of a neutral reform, both parties could not but have been aware that, with Republican Benjamin Harrison in the White House making the appointments to the new circuit courts of appeals and the Republicans likely to retain control of the Senate even in the face of a Democratic surge in the election of 1890, Republicans would sit in these new judgeships. But, with the Reed rules in place, the Republican majority could dictate the agenda, even with a few defections from its ranks. The Democrats most likely did not want to go on record with a no vote on what the public might have regarded as a much-needed reform.

With these preliminaries completed, the members of Congress could proceed with a discussion on the merits. Both Rogers and Culberson now gave testimonials on behalf of the legislation. Oates had thirty minutes to speak against the measure. Rogers yielded the bulk of his time to Culberson, who argued at length for the bill. His advocacy hammered the central points. The courts overflowed with business and needed relief. The words he chose to carry his cause show a strong desire to neutralize the impact of the addition of a new layer of courts to the judicial apparatus. Only he never used that particular loaded term. He referred to the "judicial machinery," the "judicial department," and "our judicial system."[35] These labels created the impression that the courts embodied not simply another branch of government but the very essence of good administration at the ground level.

Were the federal courts the shock troops of encroaching federal government? Culberson conceded as much when he posited that "the judicial department of the Government performs more labor than either of the other departments of the Government." He also admitted to the "judicial despotism exercised by circuit and district judges" in cases with more than five thousand dollars at stake.[36] The federal bench could wield enormous influence over society, the economy, and, when so disposed, the process of government itself. The nation needed an intermediate level of appellate courts.

The real need lay less in the courts themselves, however, than in the world they served. Culberson cited the growth of population, the economy, and the railroad networks as the irresistible engine driving judicial administrative expansion. At the time of the first law providing for the federal courts, "railroads were unknown and corporations did not breed litigation."[37] This was an admission of enormous proportions. Corporate counselors had cleverly used the removal provisions of the Civil Rights Acts to avoid the grasp of local regulations and local juries' verdicts in tort cases. Federal common law courts, judges, and juries had been more supportive. This forum shopping allowed the litigious large-scale businesses to duck local prejudice (or local conscience) as they plied their entrepreneurial activities.[38]

The aversion of big businesses to local regulations had led to a concerted campaign against one of the primary offenders, the railroads, in several areas of the country. The Interstate Commerce Act, a response to this movement, had only partially calmed the revolt. The People's, or Populist, Party (formed at the end of 1889) would soon fracture the two-party system in the farming states of the West and South.[39] But Culberson turned the proto-Populist arguments on their head. He cast aside criticisms of the additional courts as an extension of federal power and portrayed the bill as a benevolent reform. The additional judges would overthrow the "kingly power of district and circuit judges." The district and circuit judges exercised this authority without appellate review because the Supreme Court was too overburdened with cases to come to the rescue. "Such a system of jurisprudence, such unlimited judicial authority over cases . . . would not be tolerated for a day by any State in the Union." Thus, Culberson concluded the legislation did not aid powerful and remote corporations, but advanced the cause of the little person, a cunning feat of rhetorical legerdemain. He went on to say that anything else would have been "repulsive to all our ideas of even-handed justice and hostile to the genius and spirit of our institutions."[40]

Democrats were not entirely content with the prospect of a Republican appellate bench. Roger Q. Mills (D-Tex.), lawyer and several times wounded Civil War veteran, attempted to make the new appointments to the bench evenly divided between the two parties. Like the membership requirements of the Interstate Commerce Commission, the federal judiciary would contain an even number of Democrats and Republicans. He offered the reason that "there could be no greater calamity befall the American people than for the whole body of the people to come to the conclusion that the judgments of the courts were partisan and therefore corrupt."[41] Courts were political because everything in government was political. His proposal expressed another continuing theme in antibureaucracy reasoning, and it directly confuted Cannon's depiction of a neutral judiciary, not to mention Reagan's position on interstate commerce.

Breckinridge endorsed Oates's proposal on the grounds of excessive expense in the proposed appellate circuits and the preservation of a homogeneous jurisprudence arising from a single intermediate court sitting in the capital.[42] That remark brought Ezra B. Taylor (R-Ohio), lawyer, former judge, veteran, and chair of the Committee on the Judiciary, out of his seat to object to Mills's amendment. He maintained that Mills's suggestion would bring politics overtly into the judicial selection process, achieving what Taylor supposedly wanted to avoid. Congress had only recently curbed the spoils system.[43] Few persons were willing to extend the discussion surrounding the corruption of the government by partisan appointments to the judicial branch (even though they all knew that such appointments depended on political affiliation).

Rogers then offered concluding remarks. He lamented that nothing could be done about corporate forum shopping, but he denied that eliminating the "evil" of circuit riding through permanent circuit courts of appeal would produce disharmony in the law. "That great central power, the Supreme Court of the United States," would rectify any differences between the circuits, he argued. His favorable reference to a hierarchical and central authority may have been a unique admission (at least in these debates) of the importance of a single, final voice in the governance of a great nation or merely a nod to the older idea that men of character could be trusted with power. But, above all, need justified the administrative novelty. Rogers introduced into the *Record* the committee report that laid out the bare facts of the matter according to the majority, a judicial system clogged with cases.[44]

With Rogers's remarks the House voted against the amendment to limit the jurisdiction of the new courts 119 to 94, with 114 not voting. The legislation then passed the House, 131 to 13, with 183 not voting.[45] The bill could continue its journey on Capitol Hill to the Senate. There the junior senator from New York, William M. Evarts, took the legislation in hand and dictated its course.[46]

Courts and the Administration of the Laws

The House, or Rogers, bill made the circuit courts the appeals courts and added two judges to each circuit court. It eliminated the Supreme Court justices' circuit riding. The Evarts proposal retained the circuit courts and added only one judge per circuit. In addition, it added an entirely new level of courts, the circuit court of appeals with three judges each, to each circuit. Some matters could go directly to the Supreme Court; others would flow to the appellate courts. It would be up to the Supreme Court whether or not to hear these appeals from the new appellate courts.[47] The specific provisions for jurisdiction are not relevant here; it is sufficient to say that the proposal's complications most likely favored the professional lawyer specialist, not to mention the wealthier client who could afford this kind of representation.[48]

Evarts's career tracked his proposed changes in the legislation. Born in Boston on February 6, 1818, to a lawyer turned Congregationalist preacher, Evarts could trace his lineage back to the founding of the colony and, like Hoar, to whom he was also related, could claim familial links to the Shermans. Although his father's death in 1830 left his family in straitened circumstances, he attended the prestigious Boston Latin school, Yale College, and Harvard Law School.[49]

With these credentials and connections Evarts began a long, distinguished, well-compensated practice in New York City, making his mark as an orator with cogent, carefully constructed, and long arguments before appeals courts at the city and state levels as well as before the U.S. Supreme Court. At the peak of his career he earned well over seventy-five thousand dollars a year, a princely sum for the time. After a stint as an assistant district attorney in New York, from 1849 to 1853, he became an organizer in the newly founded Republican Party in 1855. The fulsome compensation he received for his legal services abroad during the Civil War helped spur the creation of the Department of Justice. After he served as one of Johnson's defense attorneys in the president's impeachment trial before the Senate, Johnson rewarded him with an appointment as U.S. attorney general. Evarts advocated enfranchisement for the freedmen but supported re-admission of un-reconstructed, former Confederate states.[50]

Firmly opposed to the so-called rule by bayonet approach to the South, Evarts found no difficulty serving on the legal team that successfully brought about Rutherford B. Hayes's ascension to the presidency in 1877. Evarts's philosophy was that of "a typical nineteenth century lawyer, believing in freedom of enterprise, in the rights of property, in due process of law, and in the American businessman." Consistent with these principles, he performed his duties as Hayes's secretary of state, president and one of the founding members of the New York State Bar Association as well as the American Bar Association, and an opponent of David Field's revolutionary reform of the civil code.[51]

Elected to the U.S. Senate in 1885, Evarts became a solid partisan for Republican policies—though with a few surprising positions. He supported the Blair bill, which he came to favor through his position as a trustee of the Peabody Fund. He argued for the Lodge Elections bill, the incorporation of the American Historical Association, and the fund-raising effort for the Howard University Law School's new building that would bear his name.[52] When the circuit courts of appeals bill came to the Senate, this thin, angular man with a sallow complexion saw it as a boon to lawyers and a capstone to the kind of state the lawyers had constructed.

On September 19, 1890, Evarts presented his version of the bill to the Senate. He had made the new circuit courts true appellate courts. Although Supreme Court Justices would still participate, they would not be part of the trial, or fact-finding, process. After a series of amendments that covered everything from the shape of the circuits to the treatment of appeals from the Indian territories, Evarts offered his own extensive remarks,[53] portraying the circuit courts of appeal as a neutral reform that relieved the Supreme Court of its overwhelming caseload. Necessity seemed to drive invention, but Evarts did not rest his case on mere necessity. The terms he used are as instructive as the general content of his arguments. Four times he referred to the "administration of justice" and three times to the "judicial establishment."[54]

A conscious advocate of a more substantial national state, he frankly portrayed the courts as the best administrators in a time for the nation which required more and more administrative expertise. With his extensive experience as a both a trial and appellate court advocate, Evarts well knew that the enforcement of laws occurred in courtrooms. Properly understood, the judiciary constituted just as much an establishment or institution of government as the other two departments, or branches. He had no doubt that the courts were part of the state. Evarts also presented his measure as a politically neutral reform to serve the interests of "jurisprudence and uniformity of decision." He repeated that phrase to counter the opposition's call for subunits of the Supreme Court to alleviate the burden on the whole court.[55]

After Evarts's presentation, George Vest spoke for those who opposed the measure. He had practiced law both before and after the Civil War in Missouri, during which he represented Missouri in the Confederacy's House of Representatives then its Senate. His oral arguments on behalf of a client suing his neighbor for shooting his dog, Drum, became part of local legend. He returned to political life in the 1870s, serving in the U.S. Senate from 1879 to 1903. As one would expect from this resume, his arguments repeated the core of the traditional rejection of professional, unelected, central power.[56] He compared the workload of federal judges unfavorably to that of state judges and denounced justices working in "the shadow of the Capitol." They were unresponsive to any constituency, and life tenure isolated them from the will of the people. They were the worst kind of administrators.[57]

Vest's solution to the high court's workload was to subdivide the Court into smaller pieces. With a smaller number of justices deliberating and multiple panels at work, they could supposedly dispose of the burgeoning caseload three to four times more quickly as before. There would be no need to create more unelected judges.[58] One may substitute the word *bureaucrats* for *judges* and get the gist of Vest's antibureaucracy sentiments.

Vest's counterproposal prompted a dense interchange on the practicability of this "scheme," its constitutionality, and its jurisdictional import. Kentucky Democrat John G. Carlisle, Hoar, Joseph N. Dolph (R-Ore.), Delaware Democrat George Gray, and Spooner all worried about the constitutionality of his proposal. Vest dismissed their concerns as cavils, derisively remarking at one point that "any lawyer would be satisfied with the decision of three judges of the Supreme Court of the United States." How the remark fit his earlier criticism of the justices he did not explain. His localism did not appeal to many in the Senate, however, nor to the professional bar organizations to which many of his audience belonged. Yet Vest's commentary revealed a great deal about the underlying sentiments of an important, if underrepresented in the Senate, portion of the country's lawyers.[59]

By this time, the beginning of the 1890s, the legal profession had begun to divide, unevenly, into two segments. An elite bar—leaders of their state bars and members of the newly established American Bar Association—dominated practice in the highest courts. They also garnered the largest fees in a new system of hourly rates for legal services. Some of these lawyers would also serve as professors in the handful of elite law schools in the United States. There, they would work a veritable revolution in legal education. Beginning at Harvard Law School, under the leadership of Christopher Columbus Langdell, new faculties and methods were replacing the nuts-and-bolts institutions with academic classrooms. The anecdote-filled lectures were losing out to Socratic dialogues informed by a scientific exploration of the principles behind the cases. In the decades to come, elite law schools would only admit college graduates and became the feeders of large law firms and corporate practices.[60] In the meantime the vast majority of attorneys, like Vest, continued to "read" law in law firms before applying for admission to the bar or attending prestigious law schools, practicing locally or beginning political careers. They resented their increasingly visible second-class status, one that (at least according to Vest) the circuit courts of appeals bill would worsen.

Veering away from Vest's proposal for a division of the Supreme Court, Dolph presented the case for the other dissenters who favored the House bill over Evarts's substitute. Dolph began his critique by admitting that the United States had simply outgrown its "judicial system." The sheer scale and scope of the nation's enterprises necessitated a change that recognized the growing irrelevance of state borders with the advent of "steam and electricity." His terms varied slightly from those Evarts had used, resembling more his compatriots' in the House. *Judicial system, judicial establishment,* and *judicial machinery* connote an impersonal, institutionalized functioning. The Supreme Court became "the balance-wheel in the vast mechanism of our dual form of government."[61]

The machinery metaphor had appeared before, but now its context was demonstrably different. This was a machine age. What was more, a politician could still refer to the wonders of technology and be seconded in his statements. While some might have found the analogizing of the court system to impersonal devices disturbing, it felt more and more appropriate as the century reached its conclusion. This was not the high tide of scientific government. It was, however, in its early stages.[62]

Dolph had no college education, entering the bar of the state of New York after study while teaching school. Service in the Civil War as a member of the "Oregon Escort" protecting emigrants against Native American resistance brought him to Oregon, where he settled down to practice law, mainly for the railroads, then served as a city attorney, a U.S. attorney, then a state senator until 1874, when he expanded his law practice. He became a U.S. senator in 1883, losing his seat in 1894. He brought to the discussion the tremendous burdens under which federal judges operated, especially in a region the size of the Pacific Northwest. Asserting that the Evarts substitute would place too great a burden on these judges, Dolph argued for the Rogers bill. To the contention that the circuit courts of appeals would not have sufficient business to occupy themselves, he wisely reminded his colleagues that, essentially, if you build it, they will come.[63]

The final statement of the day came from Morgan, whose battle against "northern aggression" had subsided from the incendiary to the quaint. Someone had laundered the Republican "bloody shirt." Survivors of the war met regularly at celebrations of their common sufferings.[64] No one held his wartime service against him. Morgan spoke in favor of the Evarts substitute. He had been around long enough to be forgiven his eccentric mix of reformism and suspicion of change. He, too, referred to the "administration of justice," but he stated obliquely that the South had reason to be suspicious, fearful, and distrustful of federal courts, an allusion to Reconstruction.[65]

The heritage of Alabama "justice" weighed heavily upon him. Its courts had gone from frontier to settled lands through Indian wars and a civil war. Administration of justice encompassed the maintenance of slavery and the dispossession of the Indians. During Reconstruction Alabama had undertaken a series of experiments in equal justice for people of color then rejected the notion during "Redemption." If these very contradictions were the essence of politics in the post-Reconstruction era, what could *administration of justice* mean? Morgan was a relic of times gone by, but he could still yearn for some kind of institutional reform in which courts would perform without fear or favor.

When the Senate reconvened on September 20, the participants sallied back and forth on a number of issues. Dolph's amendment giving appellate jurisdiction over the territories to the circuit courts elicited a lengthy discussion about whether the territorial courts could be trusted, as Evarts maintained. After those present agreed to this modification, the senator from Oregon proposed another change, altering the shape of the Pacific Coast circuit. Evarts objected, for he believed that a discussion of this kind of matter would indefinitely delay passage of any act. Almost completely blind from a degenerative ailment, for him time was growing short.[66]

The senators, however deliberative their body might be, were just as local in their outlooks as the members of the House. Where courts met, lawyers congregated, litigants gathered, businesses flourished, and money flowed. And the future held an even greater promise of wealth. With the increasing scale and scope of interstate commerce, diversity of citizenship litigation, and the amounts at issue, not to mention the ever-expanding federal criminal code book, the federal courts could expect a substantially heavier workload.

The senators remembered the old script from the Pendleton and Interstate Commerce acts. What else could explain the intervention of Republican senator John J. Ingalls from Kansas? The "efficiency of our judicial system" concerned everyone, he insisted. Reagan rose to second this view. His own circuit, the Fifth, stretching from Texas to Florida, required reorganization. He despised the "autocratic powers" of the circuit judges, whose glutted dockets impaired the "administration of justice."[67] As Evarts had warned in his exchange with Dolph, discussion over the shape of the circuits opened up a floodgate. But behind the gerrymandering of judicial circuits lay the old triumvirate: economy, efficiency, and responsiveness. It would have its say. Evarts would just have to be a little more patient.

Concerns about the jurisdiction of the new courts also arose. John W. Daniel (D-Va.), known as the "Lame Lion of Lynchburg" from a wound he received at the Battle of the Wilderness, offered an amendment to add to the appellate ambit federal felonies and matters involving the custody of a child. Although the proposal possessed no inherent centralization ramifications on its face, Daniel's language begs a closer reading. A law graduate from the University of Virginia who wrote two renowned books on legal matters and helped establish the "Lost Cause" movement, Daniel did not see the issue as simply one of reform. He put great weight on the concept of "free institutions" in a "republican form of government." Inherent in the very existence of the nation as a "republic" was the core value of liberty.[68] What this had to do with his amendment is not clear, except that it gave him his chance to connect an antebellum southern ideal of personal liberty with court reform.[69]

Vest, however, had not finished. He still opposed the creation of the circuit courts of appeals. Would not this intermediate level of scrutiny merely serve corporations seeking to delay litigation until it died? Pushed by the questioning of northern Republicans, Vest made his last stand. Paraphrasing some unnamed English judge, he asserted that "all justice should be administered in a manner acceptable to suitors; in other words, that the courts of the country should be popularized as far as possible."[70] The new judges would be bureaucrats, indifferent to the people. "It is a country based upon the will of the people. It is a country that appeals in all its laws and in all the administration of its laws to the consent and confidence and affection of the people."[71] Vest was indifferent to claims of neutrality. The courts should be accountable not to the abstractions of the law but to the popular will. The consent of the governed trumps the need for dispassionate adjudication.

Speaking past this "sentiment," Evarts continued to paint his measure's impact in beige. It was what the litigators wanted. They must be appeased. "The preponderence [*sic*] of opinion, judicial and professional, and of the community interested in litigation, is hostile to the scheme of a division of the Supreme Court into chambers." Vest replied that the rural South, the farmer, the trader, and the merchants who felt under siege by the growing reach of interstate corporations needed a champion. Having more federal courts was the antithesis of democracy. "What do the people know about the details of procedure in the Supreme Court? Who has ever made this a burning issue except the Bar Association of the United States, and that has been divided from beginning to end, and it is divided to-day?"[72]

Like punch-drunk fighters in the last rounds, the two sides in the Senate debate staggered toward votes on the amendments to the amendments. One by one they went down to defeat, with roughly half the body absent for each vote. On September 24 the senators resumed their discussion, deciding to keep the Maryland to South Carolina circuit court of appeals in Richmond rather than Baltimore. At long last they voted forty-one to six in favor of passage, with thirty-one absent. Evarts, Hoar, and Pugh received appointments to the conference committee that would reconcile the two measures.[73]

The House received the results of the conference committee on February 28, 1891, during the usual abbreviated second session that followed the November election. Made a lame-duck Congress by the Democratic surge, its Republicans met knowing that their party had lost the House but retained the Senate. Their choice was either to accept the Senate (Evarts) version or do nothing at all. Most likely, if they did nothing, the new Democratic leadership would have other priorities than the circuit courts or in any case a different approach. With the Republican majority to continue in the Senate, however, the Republican leadership knew that the new judges would be Republican. A statement from the House managers, Ezra B. Taylor and L. B. Caswell, summarized the differences between the two measures:

> The effect of the conference is to require the appointment of nine circuit judges, one in each circuit, instead of seventeen, as provided in the House bill, and to create a court of appeals, consisting of two circuit judges and the Chief Justice or associate justice of the Supreme Court assigned to the circuit, while the House bill relieved the justices from this duty. The circuit courts retain original jurisdiction for the trial of causes, while the House bill confines original trials to the district courts. No causes now on the calendar of the Supreme Court are to be remanded to the court of appeals, as provided for in the House bill.[74]

With discussion limited to thirty minutes for each side, the congressmen considered their two options.

Rogers spoke first, lamenting the Senate's substitution. He referred to the "federal judicial system" and the distribution of original jurisdictions. This language suggests he considered the judicial branch a single entity with organizational purpose, arrangement, and coherence. Primarily, he contended that the Evarts bill did not relieve the Supreme Court at all, leaving the present overload uncorrected. Circuit riding remained, draining time and resources that could be better used elsewhere. Last, it provided additional marshals who served no additional function.[75]

Culberson responded essentially with "half a loaf is better than none." Given the Senate's action and the pressing need to get something passed, he argued, the House members should hold their noses and affirm. "Shall the demand of the bar of the United States, without regard to party, be ignored?" Bringing up the issue of spoils, he asked rhetorically, "Shall the best interests of the country, so long outraged and disgraced by the law's delay, continue to be neglected because the President of the United States may fill these places with his party friends?" He was willing to answer yes while still leveling this charge of politicizing the judiciary.[76]

Oates lobbied again on behalf of a single court of appeals to preside in Washington, D.C. Using the venerable slippery slope argument, he predicted that the circuit courts would soon multiply until their numbers dwarfed the "federal judicial system." He held that only an economical plan would provide "the administration of justice between litigants and . . . protect the people against turbulence, violence, and lawlessness." Breckinridge continued, emphasizing his original point about "harmonious and national jurisprudence." After all, if the law diverges according to jurisdiction, it is no longer law. Although he asserted the need for a national law with the advent of steam travel and the telephone, he also seconded Oates's fear of multiplying courts.[77]

Richard Vaux (D-Pa.) worried that the Supreme Court was accumulating too much power. The Congress endangered the Court's standing with the people, he maintained, by making it an omnipresent force in American political life.[78] Vaux had spent most of his career as a practicing attorney in Philadelphia, working for penal reform, and served one term of elected office as mayor. His current status as a member of Congress as an appointee would end in March, for he had lost his bid to be elected in his own right. His appeal from personal experience, "I am a lawyer," nevertheless captured the essential truth of the second state approach. It was lawyers' work.[79]

A Vermont Yankee transplant now representing Wisconsin, Lucien B. Caswell, and a Missouri Republican, Nathan Frank, both practicing lawyers, spoke in favor of the conference report along the same lines as Culberson. Caswell expressed the opinion that "subsequent Congresses will find it easier to amend and improve the law" than to enact it in the first place. Frank reiterated this prediction, stating that eventually there would be "a system entirely satisfactory to the country."[80] One might wonder whether he was referring to a future Republican-controlled Congress, given the imminent Democratic takeover. The old system of spoils even in the judiciary remained deeply relevant.

Following these lackluster endorsements, "one of the most important changes in the jurisprudence of the country" came to a vote of a sort. Speaker Reed recorded 107 ayes and 62 noes. Oates called for the yeas and nays, a more formal roll call vote. This and Oates's subsequent call for tellers did not elicit sufficient numbers in the speaker's opinion, only 29 and 33, respectively, for each request. Despite an objection from Breckinridge, Reed refused both requests, thus, the House agreed to the conference report and the Evarts, or Circuit Courts of Appeals, Act became law.[81] Tallying the numbers, we find that only 169 representatives participated in this action at all—only slightly more than the fewer than half, 144, who took part in the original vote, possibly another instance of those with misgivings refusing to go on record against a supposedly neutral, much-needed reform. Similarly, we can only poll the opinions of those who spoke during the debates to discern anything more than the yeas and nays.

The end result of this twenty-year debate was the expansion of the federal court system. Although its supporters claimed that the reform would lighten the load on the Supreme Court, if anything, the amount of litigation quickened. Just like building additional lanes on a highway, the Congress only added to the traffic. The added capacity to handle legal cases furthered the use of that system. With its added capacity the national government's judiciary could extend its reach. The Congress, whether wittingly or unwittingly, had laid the necessary judicial infrastructure for the administrative state in this, the second state, era.

"Rendering Good Service" with the Second Morrill Act

On June 14, 1890, Justin Smith Morrill introduced a second appropriation in support of "colleges for the advancement of scientific and industrial education."[82] His nation, his Congress, and he, himself, had changed a great deal since he had first introduced his proposal to aid colleges. The very fact that he felt another piece of legislation was necessary leads to the conclusion that the changes had not wrought a tectonic shift in the nature of the American state. Colleges still wanted assistance. The Congress was still considering how best to aid higher education. The debate over the nature of American government continued. The principles of the second state, however, were now well embedded in the debate. In fact, they framed it. Morrill would have to demonstrate a need, argue that his means were the most limited possible, that the apparatus of government was as minimal as could be, and that the functioning of his proposal was consistent with the prevailing, persistent set of ideas behind American governance. If he did, passage was ensured.

This was not the first time Morrill had tried to supplement the funding plan that became law in 1862. In what may be seen as a backhanded compliment, he attributed its lack of success to his New Hampshire colleague's quest for common school funding. Blair's speech on common schools, "like the soul of John Brown, will be marching on and rendering good service everywhere to common schools for years to come."[83] This allusion to one of the Union's Civil War marching songs evinced a certain frustration with the process that had delayed his own bill while the Senate fruitlessly debated the Blair bill. Nevertheless, the arguments for both stemmed from the same tree.

As Garfield, Hopkins, Blair, and many others had, Morrill drew a link between his proposal and the future prosperity and survival of the country: "A popular government of the people pre-eminently requires the support of sound learning in all departments, in jurisprudence, finance, foreign relations, as well as in its home affairs and in its executive and legislative administration."[84] Literacy and numeracy were not enough. This was not a particularly second state proposition. Washington, Jefferson, and others in the antebellum period had favored aid to higher education. What was different was Morrill's characterization of the evil to be avoided.

The surplus from the tariff presented an urgent need. He warned it will "beget danger [*sic*] of heedless and possibly wild projects for massive expenditures."[85] Morrill shared the fiscally conservative fears of the first state's formulators. Large amounts of money produced extravagance that was devastating to the body public. Here was a first state idea being applied to a second state function: the sponsorship and standardization of higher education.

Morrill expressed hope for quick passage without much debate. But he would be disappointed. Education always lay at the margin of the second state—it dipped too deeply into local prerogatives. Reagan drew the line at federal supervision of education: "Mr. President, I am in hopes that that amendment will not be adopted. There can be but one main purpose in it, and that is to give the Federal Government supervision of education in the States."[86] Morrill's attempt to perfect his proposal had elicited the same problem that all plans to increase the size of the national state encountered. Sponsorship and standardization had difficulty existing without some form of supervision.

Hoar urged caution: "There is a good deal of question in my mind what would be the precise legal meaning of the word 'college.'" Besides the fact that there could be no legal meaning of the word *college*, his remark served notice to Morrill and Blair, his belated cosponsor, that the measure could not be passed without discussion. Morrill managed to get unanimous approval to have S. 3714 considered the next Thursday after the morning business. Blair had the bill and his committee's report printed in the *Record*.[87]

The lateness of the session (June 21, 1890) limited the amount of time that Morrill and Blair could allow for consideration of the merits or demerits. Now that they had been put on notice about the substantial opposition they had not expected, they had to compromise if they wanted to ensure that there would be enough time for the lower house to pass the bill. And no one could ignore the elephant in the room: race. The senators from southern states in particular were anxious about certain provisions in the legislation which might affect segregated education. Just as other proposals invariably involved slavery before the Civil War and the "Negro" question after it, the second Morrill bill to aid agricultural and mechanical arts colleges and universities had to pass the gauntlet of the race question.

Reagan went so far as to claim a cabal: "I wish to add here that it seems to be upon the theory of a great many leading men in New England, almost a New England idea, that the Constitution of the United States is to be overthrown by the enlargement of the powers of the Federal Government and by the abridgment of the powers of the States, and this is one of the means of doing it."[88] The rhetoric may have been a bit overblown, but it had the essentials right. New Englanders were playing a leading role. The legislation would expand the powers of the federal government. But he was wrong in one essential respect: the prevailing view of the Constitution in the Senate favored this enactment, and it knew no section. The great compromise of the second state now encompassed all sections.

Morgan's critique thrust to the heart of the matter in the harshest terms. He objected to the "scheme" that "the schools shall be regulated by a law passed here and by administrative measures enacted here."[89] Although the argument was about the form the national government would take, behind it lay a concern about Alabama's segregated society. By this time the southern states had almost completed their process of separating their facilities, their public spaces, their economy, and their society into two. Under the label *colored*, whites relegated African Americans to inferior, infrequent, and noticeably removed areas, schools, restrooms, sections of restaurants, if any at all, and railroad cars, among others.[90] Morgan's opposition was only the tip of the iceberg. Race was inextricable from the process, as its repeated appearances in the Second Morrill Act debate shows.

Given that race was tied to federalism, Morgan could logically make the link between his section's peculiar arrangement and elements of the proposal such as section 5, which reads, "the Secretary of the Interior is hereby charged with the proper administration of this law, through the Commissioner of Education; and they are authorized and directed, under the approval of the President, to make all *needful rules and regulations* not inconsistent with its provisions to carry this law into effect."[91] Blair's committee had attempted to make a step beyond the second state into a regulatory third state. It was a natural progression, but not an automatic or an incontestable one. First there is the gathering and dissemination of information. Then there is sponsorship of various activities. Then the Congress moves to standardize the provision of these services by sponsoring legislation. Finally, there is a concern with supervising the activities. The supervision can either be light, through the courts and congressional oversight, or heavy, through the administration of bureaucracies. Blair and his committee tried to argue for the latter. They ran into trouble not just with ardent segregationists such as Morgan and Reagan but also with members of their own party.

The senators eventually removed all references to the "commissioner of education." They replaced the wording with *secretary of the interior* even on relatively innocuous requirements involving who was to receive the reports. There seemed to be an implicit understanding that only a cabinet officer would have the appropriate rank to communicate with the states on their use of the monies. Federalism played a substantial role in this alteration of the legislation. This was not the anti-statist, states' rights federalism that had prevailed in the first state. This was the federalism of co-sovereigns. As Blair put it, "I believe that both are independent and are sovereign each within its proper sphere."[92] The compromise of the second state approach became clear in his rendition of the motivating philosophy.

The 1880s had reached their end. Blair summarized the governing ideas of this period: "The nation has the power of necessity, in self-defense it has the power, to educate those who are to be the State and are to be the nation, so that they may exercise the powers of self-government." The state could only exercise this power through sponsorship and standardization, lightly supervised. Speaking of the agricultural and mechanical arts colleges, Blair stated, "These institutions are really the nuclei where this form of education must take root and from which it must expand throughout all portions of the country."[93] Just as a tree grows out of an acorn, so would a system of higher education spread from such a limited appropriation. Blair, Morrill, Evarts, and the rest of the Senate placed their faith in this minimalist approach not only because more ambitious funding plans such as the Blair bill had failed but due to their shared commitment to the principles of the second state, in which the nation could be more active, have a more expansive apparatus, and legislate for the betterment of the country.

There was still the issue of how to deal with the South's segregated educa-

tional system. Pugh had proposed an amendment to make sure that the state legislatures were able to divide their grants between the colleges they had set up for
whites and the ones set aside for "coloreds." Hawley and Ingalls not only tolerated racial discrimination but accepted it as the best system for the South. Hawley opined "I would not do that, but that is their way." Ingalls went even farther,
supporting segregation outright: "I believe that it is inappropriate and improper,
in various ways detrimental to the best interests of both races, that coeducation
should be conducted." But even within this acceptance of racial separation he
distrusted the southern Democrats' representation of their system in positive
terms. "I do not believe they like the colored people as well as they do the white
people, and I think they must be put under bonds just the same as the Northern
people must be put under bonds to do justice," he asserted.[94] As an admirer of
Charles Sumner and an inveterate supporter of civil rights for African Americans, he wanted a proportionate share to go to both groups.[95]

On June 23, 1890, the Senate completed its hasty deliberations with the unanimity born of the accommodation that marked the end of Reconstruction and
was the hallmark of the second state approach. Morrill accepted amendments to
his bill which allowed the state legislatures to administer the funds in the way
they saw fit with no formal federal oversight except the reporting requirements.
The only restriction with regards to segregated colleges was that the distribution had to be "equitable." To accommodate black colleges such as the Tuskegee
Institute, he changed the language to include "the institution for colored students." The senators thus enshrined the wording of segregation in federal law.
With the substitution of the *secretary of the interior* for *commissioner of education*
in order to gain the good opinion of senators such as Plumb, the act would was
now "conducive to good administration." The Senate passed S. 3714 without a
tally and amended its title to reflect the fact that they had removed the railroad
lands from the funding arrangement.[96]

On August 19, 1890, S. 3714 came before the House under a special rule limiting debate to two hours. Like the Senate, the representatives were concerned
about the funding mechanism, were largely in agreement about the constitutionality of the measure, and were divided about the impact of the plan on the
state of the republic. Unlike the Senate, the representatives evinced a different
overall view of higher education. From the start speakers decried the use of federal money to help train the professional doctors, educators, and lawyers. This
distaste for federal funding of "elite" education showed the differences between
the two houses of Congress, but it also showed a lingering desire to sponsor the

more common occupations rather than the emerging professional occupations. This was not yet the expert driven society of the third state. The congressmen displayed a second state mentality—a commitment to the generalist in private life as well as public service.

Louis E. McComas (R-Md.) had charge of the bill. He allowed Joseph D. Taylor (R-Ohio) to present an amendment dedicating the funds solely for agricultural and mechanical arts education.[97] They were both college-educated lawyers, though Taylor had a more distinguished legal resume to that point. Neither should have been all that dismissive of higher education, yet the chasm between their experience and the ideas which they entered into the *Record* could not have been plainer.

McComas explained Taylor's amendment as necessary "so as to prevent the money being expended in the ordinary college training in belles-lettres and the dead languages, but to more nearly confine these schools to industrial training and agricultural education." Taylor echoed "our agricultural colleges educate young men to be doctors and lawyers and preachers and teachers and disqualify them for the farm."[98] Congress, it appears, could not look to a future of professionally educated men while remaining true to the desires of its members' constituents, especially when philosophies like that of the Grange still held sway over issues such as falling crop prices, railroad monopolies, and banks.[99]

At various times during his presentation McComas had to answer questions about why the allocation was out of public land sales and not the general treasury, how much the measure would cost, and what would happen if the money from land sales dried up. He minimized the cost of the proposal, predicted an important impact, and professed ignorance about why anyone might question the constitutionality of the project. He did not have to wait long for the Democratic side of the aisle to rebut him.

Shades of the old days lingered, as Samuel W. T. Lanham (D-Tex.) entered into the *Record* President James Buchanan's veto message from the 1859 Morrill Act. Daniel Kerr (R-Iowa) lamented the funding formula that would give to each state equally instead of proportionately, labeling it unconstitutional. Mark H. Dunnell (R-Minn.) joined him, adding that the "pittance" was not enough to help, while it would diminish the chances for farmers to buy their own land by forcing the federal government to sell the land rather than give it, for example, to his constituents. James O'Donnell (R-Mich.) weighed in with his understanding that no farmer wanted the bill but that he would vote for it if amended because he supported education bills.[100]

In the same way that the Department of Agriculture, the Department of Education, the Department of Labor, the education bills, the Pendleton Act, the Interstate Commerce Act, and the Evarts Act received considerable support from organizations dedicated to those respective causes, so the second Morrill bill had its backers. Asher G. Caruth saw a connection between these interest group efforts and those of the railroads on their companies' behalf. The "education lobby" had "haunted the corridors of this Capitol; they have stood sentinel at the door of the Committee on Education; they have even interrupted the solemn deliberations of that body by imprudent communications."[101] His effort to make the agricultural colleges into some sort of nefarious business organization stemmed from an ancient disparagement, distrust, and opposition to special interests, a shadow conspiracy of those seeking to live off the public weal.

Caruth's attempt to characterize the agricultural colleges ran into difficulty because they were by now fixtures of localism. He was unable to fend off various corrections as he became mired in the details of how every institution in each state charged its students.[102] Although he tried to salvage his argument with a reference to pork barrel politics, its members demonstrated the difficulty that anti–state enlargement advocates faced in the second state intellectual environs. The constitutional argument of Jackson, Madison, and Jefferson that Congress could not appropriate money for purposes not explicitly mentioned in the Constitution had lost its persuasive power over congressional majorities. A different mind-set prevailed which allowed for federal funding for sponsorship with a standardizing effect to follow. As long as the supervision of the effort was locally based, the additional programs could overcome older, first state principles.

The line of thought was clear. As long as the idea was to benefit a common, not elite, segment of the country, it could command bipartisan support. John A. Anderson (R-Kans.), a Presbyterian minister, not a lawyer, could speak with some authority on the topic as a former regent of the University of Kansas and president of the Kansas State Agricultural College. He explained that the colleges had "been absorbed by professional educators and . . . have turned out professional men," by which he meant "lawyers, doctors, preachers, and teachers." He believed that, once the Morrill bill was amended, these colleges would be encouraged to provide a "practical" education, "out of which the farmers of the country can make more money than they do, or out of which the girl or woman who is compelled to support herself by her own labor can make more money as a telegraph operator or printer or in other directions than without it."[103]

The House adopted Taylor's amendment without a count and rejected

Caruth's amendment to strike out the reporting requirements and the with-holding provision. By a vote of 135 to 39 the second Morrill Act passed the House. On August 20, on a motion from Blair, the Senate concurred in the House's amendment. On August 30 President Harrison signed the Second Mor-rill Act of 1890 into law.[104] With this signature the process of debate had come full circle. The debate on the Evarts Act would continue until the following year, but the culmination of a remarkable decade of conceptual development had al-ready been reached.

AS THE DEBATES over elevating the Bureau of Labor into a department, the Evarts (Circuit Courts of Appeals) Act of 1891, and the Second Morrill Act demonstrate, significant additions to the administrative state took place even as Reconstruction politics receded into distant memory. Moreover, these suppos-edly neutral reform efforts rested upon the same basic novelties that underlay the Civil War and Reconstruction agencies and departments. The interplay of interest groups, their associations, the pro-enlargement advocates both in Con-gress and the executive branch, all interacted to produce additions to the national state, though the dictates of the older antibureaucracy ethic remained in place. Lawyers' concepts, procedures, values, and interchanges allowed the congress-men to consider, modify, and ultimately pass these measures. Oddly enough, their words in the Evarts Act debate rendered the most lawyer-specific legisla-tion the most coolly administrative. Rogers's *administration*, Culberson's *judicial machinery*, Evarts and Morgan's *administrative machinery*, and Dolph's Supreme Court as a "balance-wheel" demonstrated that legal matters themselves were now devoid of the human element. Morrill's use of the doctrine of equity to jus-tify funding segregated schools seems warm by comparison.

Congress had moved firmly into new territory. It had created a more elabo-rate, expansive state as it shifted from sponsorship to supervision to standard-ization. The way opened for the Progressives. Ultimately, Congress retained the older values, while it accepted new challenges. The lawmakers, like the public they represented, could not avoid repeating the choices of earlier days. The con-gresses of the Progressive Era did not originate the paradox. They inherited it and chose to reenact it. Future generations could criticize that choice after new crises hit but found they could do no better.

The administrative mentality would have to wait for the Progressive, New Era, and New Deal eras, from the 1890s to the 1930s, but much of the prepara-tory conceptual work was already in place by 1891. Lawyers in Congress had given to lawyers in the administration of the civil service, the regulatory agencies, and the courts the opportunity to guide the state-making process in the future. The watchwords *exceptionalism, economy, democratic responsiveness,* and *efficiency* were still in play, the language reflecting ever more dimly an increasingly changing reality. Nevertheless, forced to rely on the encoded outline they had fashioned, the advocates of a more substantial national state continued the expansion of the leviathan into the new area of standardization of administration as well as sponsorship and supervision.

"To Answer Our Purposes, It Must Be Adapted"

In 1887 Woodrow Wilson championed the idea of expertise in the administration of government in an article in a fledgling academic journal, *Political Science Quarterly*. Many regard the article, "The Science of Administration," as one of the founding documents of political science,[1] but one passage in particular stands out: "to answer our purposes, it [methods of administration] must be adapted, not to a simple and compact, but to a complex and multiform state, and made to fit highly decentralized forms of government." Wilson had an ambitious program: "If we would employ it, we must Americanize it, and that not formally, in language merely, but radically, in thought, principle, and aim as well. It must learn our constitutions by heart; must get the bureaucratic fever out of its veins; must inhale much free American air."[2] In writing these words, the future president participated in and contributed to the conversation about the nature and course of the American state.

Given the fact that Wilson himself was seeking a professorship in this field, we could also conclude one of his goals was to make the case for political science as an academic discipline. The search for a legitimate, scholarly, academic basis for his position made him one of the leading young intellectuals and academics of his time. But his ideas, lauded as a vision of the future, were in fact a tribute to the already existing "second state," with its melding of expertise and the antibureaucracy ethic. He garbed that state in the raiment of American exceptionalism, the concept that the United States stands apart from the rest of the world, even as the approach he described verged closer to European models.[3] Nevertheless, in his view the federal government did not need the "bureaucratic fever" to run its new bureaus. It could regulate its railroads and its corporate empires without recourse to highly centralized, supposedly undemocratic agencies. In short he knew, even if only subconsciously, that the second state had arrived, and he knew—and what a close reading of the congressional debates reveals—how its advocates had cloaked their invention.

The wonderfully rich sources examined here demonstrate that the thought process behind an expanded national government in the United States, from 1858 to 1891, did not constitute a series of radical departures but, rather, revealed a halting, gradual, and almost self-effacing series of overlapping dramas. The recognition that the administrative apparatus of government must change did not accompany a full-blown shift in the older ideas of a limited government, the "government of states," or the "first state."

The process, in fact, allowed antibureaucracy thinking—the demand for the dispersal of power, economy, and representativeness of any new institution—to be almost as visible in the debates at the end of our period of study as at its inception. What is more, the debates show how members from different sections, parties, and interests came to share certain notions of government building. At times the extent of the consensus is astounding, and thus the advocates of each of these programs often deployed the same set of concepts as their opponents. Congressmen learned to encode novelty as the most conservative possible response to absolute exigency or as the most practical housekeeping measure to deal with pesky inefficiencies. They spoke of localities, borrowed techniques from state government, and promised that the character and piety of appointees to the new commissions, departments, and bureaus would always matter. As a result, the ideas of the second state approach exhibited a disconnect with the acts of enlarging the government. Thus, legislative inventions such as the Interstate Commerce Commission which appear to many historians as heralds of a new age of economic regulation were for their creators nothing of the sort. Everyone knew the steps to this dance; it was only a matter of who would lead.

But consensus was not the whole story, for the continuities were in constant tension with a series of complicating and evolving ideas, influences, and contexts.

Geographical section mattered. So, too, political partisanship added another dimension to the debates. Partisan rivalries for office and the spoils of office also cut across the second state mind-set. Economic issues, political scandals, and foreign policy shaped the contours of the Congress. Scheduling and congressional procedures combined with these party exigencies to influence the course of the discussion.

Finally, varieties of personal experience found their way into the debates—for example, in the educational background of representatives as well as their Civil War experiences. Perhaps the most controversial among them centered on the foreign travel of some of the participants. Some brought back from abroad an admiration of German and English administrative solutions. For others, the mere mention of foreign institutions raised hackles of American exceptionalism. Proposals had to find a way through these complications.

Above all, lawyers found ways through this thicket of conflicting interest and advocacy. Deferred to for their expertise and numerous, in every session lawyers dominated the debates over the creation of new institutions or the undertaking of a new task. By training and practice they accustomed themselves to give-and-take over details. They participated in the debates as though they were arguing a case in court, scoring points and sharing insider knowledge of the ways of lawyers. Their courtroom demeanor allowed them to criticize one another's points with professional courtesy. It was this lawyerly style that allowed the congressmen to end the day of linguistic jousting only to repeat the process the next. As lawyers, they grasped the implications of legislative initiatives. They translated for their colleagues how changes in the law could change the way that everyone lived and created a set of ideas consistent with their predispositions. In the process they infused their discourse with their professional attributes as well as into the concepts with which they were wrestling.

The fact that lawyers and their concepts and way of thinking dominated the discussion played a substantial role in this transition from the first state mind-set to that of the second state. Legal devices such as the trust, experience with administration of estates, the professional ethic of service, the centrality of courts and courtlike proceedings, the drawing on precedents to argue a policy point and a legal point, and even their very style of presenting their arguments as if to a jury or an appeals court gave them the language, if not the actual apparatus, to enable this shift. At the same time that many of them derided elites, remote power, and cosmopolitanism, their own experiences allowed them to draw on both esoteric legal knowledge and popular notions about the nature of the American state.

Closer reading of the debates reveals not only the concepts behind congressional actions but also the inch-by-inch progress by which a larger state emerged consistent with the antibureaucracy ethic of the country as well as its legislators. The Jeffersonian/Jacksonian/old republican (the first state) conception of government envisioned a small, lightly staffed, largely amateur, and highly politicized administrative apparatus for the federal government in which the victor distributed the spoils of office, all the while decrying the corruption and cupidity of its opponents. The federal government took on only the most necessary functions of order keeping described in the Constitution. Even the National Republicans', later the Whigs', advocacy of internal improvements did not include an expansion of federal power, expense, or expertise. Loose construction of the Constitution in the Hamiltonian manner might include a national bank, but that bank was largely a private affair, with no federal bureaus or bureaucrats in the vicinity.

By contrast, second state thinking about the federal government evolved to encompass a more intrusive style of government, responsible for a number of social and economic activities. Although this kind of government seems to anticipate, indeed include, elements of the regulatory administrative model of the Progressive Era and thereafter (the "third state"), two important qualifications separate the two. First, there was no clear transition from the second state to the third, any more than there was a smooth, logical, and self-conscious transition from the first state to the second. Instead, one finds overlapping layers of continuity: first state ideas appearing in the middle of debates on second state innovations; both first and second state concepts carrying over into the Progressive period. Second, the second state was not itself a transition period. Its values, honed in the cauldron of the Civil War and Reconstruction, were distinct from those of the old republican and the Progressive period to come. While not self-contained, the second state heyday deserves attention for itself—for its creative power and its limitations.

In the initial debates over the Morrill Act antebellum conceptions of the state dominated the contributions of southern representatives, who struggled with the idea of sponsorship. The plan was not original in method, but the goal was substantially different from the piecemeal efforts Congress had accepted in the first state's set of precepts. In particular, constitutional interpretation—the very nature of the government—came into question. Despite these difficulties, the congressmen groped their way toward a group of legal terms that enabled them to make the leap into a new approach. Only President Buchanan's veto prevented them from carrying out their vision, but they had already laid the foundation for further action.

In the second debate on the Morrill Act and the discussion of the creation of a Department of Agriculture during the first years of the war, antebellum conceptions persisted, even though their southern advocates had departed. The fear of foreign competition, the need to shore up a vital constituency, and wartime demands led Congress to act. Nevertheless, the federal government committed itself to a limited form of sponsorship of higher education and agriculture. Advocates of these additional programs had finessed the bureaucratic implications by giving the states a choice. The Department of Agriculture began its existence with a small budget and a commissioner at its head. Congress shrank from making a total commitment to the establishment of a cabinet level department until 1889. But the new task of supervision had plagued the debate. Having committed the national government to sponsoring two fields of endeavor—higher education and agriculture—they now had to deal with the attendant task of supervising the activity. Shrinking from the implications, they compromised by imposing additional restrictions on how the programs would be run. This was still congressional government, to use Woodrow Wilson's phrase. Events conspired against this fragile compromise.

Later in the war, when the federal government had grown larger and more expensive, the Freedmen's Bureau debates indicated how limited the congressmen's conception of the state remained while they accommodated their thinking to a different social, political, and economic landscape. The advance of Union armies had created another crisis: what to do with the freedmen. The Congress's goals might have been expansive, including federal supervision for a limited time of reconstructed states and southern localities, but the means the congressmen assayed to reach these goals remained consistent with antebellum ideas of the state. Ultimately, the leaders in Congress took the Freedmen's Bureau away from the radicals and made it consistent in both origins and conceptualization with the antibureaucracy traditions. The second state compromise with power allowed sponsorship and supervision but only with limited means. Congress was still uncomfortable with the new way of thinking.

The same was true of the rise and fall of the Department of Education, even though the debate now included Union Civil War veterans and took place during the supposed reign of the Radical Republicans. Despite these setbacks, those supporting a larger role for the national government had succeeded in introducing another new task to the state's repertoire: standardization. The Bureau of Education was only one instance among many of second state thinking about how to govern the country.

The creation of the Department of Justice featured the language of economy, efficiency, and reform borrowed from the older terminology, but it also represented this same breakthrough in the character of congressional thinking about the proper place of the state. The scandal of mounting legal bills from outside attorneys and ever-increasing legal work might not seem like much of a crisis, but its apparent minor status hides its larger ramifications. The debate over the Department of Justice cemented the concept of standardizing an activity, in this case law enforcement. This "second pillar" of its creators' republican state concept fit naturally into the architecture of ideas that now included ongoing federal supervision and sponsorship that the Congress built into the Morrill Act and the Department of Agriculture. What was more, it gave to lawyers an open, central, and prominent role in the management of the administrative apparatus. With the Department of Justice, would-be creators of additional institutions had found the model for the three great administrative innovations of the 1880s: the civil service, the Interstate Commerce Commission, and the circuit courts of appeal established by the Evarts Act.

The triumph of the second state mind-set should not blind us to the very real restraints on congressional enactments in this period. Even failures to approve proposals show a great deal about the development of congressional thought. Aid to common schools came up most significantly with the Hoar bill, the Perce bill, and, famously, the Blair bill. The very evolution of these plans impacted congressional thinking. From the supervisors in the Hoar bill to the land grants of the Perce bill to the emergency ten-year allocation in the Blair bill, the senators and representatives quarreled, waxed eloquent, and occasionally agreed about the nature of the republic, the proper means to enact policy, and their place in the process. Coalitions of thought emerged from these discussions which contributed to the increasing preeminence of second state principles in the 1880s.

The supporters of the Pendleton Act, the Bureau (later Department) of Labor, the Interstate Commerce Act, and the Evarts Act all characterized the legislation in the language that the proposers of the earlier measures had pioneered. Some southern representatives and Democrats could go on record in support of these initiatives precisely because they were couched in the second state conceptual framework. Even those who opposed novelties such as rate-making powers and circuit courts conceded the preeminence and the legitimacy of the courts as administrative adjudicators. As lawyers themselves, they could do little else.

At the same time, these were critical departures from the supervisory and sponsorship policies of the first Morrill Act and the Department of Justice, respectively. Each in turn was prompted by a perceived crisis in the civil service system, labor relations, railroad rates, and the overflow in the federal courts. The Pendleton Act sought the limitation of the democratic patronage system in favor of examinations such as those taken by applicants for admission to the bar. The Bureau of Labor satisfied the need for information collection and dissemination as well as giving a voice to its constituency. The ICC was the first, though hesitant, foray into regulation. The Evarts Act abandoned the old system of courts in favor of a more elaborate circuit court arrangement. From the arguments both for and against the legislation, the Congress acknowledged its accession to the precepts of the second state. Information gathering and dissemination, limited financial support, an ethic of service to Congress, and lawyer-like personnel attributes characterized the building blocks of the nonbureaucratic bureaucracy. Standardization had taken its place alongside sponsorship and supervision.

It was very fitting, therefore, when Congress debated a second Morrill Act. It had come full circle in many ways, arriving, however, at a different place. Although the voices of limited government continued to resound in both chambers of the Capitol, the prevailing set of ideas included funding the land grant colleges, even though the monies came out of a shrinking resource. They still had trouble providing for the supervision of the money. They still had to accommodate the older federal structures. They still could not easily reconcile themselves to a substantial commitment. They still worried about local distinctiveness. Nevertheless, they had gone past the sectional rivalry by recognizing the Jim Crow South. The second state mentality had lost its novelty and had become de rigueur.

Future generations of congressmen and women would build on this legacy just as these Congresses had built on the intellectual foundations of the first state paradigm. The problems inherent with a regulatory agency such as the Interstate Commerce Commission would be met with new compromises—with a third state mentality that accepted the dictates of progressive governance. If we were to trace out developments, we might find a fourth state—one of national security in the wake of the Cold War. It was not that the Congress had abandoned the first, second, and third states' ways of thinking. They continued to apply. Congress still doled out benefactions to constituents as in the first state conception. Individual representatives and senators sought ways to sponsor, supervise, and standardize activities, as with the second state approach. Regulatory agencies and welfare programs survived. But now they could reconcile themselves to other functions.

In a way it was destined to happen. A legalistic and antibureaucratic political culture could not fathom a different kind of state. Conceptual persistence is a part of human psychology. The U.S. second state, like its predecessor and successors, was like a bound leviathan. The paradox of national government expansion in the United States both emerged from and was represented in the congressional debates between 1858 and 1891. That they would repeat these debates was a choice made, a reaffirmation, and a peculiar outgrowth of the nature of the discussion. When unitary, authoritative, and universalistic bureaucracies are perceived as the greater threat, the United States must accept the consequences. The politics of post-9/11 America may or may not be new, but the supposed dilemma is perennial. Opinion shapers in Congress and outside of those halls will always pose the issue as a choice between freedom and tyranny. As long as that preconception exists, we will see these debates again, along with the crises that provoke them.

Acknowledgments

My efforts in this inquiry involved the full scope of my academic training in three different disciplines: history, political science, and law. As such, I have accumulated debts to a wide range of people. The conceptual beginnings of this project began at Rutgers College in New Brunswick, New Jersey. I thank my advisors there, Kenneth Finegold in political science and James Reed in history, for their invaluable guidance. Another phase of the work continued at Harvard Law School, where several professors, including Morton Horwitz, took a confused undergraduate and made him a more disciplined legal scholar. To them I owe more than I can calculate.

For this work itself, I must pay tribute to several sources of financial support: the U.S. Department of Education's Jacob Javits Fellowship; the trustees, graduate board, and history department at the Johns Hopkins University for a university fellowship; the New York University School of Law and its Samuel I. Golieb Fellowship; and the state of Maryland's graduate scholarship program. My employer, Seton Hall University, and my colleagues and friends at the Hall also deserve praise for their support of my work. Maxine Lurie, chair of the history department, and Molly Smith, dean of the College of Arts and Sciences, were unstinting in their support.

I am particularly indebted to those who have taken the time and effort to read drafts and give me the benefit of their wisdom including, but not limited to, William E. Nelson and the members of the New York University School of Law Legal History Colloquium; James Vorenberg, the commentator on my panel's papers at the American Society for Legal History conference in Cincinnati, Ohio, in November 2005; the participants in the Faculty Research Forum at Seton Hall; my dissertation committee at the Johns Hopkins University, including Matthew Crenson, Joseph Cooper, and Steven Hanke; the members of the Johns Hopkins American History seminar; and Ronald G. Walters, my indefatigable second reader at the Johns Hopkins University Press. I must make particular mention of the immense editorial efforts of Mark Summers at the University of

Kentucky–Lexington. His close read, pages of comments, suggestions, references, and critical analysis made a seminal impact. Chuck Grench, senior editor at the University of North Carolina Press, Daniel R. Ernst of the Georgetown University Law Center, and Ballard C. Campbell of Northeastern University provided much assistance with an earlier version of the manuscript. Joel H. Silbey, President White Professor of History, Emeritus, Cornell University, helped me to perfect the most recent version. Special thanks must go to James E. Gillispie in the Milton S. Eisenhower Library's government publications division for his invaluable assistance and the rest of the staff at the Johns Hopkins University Sheridan Libraries for their aid in my researches as well as the libraries of Seton Hall University, the University of Pennsylvania, and Rutgers–The State University of New Jersey, including Anne Dalesandro and Mary McGovern of the Rutgers School of Law–Camden Law Library.

I must give all the appreciation I have and more to my parents, N.E.H. Hull and Peter Charles Hoffer—of Rutgers Camden Law School and the University of Georgia history department, respectively—without whose unqualified support nothing would have been possible. My father's persistence, advice, editing, and near constant willingness to engage in conversation for the umpteenth time about this work went beyond the call of duty. To my graduate advisor, Louis Galambos, whose immense reserves of patience, skill, knowledge, and editorial abilities were taxed to the limit by my demands, I owe the deepest gratitude and affection. To Robert J. Brugger, this book's editor and my mentor for many years, I owe a debt hard to express and harder to repay. Finally, I thank Elizabeth Gratch for the grueling task of correcting my many style and language difficulties. For the remaining errors despite all of this assistance, I take full responsibility.

Notes

INTRODUCTION: "Badly in Detail but Well on the Whole"

1. For Carl Schurz's life story, see Hans L. Trefousse, *Carl Schurz: A Biography* (Knoxville: University of Tennessee Press, 1982); and Claude Moore Fuess, *Carl Schurz: Reformer* (New York: Dodd, Mead, 1932).

2. Carl Schurz, *The Reminiscences of Carl Schurz* (London: J. Murray, 1909), 3:278–79; italics added.

3. For Greeley's deceptively maverick career, see Glyndon G. Van Deusen, *Horace Greeley: Nineteenth-Century Crusader* (Philadelphia: University of Pennsylvania Press, 1953), 98–99; Suzanne Schulze, *Horace Greeley: A Bio-Bibliography* (Westport, Conn.: Greenwood Press, 1992), 19, 22, 26, 40, 45; Henry Luther Stoddard, *Horace Greeley: Printer, Editor, Crusader* (New York: G. P. Putnam's Sons, 1946), 91–93.

4. Horace Greeley, Letter to J. Tarbell, Mar. 23, 1870, in J. Tarbell, "Horace Greeley's Practical Advice," *Magazine of American History with Notes and Queries* (New York), 18 (July–Dec. 1887): 423–25, 424–25.

5. George M. Fredrickson, *The Inner Civil War: Northern Intellectuals and the Crisis of the Union* (New York: Harper & Row, 1965), 9–10. Fredrickson uses the term to describe the ideas of one part of the intelligentsia while I maintain that it is shared by the vast majority. For "anti-bureaucracy," see Ellis W. Hawley, "The New Deal State and the Anti-Bureaucratic Tradition," in *The New Deal and Its Legacy: Critique and Reappraisal*, ed. Robert Eden (New York: Greenwood Press, 1998), 77–92.

6. Richard Franklin Bensel, *Yankee Leviathan: The Origins of Central State Authority in America, 1859–1877* (1990; rpt., New York: Cambridge University Press, 1995), 116–92.

7. Felix Frankfurter, *Felix Frankfurter Reminisces: An Intimate Portrait as Recorded in Talks with Dr. Harlan B. Phillips* (New York: Reynal, 1962), 104. For Frankfurter's life and philosophy *see* H. N. Hirsch, *The Enigma of Felix Frankfurter* (New York: Basic Books, 1981), 12–24; Michael Parrish, *Felix Frankfurter and His Times: The Reform Years* (New York: Free Press, 1982), 5–59; Melvin I. Urofsky, *Felix Frankfurter: Judicial Restraint and Civil Liberties* (Boston: Twayne Publishers, 1991), 1–8.

8. Frankfurter, *Reminisces*, 104.

9. The term *administrative state* originated with Dwight Waldo's *The Administrative State* (New York: Ronald Press, 1948), cited in William D. Richardson, *Democracy, Bureaucracy, and Character: Founding Thoughts* (Lawrence: University Press of Kansas, 1997), 5 n. 14.

10. The term *bureaucracy*, which for the purposes of this work means rule by bureaucrats, has a long, complex history. See Martin Albrow, *Bureaucracy* (New York: Praeger, 1970).

11. Robert A. Divine, et al., *America: Past and Present*, 6th ed. (New York: Longman, 2002), 2:640; Pauline Maier, et al., *Inventing America: A History of the United States* (New York: W.W. Norton, 2003), 2:689; Mark C. Carnes and John A. Garraty, *The American Nation: A History of the United States*, 11th ed. (New York: Longman, 2003), 2:572; John M. Murrin et al., *Liberty, Equality, Power: A History of the American People*, 3rd ed. (Fort Worth, Tex.: Harcourt, 2002), 2:711. In *Building a New American State: The Expansion of National Administrative Capacities, 1877–1920* (1982; rpt., New York: Cambridge University Press, 1995) Stephen Skowronek proposes that the state of parties and courts gave way to the administrative state in the Progressive Era and is the dominant view in state-building literature in political science.

12. Michael G. Kammen, *People of Paradox* (New York: Knopf, 1973); Seymour Martin Lipset, *American Exceptionalism: A Double Edged Sword* (New York: W. W. Norton, 1996); Dorothy Ross, *The Origins of American Social Science* (1991; rpt., New York: Cambridge University Press, 1997), xiv–xix.

13. For another example of work that analyzes congressional debates for their own worth, see David P. Currie's volumes on *The Constitution in Congress* (Chicago: University of Chicago Press, 1997–).

14. I must thank Tony Alan Freyer for suggesting the Evarts Act as a proper topic for a consideration of state building in this period. He was absolutely correct that courts, and the Evarts Act in particular, should be included in this inquiry.

15. I calculated this total not from the pages of the *Globe* and *Record* (they are larger than the standard page) but from an estimate of the average words per page and assumed 250 words per page.

16. *Congressional Globe*, vols. 27, 28, 32, 34, 35, 36, 37, 39, 40, 42, 43, 45 (Washington, D.C.: Blair & Rives, 1858–73); *Congressional Record: Proceedings and Debates of the United States Congress*, vols. 14, 17, 18, 21, 22 (Washington, D.C.: U.S. Government Printing Office, 1884–91).

17. A part of what many historiographers call "consensus history." Gary B. Nash, Charlotte Crabtree, and Ross E. Dunn, *History on Trial: Culture Wars and the Teaching of the Past*, rev. ed. (New York: Vintage, 2000), 56–58.

18. The "state" as a leviathan is a popular one in the literature on state building. The original inspiration is from Thomas Hobbes's classic work, *Leviathan* (1651), edited with an introduction by C. B. MacPherson (1968; rpt., London: Penguin Books, 1985).

PROLOGUE: "The Great, Noisy, Reedy, Jarring Assembly"

1. *We, the People: The Story of the United States Capitol, Its Past and Its Promise* (Washington, D.C.: U.S. Capitol Historical Society in cooperation with the National Geographic Society, 1976), 43; Edward Dicey, *Spectator of America, Edited with an Introduction by Herbert Mitgang* (Chicago: Quadrangle Books, 1971), 66–67.

2. Carl Abbott, *Political Terrain: Washington, D.C., from Tidewater Town to Global Metropolis*, (Chapel Hill: University of North Carolina Press, 1999), 64, 66.

3. Allan G. Bogue, *The Earnest Men: Republicans of the Civil War Senate* (Ithaca: Cornell University Press, 1981), 26.

4. Dicey, *Spectator of America*, 69.

5. Anthony Trollope, *North America*, edited with an introduction, notes, and new ma-

terials by Donald Smalley and Bradford Allen Booth (New York: Alfred A. Knopf, 1951), 329.

6. William C. Allen, *History of the United States Capitol: A Chronicle of Design, Construction, and Politics* (Washington, D.C.: U.S. Government Printing Office, 2001), 329.

7. Bogue, *Earnest Men*, 28–29.

8. Barnet Baskerville, *The People's Voice: The Orator in American Society* (Lexington: University Press of Kentucky, 1979), 92–93.

9. Allen, *History of the United States Capitol*, 215–87.

10. Glenn Brown, *History of the United States Capitol, Two Volumes in One* (New York: Da Capo Press, 1970), vol. 2 (Washington, D.C.: Government Printing Office, 1903), 126–31.

11. *The Capitol: A Pictorial History of the Capitol and of the Congress*, 9th ed. (Washington, D.C.: U.S. Government Printing Office, 1988), 107.

12. Dicey, *Spectator of America*, 71.

13. Trollope, *North America*, 329.

14. *New York Graphic*, Jan. 24, 1876.

15. Frank G. Carpenter, *Carp's Washington*, arranged and edited by Frances Carpenter (New York: McGraw-Hill, 1960), 13, 17.

16. Dicey, *Spectator of America*, 70.

17. *Chicago Tribune*, Jan. 31, 1870.

18. Ernest Duvergier De Hauranne, *A Frenchman in Lincoln's America*, trans. Ralph H. Bowen, ed., Bowen and Albert Krebs (Chicago: Lakeside Press, 1975), 1:55.

19. Dicey, *Spectator of America*, 73.

20. Dicey, *Spectator of America*, 70–71.

21. Dorothy Ross, *Origins of American Social Science* (New York: Cambridge University Press, 1991, 1997), xviii–xix, esp. n. 3; Mary P. Ryan, *Civic Wars: Democracy and Public Life in the American City during the Nineteenth Century* (Berkeley: University of California Press, 1997), 3–15 and accompanying notes.

22. A list of horribles which can be greatly extended: *Nation*, May 1, 1879; *Cincinnati Commercial*, Apr. 20, 1866, and June 20, 1874; *Washington Star*, Mar. 14, 1875.

23. Mark Wahlgren Summers, *The Press Gang: Newspapers and Politics, 1865–1878* (Chapel Hill: University of North Carolina Press, 1994), 26.

24. For a contemporary account, see Woodrow Wilson, *Congressional Government: A Study in American Politics* (Boston: Houghton Mifflin, 1885), 91.

25. Alvin M. Josephy Jr., *On the Hill: A History of the American Congress, From 1789 to the Present* (1975; rpt., New York: Simon & Schuster, 1979), 166.

26. See William S. Blatt, "Interpretive Communities: The Missing Element in Statutory Interpretation," *Northwestern University Law Review* 95 (Winter 2001): 629–43; *generally* William D. Popkin, *Statutes in Court: The History and Theory of Statutory Interpretation* (Durham, N.C.: Duke University Press, 1999).

27. Popkin, *Statutes in Court*, 64–113.

28. Allan G. Bogue, Jerome M. Clubb, Carroll R. McKibbin, and Santa A. Traugott, "Members of the House of Representatives and the Processes of Modernization, 1789–1960," *Journal of American History* 62(2) (Sept. 1976): 275–302, 284–85.

29. Alexis de Tocqueville, *Democracy in America* ed. J. P. Mayer (1837; rpt., New York: Viking, 1969), 164, 264.

30. See generally Mary Ann Glendon, *A Nation under Lawyers* (New York: Farrar, Straus and Giroux, 1994); and Anthony T. Kronman, *The Lost Lawyer: Failing Ideals of the Legal Profession* (Cambridge: Belknap Press of Harvard University Press, 1993).

31. Peter Charles Hoffer, *Law and People in Colonial America*, 2nd ed. (Baltimore: Johns Hopkins University Press, 1998), 131–33.

32. Frankfurter, *Reminisces*, 104.

33. See, among others, Robert Kagan, *Adversarial Legalism: The American Way of Law* (Cambridge: Harvard University Press, 2001).

34. E.g., Christopher Tomlins, "Framing the Field of Law's Disciplinary Encounters: A Historical Narrative," *Law and Society Review* 34 (2000): 911–67.

35. Guyora Binder and Robert Weisberg, *Literary Criticisms of Law* (Princeton: Princeton University Press, 2000), 39 ff.

36. See, e.g., Robert W. Cover, *Justice Accused: Anti-Slavery and the Judicial Process* (New Haven: Yale University Press, 1975), 137–47.

37. James Farr, "The Americanization of Hermeneutics: Francis Lieber's *Legal and Political Hermeneutics*," in Gregory Leyh, *Legal Hermeneutics: History, Theory, and Practice* (Berkeley: University of California Press, 1992), 102 n. 18, for Lieber's Prussian difficulties.

38. Margaret Susan Thompson, *The "Spider Web": Congress and Lobbying in the Age of Grant* (Ithaca: Cornell University Press, 1985), 16–21.

39. Michele Landis Dauber, "The Sympathetic State," in Forum: "'Overtaken by a Great Calamity': Disaster Relief and the Origins of the American Welfare State," *Law and History Review* 23(2) (Summer 2005): 399–400.

40. Lawrence Friedman, *A History of American Law*, 2nd ed. (New York: Simon & Schuster, 1985), 218, 221.

ONE: A "Government of States"

1. Although the conception of the "cosmopolitan progressive" embodies much of what I intend to describe, unlike the originator of this term, I believe the transatlantic conversation was continuous from the colonial period onward and reformist minded persons had always sought the potency of European based ideas and institutions. See Daniel T. Rodgers, *Atlantic Crossings: Social Politics in a Progressive Age* (Cambridge: Belknap Press of Harvard University Press, 1998).

2. Leonard Curry, *Blueprint for Modern America: Nonmilitary Legislation of the First Civil War Congress* (Nashville: Vanderbilt University Press, 1968), 9; Harold M. Hyman, *American Singularity: The 1787 Northwest Ordinance, the 1862 Homestead and Morrill Acts, and the 1944 G.I. Bill*, Richard B. Russell Lectures, no. 5 (Athens: University of Georgia Press, 1986); Allan Nevins, *The State Universities and Democracy* (Urbana: University of Illinois Press, 1962), 22; Roland R. Renne, *Land-Grant Institutions, the Public, and the Public Interest* (*The Annals of the American Academy of Political and Social Science*, special edition, vol. 331, Sept. 1960, 46–51), 48; Heather Cox Richardson, *The Greatest Nation of the Earth: Republican Economic Policies during the Civil War* (Cambridge: Harvard University Press, 1997), 1–7.

3. See generally Forrest McDonald, *Novus Ordo Seclorum: The Intellectual Origins of the Constitution* (Lawrence: University Press of Kansas, 1986); Jack Rakove, *Original Meanings: Politics and Ideas in the Making of the Constitution* (New York: Vintage, 1997).

4. David Madsen, *The National University: Enduring Dream of the USA* (Detroit: Wayne State University Press, 1966), 9–66.

5. For the beginnings of the divide between the strong federalists and the weak federalists' factions, see E. Wayne Carp, *To Starve the Army at Pleasure: Continental Army Administration and American Political Culture, 1775–1783* (Chapel Hill: University of North Carolina Press, 1984), 221–22.

6. Jack P. Greene, *The Intellectual Construction of America: Exceptionalism and Identity from 1492–1800* (Chapel Hill: University of North Carolina Press, 1993), 167–99.

7. Alfred Charles True, *A History of Agricultural Education in the United States, 1785–1925*, U.S. Department of Agriculture Miscellaneous Publication no. 36 (Washington, D.C.: U.S. Government Printing Office, 1929), 1–102; William Edwin Sawyer, "The Evolution of the Morrill Act of 1862" (Ph.D. diss., Boston University, 1948), 15–115.

8. Edmund J. James, *The Origin of the Land Grant Act of 1862 (The So-called Morrill Act) and Some Account of Its Author Jonathan B. Turner*, University Studies 4(1) (Nov. 1910) (Urbana-Champaign: University of Illinois Press, 1910); Karl-Ernst Jeismann, "American Observations Concerning the Prussian Educational System in the Nineteenth Century," in Henry Geitz, Jurgen Heideking, and Jurgen Herbst, *German Influences on Education in the United States to 1917* (Cambridge: Cambridge University Press, 1995), 35–39; and Roger L. Williams, *The Origins of Federal Support for Higher Education: George W. Atherton and the Land-Grant College Movement* (University Park: Pennsylvania State University Press, 1991).

9. Perry Anderson, *Lineages of the Absolutist State* (London: N.L.B., 1974), 240–46, 265–77; Charles E. McClelland, *State, Society, and University in Germany, 1700–1914* (Cambridge: Cambridge University Press, 1980), 56–57, 73, 98, 142–45; James Van Horn Melton, *Absolutism and the Eighteenth-Century Origins of Compulsory Schooling in Prussia and Austria* (Cambridge: Cambridge University Press, 1988), 234–39; Karl A. Schleunes, *Schooling and Society: The Politics of Education in Prussia and Bavaria, 1750–1900* (Oxford: Oxford University Press in U.K., St. Martin's Press in U.S.A., 1989), 1–7.

10. Robert D. Mitchell, "The Formation of Early American Cultural Regions: An Interpretation," in *European Settlements and Development in North America: Essays on Geographical Change in Honor and Memory of Andrew Hill Clark*, ed. James R. Gibson (Toronto: University of Toronto Press, 1978), 66–90.

11. See, e.g., Joyce Chaplin, *An Anxious Pursuit: Agricultural Innovation and Modernity in the Lower South, 1763–1815* (Chapel Hill: University of North Carolina Press, 1993); Edgar W. Knight, *Public Education in the South* (Boston: Athenaeum Press, 1922), 264–65.

12. George Donald Merrill, "Land and Education: The Origin and History of Land Grants for the Support of Education" (Ed.D. diss., University of Southern California, 1965), 141; Paul Westmeyer, *A History of American Higher Education* (Springfield, Ill.: Thomas, 1952), on Tappan, see 31–32; generally, see 29–40.

13. Jurgen Herbst, *And Sadly Teach: Teacher Education and Professionalization in American Culture* (Madison: University of Wisconsin Press, 1989), 15–31, 55–56.

14. Lawrence A. Cremin, *American Education: The National Experience, 1783–1876* (New York: Harper & Row, 1980), 126–27; Richard Hofstadter and C. DeWitt Hardy, *The Development and Scope of Higher Education in the United States* (New York: Columbia University Press, 1952), 13–14, 23–28.

15. True, *History of Agricultural Education*, 88–97.

16. See, e.g., David M. Potter, *The Impending Crisis, 1848–1861*, comp. and ed. Don E. Fehrenbacher (New York: Harper & Row, 1976), 24, 289.

17. William Freehling, *Prelude to Civil War: The Nullification Crisis in South Carolina, 1816–1836* (New York: Harper & Row, 1966), 159–73; and Don E. Fehrenbacher, *The Dred Scott Case: Its Significance in American Law and Politics* (New York: Oxford University Press, 1981), 46–47.

18. See, e.g., Herbert Hovenkamp, *Enterprise and American Law, 1837–1936* (Cambridge: Harvard University Press, 1991), 80.

19. See, e.g., J. Willard Hurst, *Law and the Conditions of Freedom in the Nineteenth-Century United States* (Madison: University of Wisconsin Press, 1959), 3–32; and, for a description of the change in the jurisprudence of property, see Morton J. Horwitz, *The Transformation of American Law, 1780–1860* (Cambridge: Harvard University Press, 1977), 31–62.

20. Richard Bernstein, *Thomas Jefferson* (New York: Oxford University Press, 2003), xii.

21. For a general introduction to the topic, see Melvin I. Urofsky and Paul Finkelman, *A March of Liberty: The Constitutional History of the United States*, 2nd ed. (New York: Oxford University Press, 2002), 133–34.

22. William J. Novak, *The People's Welfare: Law and Regulation in Nineteenth-Century America* (Chapel Hill: University of North Carolina Press, 1996); Harry N. Scheiber, "Regulation, Property Rights, and Definition of 'The Market': Law and the American Economy," *Journal of Economic History* 41(1) (Mar. 1981): 103–9; and Scheiber, "Federalism in the American Economic Order, 1789–1910," *Law and Society Review* 10(1) (1975): 57–117.

23. For the existence of some kind of national planning for the economy, see Frank Bourgin, *The Great Challenge: The Myth of Laissez-Faire in the Early Republic* (New York: G. Braziller, 1989); Carter Goodrich, "National Planning of Internal Improvements," *Political Science Quarterly* 63(1) (1948): 16–44; for the land grants and pensions impact on national development, see Laura Jensen, *Patriots, Settlers, and the Origins of American Social Policy* (Cambridge: Cambridge University Press, 2003).

24. Benjamin Horace Hibbard, *A History of the Public Land Policies* (New York: Macmillan, 1924), 311–23; Merrill, "Land and Education."

25. For a history of land policy debates at the national level through the Jacksonian period, see Daniel Feller, *The Public Lands in Jacksonian Politics* (Madison: University of Wisconsin Press, 1984); Merrill, "Land and Education," 101–32.

26. Leonard D. White, *The Jacksonians: A Study in Administrative History, 1829–1861* (New York: Macmillan, 1954), 533.

27. James, "The Origin of the Land Grant Act of 1862," 26–27, arguing Jonathan Baldwin Turner of Illinois was the author; Merrill, "Land and Education," 162, arguing the act was the result of many influences; Sawyer, "Evolution of the Morrill Act," 113.

28. Morrill's biographical information is from Randal Leigh Hoyer, *The Gentleman From Vermont: The Career of Justin S. Morrill in the United States House of Representatives* (Ph.D. diss., Michigan State University, 1974); William B. Parker, *The Life and Public Services of Justin Smith Morrill* (1924; rpt., New York: Da Capo Press, 1971); Carl R. Woodward, "Justin Morrill of Vermont: The Heritage of a Country-bred Statesman," *New England Galaxy* 5(4) (1964): 37–46.

29. See, e.g., John Mack Faragher, *Sugar Creek: Life on the Illinois Prairie* (New Haven: Yale University Press, 1986).

30. Coy F. Cross II, *Justin Smith Morrill: Father of the Land-Grant Colleges* (East Lansing: Michigan State University Press, 1999), 5, 9–12.

31. Parker, *Gentleman from Vermont*, 41.

32. Cross, *Father of the Land-Grant Colleges*, 25–43.

33. Cross, *Father of the Land-Grant Colleges*, 79–80.

34. From "A Bill Donating Lands to the Several States" (and-grant college bill), *Congressional Globe*, 35th Cong., 1st sess., Apr. 20, 1858, vol. 27 (Washington, D.C.: Blair & Rives, 1858), 1697.

35. For the state of the Republican ideology and rhetoric in this period, see Eric Foner, *Free Soil, Free Labor, Free Men: The Ideology of the Republican Party before the Civil War* (Oxford: Oxford University Press, 1970); William Gienapp, *The Origins of the Republican Party, 1852–1856* (Oxford: Oxford University Press, 1987); Richard L. McCormick, *The Party Period and Public Policy: American Politics from the Age of Jackson to the Progressive Era* (Oxford: Oxford University Press, 1986), 168.

36. William David Zimmerman, "The Morrill Act and Liberal Education," *Liberal Education* 50(3) (1964): 395–401, 400.

37. *Congressional Globe*, 35th Cong., 1st sess., vol. 27 (hereafter abbreviated as 27 C.G.), Apr. 22, 1858, 1697.

38. For a history of the General Land Office until 1837, see Malcolm J. Rohrbough, *The Land Office Business: The Settlement and Administration of American Public Lands, 1789–1837* (Oxford: Oxford University Press, 1968); for a recounting of its creation and reorganization, see Lloyd Milton Short, *The Development of National Administrative Organization in the United States*, Institute for Government Research, Studies in Administration (Baltimore: Johns Hopkins Press, 1923), 147–49.

39. White, *Jacksonians*, 421–24. For a description of Jacksonian tussles with the General Land Office bureaucracy, see Matthew A. Crenson, *The Federal Machine: Beginnings of Bureaucracy in Jacksonian America* (Baltimore: Johns Hopkins University Press, 1975), 115–31.

40. Steven Skowronek, *Building a New American State*, 24–31.

41. See Frederick S. Calhoun, *The Lawmen: United States Marshals and Their Deputies, 1789–1989* (Washington, D.C.: Smithsonian Institution Press, 1989); William Gillette, *Retreat from Reconstruction, 1869–1879* (Baton Rouge: Louisiana State University Press, 1979), 31–33.

42. 27 C.G., 1692.

43. For the history of the U.S. House of Representatives, see George B. Galloway, *History of the House of Representatives* (1961; rpt., New York: Crowell, 1962); Barbara R. de Boinville, ed., *Origins and Development of Congress* (1976; rpt., Washington, D.C.: Congressional Quarterly, 1982); and Joseph Cooper, *The Origins of the Standing Committees and Development of the Modern House* (Houston: Rice University Press, 1971).

44. Boinville, *Origins and Development*, 111–12; Galloway, *History of the House*, 101–5.

45. Galloway, *History of the House*, 296.

46. 27 C.G., 1692.

47. See, e.g., Joseph Conforti, *Imagining New England: Explorations of Regional Identity*

from the Pilgrims to the Mid-Twentieth Century (Chapel Hill: University of North Carolina Press, 2001); William J. Gilmore, *Reading Becomes a Necessity of Life: Material and Cultural Life in Rural New England, 1780–1835* (Knoxville: University of Tennessee Press, 1989), 372–73.

48. 27 C.G., 1693–96.

49. R. Freeman Butts and Lawrence Cremin, *A History of Education in American Culture* (New York: Henry Holt, 1953), 191–94; Rush Welter, *Popular Education and Democratic Thought in America* (New York: Columbia University Press, 1962), 36–37.

50. Richard D. Brown, *Modernization: The Transformation of American Life, 1600–1865* (New York: Hill & Wang, 1976), 131–32, 137–45; *Knowledge Is Power: The Diffusion of Information in Early America, 1700–1865* (New York: Oxford University Press, 1989), 217, 287–89.

51. 27 C.G., 1697.

52. 27 C.G., 1696.

53. U.S. Constitution.

54. 27 C.G., 1696–97.

55. 27 C.G., 1697.

56. 27 C.G., 1740.

57. 27 C.G., 1741.

58. See, e.g., Freehling, *Prelude to Civil War,* x; Alexander Saxton, *The Rise and Fall of the White Republic: Class Politics and Mass Culture in Nineteenth-Century America* (1990; rpt., New York: Verso, 1996), 23–25, 140–54.

59. 27 C.G., 1742.

60. 27 C.G., 1742.

61. But a combination typical of the religious press of the day, as it happened. See, e.g., Nathan O. Hatch, *The Democratization of American Christianity* (New Haven: Yale University Press, 1989), 135.

62. 27 C.G., 1742.

63. For the history of the U.S. Senate, see *Origins and Development of Congress,* 191–221; George H. Haynes, *The Senate of the United States: Its History and Practice,* 2 vols. (Boston: Houghton Mifflin, 1938).

64. *Members of Congress since 1789* (Washington, D.C.: Congressional Quarterly, 1981), 169.

65. *Origins and Development,* 220.

66. *Members of Congress,* 177.

67. 27 C.G., 2229.

68. William LaPiana, *Logic and Experience: The Origin of Modern American Legal Education* (New York: Oxford University Press, 1994), 41–42; Robert Stevens, *Law School: Legal Education in America from the 1850s to the 1980s* (Chapel Hill: University of North Carolina Press, 1983), 7–9, 25, 26.

69. William R. Johnson, *Schooled Lawyers: A Study of the Clash of Professional Cultures* (New York: New York University Press, 1978), 8–11; LaPiana, *Logic and Experience,* 47–48, 51; Stevens, *Law School,* 15 n. 46.

70. Joseph Story, *Autobiography,* reprinted in William Story, *Miscellaneous Writings of Joseph Story* (1851), in *The History of Legal Education in the United States: Commentaries and Primary Sources,* ed. Steve Sheppard (Pasadena, Calif.: Salem Press, 1999), 1:128; see also

"Autobiographical Letter to William Story," Jan. 23, 1831, in *The Miscellaneous Writings of Joseph Story . . .*, ed. William W. Story (Boston: C. C. Little and J. Brown, 1852), n. 16, in R. Kent Newmyer, *Joseph Story* (Chapel Hill: University of North Carolina Press, 1984), 41.

71. Bernard Schwartz, *The Law in America: A History* (New York: McGraw-Hill, 1974), 80.

72. Linda Przybyszewski, *The Republic according to John Marshall Harlan* (Chapel Hill: University of North Carolina Press, 1999), 186.

73. Gerard W. Gawalt, *The Promise of Power: The Emergence of the Legal Profession in Massachusetts, 1760–1840* (Westport, Conn.: Greenwood Press, 1979), 5–6, 185; Perry Miller, *The Life of the Mind in America from the Revolution to the Civil War* (New York: Harcourt, Brace & World, 1965), 109; Phillip S. Paludan, "The American Civil War Considered as a Crisis in Law and Order," *American Historical Review* 77(4) (Oct. 1972): 1013–1034, 1024.

74. M. H. Hoeflich, "Lawyers, Fees, and Anti-Lawyer Sentiment in Popular Art, 1800–1925," *Green Bag*, 2nd ed., 4 (Winter 2001): 156; Marc Galanter, "Predators and Parasites, Lawyer-Bashing and Civil Justice," *Georgia Law Review* 28 (Spring 1994): 658; and generally Maxwell Bloomfield, *American Lawyers in a Changing Society, 1776–1876* (Cambridge, Massachusetts, 1976).

75. *See generally* Michael Kammen, *People of Paradox* (New York: Knopf, 1973); David Ray Papke, *Heretics in the Temple: Americans Who Reject the Nation's Legal Faith* (New York: New York University Press, 1998), 4–15; Gerald W. Gawalt, *The Promise of Power: The Emergence of the Legal Profession in Massachusetts, 1760–1840* (Westport, Conn.: Greenwood, 1979), 135–43; Russell G. Pearce, "Lawyers as America's Governing Class," *University of Chicago Law School Roundtable* 8 (2001): 387–89; Skowronek, *Building a New American State*, 32–34.

76. 27 C.G., 2230.

77. *Congressional Globe*, 35th Cong., 2nd sess., vol. 28 (hereafter abbreviated as 28 C.G.) 712.

78. Hans L. Trefousse, *Benjamin Franklin Wade: Radical Republican from Ohio* (New York: Twayne Publishers, 1963), 7, 180.

79. 28 C.G., 712.

80. 28 C.G., 712, 713.

81. 28 C.G., 713, 714–15.

82. 28 C.G., 714–15.

83. 28 C.G., 715–16, 717.

84. 28 C.G., 718.

85. Robert W. Young, *Senator James Murray Mason: Defender of the Old South* (Knoxville: University of Tennessee Press, 1998), xiii.

86. Young, *Mason*, 33–34, xii–xiii.

87. 28 C.G., 718, 719.

88. For a history of states' rights, see Forrest McDonald, *States' Rights and the Union: Imperium in Imperio, 1776–1876* (Lawrence: University Press of Kansas, 2000).

89. 28 C.G., 719–20.

90. 28 C.G., 720.

91. Michael F. Holt, *The Rise and Fall of the American Whig Party: Jacksonian Politics*

and the Onset of the Civil War (New York: Oxford University Press, 1999), 68–70; Daniel Walker Howe, *The Political Culture of the American Whigs* (Chicago: University of Chicago Press, 1979), 16.

92. 28 C.G., 720.

93. Richard H. Sewell, *John P. Hale and the Politics of Abolition* (Cambridge: Harvard University Press, 1965), 1–104.

94. For an assessment of Hale in the Senate, see Bogue, *Earnest Men*, 86–87.

95. 28 C.G., 721.

96. 28 C.G., 721.

97. William J. Cooper Jr., *Jefferson Davis, American* (New York: Alfred A. Knopf distributed by Random House, 2000), 281.

98. 28 C.G., 722.

99. Cooper, *Davis, American*, 42–63, 127–57 193–94; William C. Davis, *Jefferson Davis: the Man and His Hour* (New York: HarperCollins, 1991), 39–70, 222–55; Clement Eaton, *Jefferson Davis* (New York: Free Press, 1977), 57–66, 82–88, 92–93, 101.

100. 28 C.G., 722.

101. For his experience at Transylvania University, a premier institution at the time in the South, see Clement Eaton, *Jefferson Davis* (New York: Free Press, 1977), 7.

102. 28 C.G., 722.

103. U.S. Constitution, art. 6, cl. 2 and 3.

104. 28 C.G., 722, 723.

105. 28 C.G., 723, 724.

106. 28 C.G., 724.

107. 28 C.G., 724.

108. Peter Charles Hoffer, *The Law's Conscience: Equitable Constitutionalism in America* (Chapel Hill: University of North Carolina Press, 1990), 78, 126–29.

109. 28 C.G., 724.

110. 28 C.G., 784.

111. 28 C.G., 785.

112. 28 C.G., 785.

113. For an interpretation that emphasizes the latter, see Joanna D. Cowden, *"Heaven Will Frown on Such a Cause as This": Six Democrats Who Opposed Lincoln's War* (Lanham, Md.: University Press of America, 2001), 67–86.

114. 28 C.G., 786.

115. 28 C.G., 786–87.

116. Roy F. Nichols, *The Disruption of the American Democracy* (New York: Macmillan, 1948), 33–34; Michael F. Holt, *The Political Crisis of the 1850s* (New York: W. W. Norton, 1978), 236–37.

117. 28 C.G., 853, 852, 851, 852.

118. 28 C.G., 852.

119. 28 C.G., 854.

120. 28 C.G., 855.

121. 28 C.G., 857.

122. For Franklin Pierce's similar message, see Robert H. Bremner, *American Philanthropy* (1960; rpt., Chicago: University of Chicago Press, 1982), 69–70.

123. 28 C.G., 1412–13.

124. Philip Shriver Klein, *President James Buchanan: A Biography* (University Park: Pennsylvania State University Press, 1962, 1978), 346; Elbert B. Smith, *The Presidency of James Buchanan* (Lawrence: University Press of Kansas, 1975), 60; McPherson, *Battle Cry of Freedom*, 194; and Potter, *Impending Crisis*, 394.

125. 28 C.G., 1414.

TWO: "The Object of a Democratic Government"

1. *Members of Congress since 1789* (Washington, D.C.: Congressional Quarterly, 1981), 177. For a detailed description of the Civil War Republican Senators and the working and living conditions for congressmen during the war, see Alan G. Bogue, *The Earnest Men: Republicans of the Civil War Senate* (Ithaca: Cornell University Press, 1981), 25–60.

2. For in-depth examinations of the war-time Congress's actions, see Richard Franklin Bensel, *Yankee Leviathan: The Origins of Central State Authority in America* (Cambridge: Cambridge University Press, 1990); Leonard P. Curry, *Blueprint for a Modern America* (Nashville: Vanderbilt University Press, 1968); Heather Cox Richardson, *The Greatest Nation of the Earth: Republican Economic Policies during the Civil War* (Cambridge: Harvard University Press, 1997).

3. Trefousse, *Benjamin Franklin Wade*, 157.

4. Josephy, *On the Hill*, 214–17.

5. Leonard D. White, *The Republican Era: 1869–1901: A Study in Administrative History* (New York: Free Press, 1958), 232.

6. Wayne D. Rasmussen and Gladys L. Baker, *The Department of Agriculture; Praeger Library of U.S. Government Departments and Agencies* (New York: Praeger, 1972), 5–6; Richardson, *Greatest Nation of the Earth*, 149–51.

7. *Members of Congress since 1789*, 177, 169.

8. Josephy, *On the Hill*, 207–8; Richardson, *Greatest Nation of the Earth*, 141.

9. *Congressional Globe*, 37th Cong., 2nd sess., vol. 32 (hereafter abbreviated as 32 C.G.), 210.

10. Allan G. Bogue, *The Earnest Men: Republicans of the Civil War Senate* (Ithaca: Cornell University Press, 1981), 25; William E. Gienapp, *The Origins of the Republican Party, 1852–1856* (New York: Oxford University Press, 1987), 189–237; Richard L. McCormick, *The Party Period and Public Policy: American Politics from the Age of Jackson to the Progressive Era* (New York: Oxford University Press, 1986), 168; Earl Maltz, *Civil Rights, The Constitution, and Congress, 1863–1869* (Lawrence: University Press of Kansas, 1990), 42.

11. 32 C.G., 217.

12. 32 C.G., 217.

13. 32 C.G., 217.

14. 32 C.G., 217.

15. See David Montgomery, *Beyond Equality: Labor and the Radical Republicans, 1862–1872* (New York: Knopf, 1969); Richardson, *Greatest Nation of the Earth*; for the Democrats during the war, see Jean Harvey Baker, *Affairs of Party: The Political Culture of Northern Democrats in the Mid-Nineteenth Century* (Ithaca: Cornell University Press, 1983); Leonard P. Curry, "Congressional Democrats, 1861–1863," *Civil War History* 12 (Sept. 1966): 213–29; and Joel H. Silbey, *A Respectable Minority: The Democratic Party in the Civil War Era, 1860–1868* (New York: W. W. Norton, 1977).

16. Edward Magdol, *Owen Lovejoy: Abolitionist in Congress* (New Brunswick, N.J.: Rutgers University Press, 1967), 353–54.

17. 32 C.G., 217.

18. 32 C.G., 217.

19. Dorothy Ross, *The Origins of American Social Science* (New York: Cambridge University Press, 1991, 1997), 22–50.

20. 32 C.G., 218.

21. 32 C.G., 855.

22. See, e.g., Silbey, *Respectable Minority*, 27, 70, 81–83; Richardson, *Greatest Nation of the Earth*, 150–51.

23. 32 C.G., 855, 856.

24. 32 C.G., 856–57.

25. 32 C.G., 1690.

26. 32 C.G., 1690.

27. Martin D. Joachim, "Governor Joseph A. Wright, Librarian," *Indiana Magazine of History* 78(3) (Sept. 1982): 242–48.

28. 32 C.G., 1690–91.

29. 32 C.G., 1691.

30. 32 C.G., 1692.

31. 32 C.G., 1755.

32. 32 C.G., 1755.

33. 32 C.G., 1690–1692.

34. Howe, *Political Culture of American Whigs*, 86–91; Trefousse, *Wade*, 27–28.

35. 32 C.G., 1755–56.

36. E.g., Anthony Downs, *Inside Bureaucracy* (Boston: Rand Corp., 1967).

37. The slippery slope argument is called a logical fallacy because it is deductively invalid. In this case Congress could at any time not grant requests for additional monies. Congress does not yield this ability when it creates a new department, but it does take on the burden of bureaucratic lobbying, a well-understood phenomenon.

38. 32 C.G., 1756.

39. 32 C.G., 1916, 2013, 2014.

40. 32 C.G., 2014.

41. Rasmussen and Baker, *Department of Agriculture*, 11.

42. 32 C.G., 2015.

43. 32 C.G., 2015, 2016.

44. Charles A. Jellison, *Fessenden of Maine: Civil War Senator* (Syracuse, N.Y.: Syracuse University Press, 1962), vi.

45. 32 C.G., 2016.

46. Bogue, *Earnest Men*, 79–82.

47. 32 C.G., 2016, 2017.

48. Fred A. Shannon, *The Farmer's Last Frontier: Agriculture, 1860–1897* (New York: Farrar and Rinehart, 1945), 268–91; White, *Republican Era*, 232–57.

49. 32 C.G., 2248.

50. Mark W. Summers, *The Plundering Generation: Corruption and the Crisis of the Union, 1849–1861* (New York: Oxford University Press, 1987), 109, 152–55.

51. Leverett W. Spring, "The Career of a Kansas Politician," *American Historical Review* 4(1) (Oct. 1898): 80–104; Michael Les Benedict, *A Compromise of Principle: Congres-

sional Republicans and Reconstruction, 1863–1869 (New York: W. W. Norton, 1974), 65–66.

52. 32 C.G., 2248, 2249.
53. 32 C.G., 1862.
54. 32 C.G., 2394.
55. Josephy, *On the Hill,* 216.
56. 32 C.G., 2395, 2396.
57. 32 C.G., 2625.
58. See, e.g., Richard Hofstadter, *Anti-Intellectualism in American Life* (New York: Knopf, 1963), 166–68, 306–9.
59. 32 C.G., 2626.
60. 32 C.G., 2626.
61. 32 C.G., 2626.
62. 32 C.G., 2626.
63. 32 C.G., 2626.
64. 32 C.G., 2626.
65. 32 C.G., 2627.
66. 32 C.G., 2627.
67. 32 C.G., 2627.
68. 32 C.G., 2628.
69. 32 C.G., 2628.
70. 32 C.G., 2629.
71. 32 C.G., 2632.
72. Eric Foner, *Politics and Ideology in the Age of the Civil War* (New York: Oxford University Press, 1980), 10; Richardson, *Greatest Nation of the Earth;* 5–6, 256.
73. 32 C.G., 2632.
74. 32 C.G., 2632.
75. 32 C.G., 2632.
76. 32 C.G., 2633.
77. 32 C.G., 2633.
78. 32 C.G., 2633.
79. 32 C.G., 2634.
80. 32 C.G., 2769.
81. 32 C.G., 2769, 2770.
82. For a pro-Western view of this, see Paul Wallace Gates, *The Wisconsin Pine Lands of Cornell University: A Study in Land Policy and Absentee Ownership* (Ithaca: Cornell University Press, 1943).
83. Coy F. Cross, II, *Justin Smith Morrill: Father of the Land-Grant Colleges* (East Lansing: Michigan State University Press, 1999), 85.
84. Walter S. Bowen and Harry Edward Neal, *The United States Secret Service* (Philadelphia: Chilton Co., 1960), 10–17, for a friendly view that reports that Lincoln approved the creation of the Secret Service; David Ralph Johnson, *Illegal Tender: Counterfeiting and the Secret Service in Nineteenth-Century America* (Washington, D.C.: Smithsonian Institution Press, 1995), esp. 65–77, for a scholar's view that discredits the official version; *Excerpts from the History of the United States Secret Service, 1865–1975* (reprinted from the Service Star, Department of the Treasury, United States Secret Service, 1978), 7–9;

Marcia Roberts, *Moments in History* (Department of the Treasury, United States Secret Service, c. 1991), 4–8.

85. Bensel, *Yankee Leviathan*, 414–15 (posits a permanent change only in industrial policy); Curry, *Blueprint for a New Nation*, 4, 250 (emphasizes the change in the direction of federal policy-making); Morton Keller, *Affairs of State: Public Life in Nineteenth Century America* (Cambridge: Belknap Press of Harvard University Press, 1977), 33 (argues that it was a limited expansion of national authority); Nelson, *Roots of American Bureaucracy*, 73–79 (observes a transformation in jurisprudence as well as institutions); Richardson, *Greatest Nation of the Earth*, 256 (perceives a semi-tragic legacy of a flawed theory); Skowronek, *Building a New American State*, 30, 39 (maintains it was only an enlargement of the state of courts and parties).

THREE: "A Government of Law"

1. For an overview of the scholarship, see Eric Foner, *Reconstruction: America's Unfinished Revolution, 1863–1877* (New York: Harper & Row, 1988), xix–xxiv; James M. McPherson, afterword, in Paul A. Cimbala and Randall M. Miller, *The Freedmen's Bureau and Reconstruction, Reconsiderations* (New York: Fordham University Press, 1999), 343–47.

2. Herman Belz, *A New Birth of Freedom: The Republican Party and Freemen's Rights, 1861–1866* (Westport, Conn.: Greenwood, 1976); Charles Fairman, *Reconstruction and Reunion, 1864–1868* (New York: Macmillan, 1971); Harold M. Hyman and William M. Wiecek, *Equal Justice under Law: Constitutional Developments, 1835–1875* (New York: Harper & Row, 1982).

3. The pervasive racism of the day is documented, for the Democrats, in Joel H. Silbey, *A Respectable Minority: The Democratic Party in the Civil War Era, 1860–1868* (New York: W. W. Norton, 1977) 27, 81–83; and Jean Baker, *Affairs of Party: The Political Culture of Northern Democrats in the Mid-Nineteenth Century* (Ithaca: Cornell University Press, 1983), 213, 249–58.

4. And of course it illustrates a myriad of other concerns inside and outside of government. See, e.g., Paul Moreno, "Racial Classifications and Reconstruction Legislation" *Journal of Southern History* 61 (1995): 271–304.

5. As very limited, see Leonard D. White, *The Republican Era: 1869–1901: A Study in Administrative History* (New York: Free Press, 1958), vii, 2; Richard Franklin Bensel, *Yankee Leviathan: The Origins of Central State Authority in America, 1859–1877* (1990; rpt., New York: Cambridge University Press, 1995), 413–15, 435–36; as a substantial departure, see Heather Cox Richardson, *The Death of Reconstruction: Race, Labor, and Politics in the Post Civil War North, 1865–1901* (Cambridge: Harvard University Press, 2001), 21–22, 30–32.

6. On the commission, see Eric Foner, *Reconstruction: America's Unfinished Revolution, 1863–1877* (New York: Harper & Row, 1988, 1989), 68–69; William S. McFeely, *Yankee Stepfather: General O. O. Howard and the Freedmen* (New Haven: Yale University Press, 1968), 20–21.

7. McFeely, *Yankee Stepfather*, 84–86.

8. Allan G. Bogue, "Historians and Radical Republicans: A Meaning for Today," *Journal of American History* 70(1) (June 1983): 7–34.

9. On Lincoln's policy of limited means for conservative ends, see James M. McPher-

son, *Abraham Lincoln and the Second American Revolution* (New York: Oxford University Press, 1991), 31–41.

10. Willie Lee Rose, *Rehearsal for Reconstruction: The Port Royal Experiment* (Indianapolis: Bobbs-Merrill, 1964); McFeely, *Yankee Stepfather*, 50–56.

11. McFeely, *Yankee Stepfather*, 20–22; David Herbert Donald, *Charles Sumner and the Rights of Man* (New York: Knopf, 1970), 16–17.

12. *Congressional Globe*, 38th Cong., 1st sess., vol. 34 (hereafter abbreviated as 34 C.G.), 567. The label is inaccurate for fully half those persons were female. The constant reference to only the male population in debate signifies a gendered reading of the situation. Because their conceptual reference was most likely also male, their assumptions about the character of the freedmen, their predictions about their future behavior and their fitness to enter American society as equals, center on decidedly male idealizations both positive and negative. I will note this phenomena only as it relates to ideas on additions to the U.S. state so the reader interested in this point will have to look to other scholars for a deeper analysis of this particular phenomenon.

13. 34 C.G., 567, 569–70.

14. 34 C.G., 568. His mention of European developments is yet another instance of the transatlantic dialogue.

15. 34 C.G., 569, 570.

16. 34 C.G., 570–71.

17. Mary K. Bonsteel Tachau, *Federal Courts in the Early Republic: Kentucky, 1789–1816* (Princeton: Princeton University Press, 1978), 167.

18. Morton J. Horwitz, *The Transformation of American Law, 1780–1860* (Cambridge: Harvard University Press, 1977), 259–61; on the importance of land law in the nineteenth century, see Lawrence Friedman, *A History of American Law*, 2nd ed. (New York: Simon & Schuster, 1985). On the idea of property and its connection to land, see William B. Scott, *In Pursuit of Happiness: American Conceptions of Property from the Seventeenth to the Twentieth Centuries* (Bloomington: Indiana University Press, 1977), 114–32.

19. 34 C.G., 571.

20. Eric Foner, *Free Soil, Free Labor, Free Men: The Ideology of the Republican Party before the Civil War* (Oxford: Oxford University Press, 1970), 38.

21. 34 C.G., 571–73.

22. 34 C.G., 571–73, quote on 572.

23. David Lindsey, *"Sunset" Cox: Irrepressible Democrat* (Detroit: Wayne State University Press, 1959), 81.

24. 34 C.G., 708, 709.

25. 34 C.G., 712.

26. Lindsey, *"Sunset" Cox*, 3–11.

27. 34 C.G., 760.

28. See, e.g., Nicholas V. Riasanovsky, *A History of Russia*, 4th ed. (New York: Oxford University Press, 1984), 371–78.

29. 34 C.G., 761.

30. 34 C.G., 761, 762, 763.

31. Mark Wahlgren Summers, *The Press Gang: Newspapers and Politics, 1865–1878* (Chapel Hill: University of North Carolina Press, 1994), 49, 114.

32. 34 C.G., 762.

33. Mark Summers to the author, June 10, 2003. I could not have said it better.

34. 34 C.G., 772.

35. Ira V. Brown, "William D. Kelley and Radical Reconstruction," *Pennsylvania Magazine of History and Biography* 85 (July 1961): 316–29, 318–19.

36. *Baltimore American*, Dec. 10, 1890; *Nation*, Dec. 29, 1881; *New York World*, Feb. 10, 1866; *Chicago Tribune*, Feb. 9, 1869.

37. Brown, "Kelley," 319, 324; see U.S. Constitution, art. 4, sec. 4.

38. Both quotes from 34 C.G., 772.

39. G. Edward White, *The American Judicial Tradition: Profiles of Leading American Judges* (New York: Oxford University Press, 1976), 63 (on judges' "public utilitarian calculus of the moment.").

40. 34 C.G., 773.

41. 34 C.G., 774.

42. 34 C.G., 774.

43. On Indians as "wards" of the state, generally, see, e.g., Wilcomb E. Washburn, *Red Man's Land, White Man's Law* (Norman: University of Oklahoma Press, 1995); Petra Shattuck and Jill Norgren, *Partial Justice: Federal Indian Law in a Liberal Constitutional System* (New York: Berg, 1991).

44. 34 C.G., 775.

45. 34 C.G., app., 55.

46. 34 C.G., app., 51, 52.

47. 34 C.G., 888.

48. 34 C.G., 889.

49. Michael Les Benedict, *A Compromise of Principle: Congressional Republicans and Reconstruction, 1863–1869* (New York: W. W. Norton, 1974), 21–40; Foner, *Unfinished Revolution*, 234–38, 451.

50. 34 C.G., 890.

51. 34 C.G., 890, 891.

52. 34 C.G., 894.

53. All information on the vote from 34 C.G., 895.

54. 34 C.G., 2798, 2799.

55. 34 C.G., 2800.

56. Allan G. Bogue, *The Earnest Men: Republicans of the Civil War Senate* (Ithaca: Cornell University Press, 1981), 82–85; David Donald, *Charles Sumner and the Coming of the Civil War* (New York: Knopf, 1960), 211–19, 119; *Charles Sumner and the Rights of Man* (New York: Knopf, 1970), 152, 201–3.

57. 34 C.G., 2798, 2801.

58. 34 C.G., 2802, 2803.

59. 34 C.G., 2803.

60. 34 C.G., 2803.

61. 34 C.G., 2931.

62. 34 C.G., 2932.

63. For general developments along these lines in France, see Bernard Silberman, *Cages of Reason: The Rise of the Rational State in France, Japan, the United States, and Great Britain* (Chicago: University of Chicago Press, 1993), 92–93, 113–19; Rudolf Vierhaus, "The Prussian Bureaucracy Reconsidered," in *Rethinking Leviathan: The Eighteenth Cen-*

tury State in Britain and Germany, ed. John Brewer and Eckhart Hellmuth (Oxford: Oxford University Press, 1999), 158.

64. Daniel P. Carpenter, *The Forging of Bureaucratic Autonomy: Reputations, Networks, and Policy Innovation in Executive Agencies, 1862–1928* (Princeton: Princeton University Press, 2001), 44–45; see also Patricia Wallace Ingraham, *The Foundation of Merit: Public Service in American Democracy* (Baltimore: Johns Hopkins University Press, 1995), 17–23; Paul P. Van Riper, *History of the United States Civil Service* (Evanston, Ill.: Row, Peterson and Co., 1958), 30–56.

65. 34 C.G., 2933–34.

66. 34 C.G., 3299–3301.

67. 34 C.G., 3300–2.

68. 34 C.G., 3302.

69. 34 C.G., 3304–9.

70. U.S. Constitution, art. 3, sec. 3, cl. 2; for Trumbull's biography, see David Osborn, "Trumbull, Lyman," *ANB,* 21:877–79; Mark M. Krug, *Lyman Trumbull: Conservative Radical* (New York: A. S. Barnes, 1965), 23–72; Ralph J. Roske, *His Own Counsel: The Life and Times of Lyman Trumbull* (Reno: University of Nevada Press, 1979).

71. 34 C.G., app., 133, 3327.

72. 34 C.G., 3328, 3329.

73. 34 C.G., 3330–33.

74. Karen O'Connor and Larry J. Sabato, *American Government: Continuity and Change* (New York: Longman, 2003), 321.

75. 34 C.G., 3334.

76. 34 C.G., 3346, 3347.

77. Summers, *Era of Good Stealings* (New York: Oxford University Press, 1993), 20–21, 91–98.

78. 34 C.G., 3349, 3350.

79. *Congressional Globe,* 38th Cong., 2nd sess., vol. 35 (hereafter abbreviated as 35 C.G.), 79–80.

80. 35 C.G., 563.

81. 35 C.G., 563, 564, 566.

82. 35 C.G., 689.

83. 35 C.G., 689.

84. All quotes from Schenck from 35 C.G., 691.

85. 35 C.G., 692.

86. 35 C.G., 694.

87. 35 C.G., 767.

88. 35 C.G., 786.

89. For military tribunals in this period, see, e.g., Dylan C. Penningroth, *The Claims of Kinfolk: African American Property and Community in the Nineteenth Century South* (Chapel Hill: University of North Carolina Press, 2003), 112.

90. 35 C.G., 961.

91. 35 C.G., 988.

92. 35 C.G., 988–90.

93. 35 C.G., 1182.

94. 35 C.G., 1307–8, 1348, 1402.

95. *Congressional Globe*, 39th Cong., 1st sess., vol. 36 (hereafter abbreviated as, 36 C.G.), 314–23 (Senate); 512–18 (House, after Senate approval).

96. 36 C.G., 339–49, 362–75, 415–21 (Senate), 627–33 (House).

97. 36 C.G., 342; italics added.

98. 36 C.G., 421 (Senate vote); 688 (House vote).

99. 36 C.G., 993.

100. 36 C.G., 2772–2880, 2808–9, 2877–78 (House); 3409–13 (Senate).

101. 36 C.G., 2878, 3413 (Senate vote).

102. 36 C.G., 3842 (Senate); 3850 (House).

103. Foner, *Unfinished Revolution*, 277.

104. On personnel numbers, see John H. Cox and LaWanda Cox, "General O. O. Howard and the 'Misrepresented Bureau,'" *Journal of Southern History* 19 (Nov. 1953): 442; and contemporary reputation, 428–29; Foner, *Unfinished Revolution*, 142–43.

FOUR: The "Two Great Pillars" of the State

1. John H. Cox and LaWanda Cox, "General O. O. Howard and the 'Misrepresented Bureau,'" *Journal of Southern History* 19 (Nov. 1953): 454; William S. McFeely, *Yankee Stepfather: General O. O. Howard and the Freedmen* (New Haven: Yale University Press, 1968), 301.

2. For a brief overview and citations on the Freedmen's Bureau's effort in this area, see Adam Fairclough, "'Being in the Field of Education and Also Being a Negro . . . Seems Tragic': Black Teachers in the Jim Crow South," *Journal of American History* 87(1) (June 2000), 65–91 nn. 2, 5, 9, 17.

3. Donald R. Warren, *To Enforce Education: A History of the Founding Years of the U.S. Office of Education* (Detroit: Wayne State University Press, 1974), 25–30.

4. E.g., Edward H. Reisner, *Nationalism and Education since 1789: A Social and Political History of Modern Education* (New York: Macmillan, 1923), 357.

5. Warren, *To Enforce Education*, 33–34.

6. Edith Nye MacMullen, *In the Cause of True Education: Henry Barnard and Nineteenth Century School Reform* (New Haven: Yale University Press, 1991), 1–242.

7. Warren, "The U.S. Department of Education: A Reconstruction Promise to Black Americans," *Journal of Negro Education* 43(4) (1974): 437–51, 439–41; *To Enforce Education*, 59–62; Rush Welter, *Popular Education and Democratic Thought in America* (New York: Columbia University Press, 1962), 141–47.

8. Warren, *To Enforce Education*, 65–66.

9. Warren, *To Enforce Education*, 52, 66–68.

10. Gordon Canfield Lee, *The Struggle for Federal Aid, First Phase: A History of the Attempts to Obtain Federal Aid for the Common Schools, 1870–1890* (1949; rpt., New York: AMS Press, 1972), 23; Warren, *To Enforce Education*, 63–64.

11. Allan Peskin, "The Short, Unhappy Life of the Federal Department of Education," *Public Administration Review* 33 (Nov.–Dec. 1973): 572–75, 572.

12. *Congressional Globe*, 39th Cong., 1st sess., vol. 36 (hereafter abbreviated as, 36 C.G.), 2966.

13. Peskin, *Garfield: A Biography* (Kent, Ohio: Kent State University Press, 1978), 68, 224, 23.

14. 36 C.G., 2966.

15. Peskin, *Garfield*, 1–23, 119–48, 167–219.

16. See, e.g., George M. Fredrickson, *The Inner Civil War: Northern Intellectuals and the Crisis of the Union* (New York: Harper & Row, 1965), 184–88; Morton Keller, *Affairs of State: Public Life in Nineteenth Century America* (Cambridge: Belknap Press of Harvard University Press, 1977), 42, 106.

17. 36 C.G., 2966.

18. 36 C.G., 2967.

19. Susan-Mary Grant, *North over South: Northern Nationalism and American Identity in the Antebellum Era* (Lawrence: University Press of Kansas, 2000); Rogan Kersh, *Dreams of a More Perfect Union* (Ithaca: Cornell University Press, 2001), 208–19; Melinda Lawson, *Patriot Fires: Forging a New American Nationalism in the Civil War North* (Lawrence: University Press of Kansas, 2002), 184–85; Paul C. Nagel, *This Sacred Trust: American Nationality, 1798–1898* (New York: Oxford University Press, 1971).

20. 36 C.G., 2967–68.

21. 36 C.G., 2968.

22. Peskin, *Garfield*, 46; John D. Hicks, "The Political Career of Ignatius Donnelly," *Mississippi Valley Historical Review* 8(1–2) (June–Sept. 1921): 80–132; and Martin Ridge, *Ignatius Donnelly: The Portrait of a Politician* (Chicago: University of Chicago Press, 1962), 1–100 ff.

23. Ridge, *Donelly*, 100.

24. 36 C.G., 2968.

25. 36 C.G., 3044; italics added.

26. 36 C.G., 3045, 3046.

27. 36 C.G., 3047.

28. 36 C.G., 3047.

29. 36 C.G., 3048.

30. 36 C.G., 3049.

31. 36 C.G., 3050–51.

32. 36 C.G., 3051, 3269–70.

33. 37 C.G., 1842.

34. 37 C.G., 1843.

35. 37 C.G., 1843.

36. 37 C.G., 1843–44.

37. 37 C.G., 1844.

38. 37 C.G., 1893.

39. For more about Barnard's tenure at the Department, later Bureau, of Education, see MacMullen, *In the Cause*, 261–76; Darrell Hevenor Smith, *The Bureau of Education: Its History, Activities and Organization*, Institute for Government Research (IGR), Service Monographs of the United States Government, 14 (Baltimore: IGR, 1923), 9–10; Warren, *To Enforce Education*, 98–126.

40. MacMullen, *In the Cause*, 259–79.

41. Warren, "U.S. Department of Education," 449–50.

42. *Congressional Globe*, 40th Cong., 2nd sess., vol. 39 (hereafter abbreviated as 39 C.G.), 1139.

43. Hans L. Trefousse, *Thaddeus Stevens: Nineteenth Century Egalitarian* (Chapel Hill: University of North Carolina Press, 1997), 78.

44. Ridge, *Donnelly*, 99.

45. 39 C.G., 1139.

46. 39 C.G., 1139.

47. 39 C.G., 1140.

48. 39 C.G., 1140.

49. Wood at 39 C.G., 1140.

50. 39 C.G., 1140–41.

51. *Congressional Globe*, 40th Cong., 3rd sess., vol. 40 (hereafter abbreviated as 40 C.G.), 1541.

52. 40 C.G., 1541.

53. 40 C.G., 1541.

54. 40 C.G., 1542.

55. 40 C.G., 1542.

56. White, *Republican Era*, 175–76.

57. William Gillette, *Retreat from Reconstruction, 1869–1876* (Baton Rouge: Louisiana State University Press, 1979), 31–33.

58. Homer Cummings, attorney general of the United States, and Carl McFarland, special assistant to the attorney general of the United States, *Federal Justice: Chapters in the History of Justice and the Federal Executive* (New York: Macmillan, 1937), 218–21; Albert George Langeluttig, *The Department of Justice of the United States* (Johns Hopkins University Dissertation, Institute for Government Research reprint, Baltimore, Maryland, 1927), 8–9.

59. Robert M. Goldman, *"A Free Ballot and a Fair Count": The Department of Justice and the Enforcement of Voting Rights in the South, 1877–1893* (New York: Fordham University Press, 2001), 37.

60. *Congressional Globe*, 41st Cong., 2nd sess., vol. 42 (hereafter abbreviated as 42 C.G.), 2994.

61. 42 C.G., 2995.

62. Huston, *Department of Justice*, 15.

63. 42 C.G., 3034–35.

64. 42 C.G., 3036.

65. Paul A. C. Koistinen, *Beating Plowshares into Swords*, vol. 1: *The Political Economy of American Warfare, 1606–1865* (Lawrence: University Press of Kansas, 1996), 195–96.

66. 42 C.G., 3037.

67. 42 C.G., 3039, 3038.

68. See later discussion for Evarts's biography.

69. 42 C.G., 3038.

70. 42 C.G., 3065.

71. 42 C.G., 3067, 3207.

72. 42 C.G., 3207, 4490.

73. See Robert J. Kaczorowski, *The Politics of Judicial Interpretation: The Federal Courts, Department of Justice and Civil Rights, 1866–1876* (Dobbs Ferry, N.Y.: Oceana Publications, 1985), 79–115; William S. McFeely, "Amos T. Akerman: The Lawyer and Racial Justice," in *Region, Race, and Reconstruction: Essays in Honor of C. Vann Woodward*, ed. J. Morgan Kousser and James M. McPherson (New York: Oxford University Press, 1982), 404–11; Ross A. Webb, "Benjamin H. Bristow: Civil Rights Champion, 1866–1872," *Civil War History* 15 (Mar. 1969): 39–53, 46–52.

74. Daniel W. Crofts, "The Blair Bill and the Elections Bill: The Congressional Af-

termath to Reconstruction" (Ph.D. diss., Yale University, 1968), 1–6; Alfred H. Kelly, "The Congressional Controversy over School Segregation, 1867–1875," *American Historical Review* 64(3) (Apr. 1959): 537–63, 538–42.

75. Richard E. Welch Jr., *George Frisbie Hoar and the Half-Breed Republicans* (Cambridge: Harvard University Press, 1971), 23–25.

76. Crofts, *Blair Bill and the Elections Bill,* 23–28.

77. Walter J. Fraser Jr., "John Eaton, Jr., Radical Republican: Champion of the Negro and Federal Aid to Education, 1869–1882," *Tennessee Historical Quarterly* 25(3) (Fall 1966): 239–60, 240.

78. Donald R. Warren, "The U.S. Department of Education: A Reconstruction Promise to Black Americans," *Journal of Negro Education* 43(4) (1974): 447.

79. Fraser, "Eaton, Radical Republican," 241, 242–45.

80. For a critical view, see Warren, *To Enforce Education,* 163–65; for a positive assessment, see Smith, *Bureau of Education,* 10–12.

81. Warren, *To Enforce Education,* 155–56.

82. Fraser, "Eaton, Radical Republican," 250–53; Warren, *To Enforce Education,* 163–64; Smith, *Bureau of Education,* 11–12.

83. Frederick H. Gillett, *George Frisbie Hoar* (Boston: Houghton Mifflin, 1934), 1–2; Duane Lee Vandenbusche, *Aspects of Domestic Issues in the Senatorial Career of George Frisbie Hoar* (Ed.D. diss., Oklahoma State University, 1964) 2–6; Welch, *Hoar and the Half-Breeds,* 5–6.

84. Vandenbusche, "Aspects," 5; Welch, *Hoar and the Half-Breeds,* 9–20.

85. Gillett, *Hoar,* 39–40, 118;Vandenbusche, "Aspects," 12, 149–53; Welch, *Hoar and the Half-Breeds,* 1–4, 28–29, 33–34.

86. Gillett, *Hoar,* 180.

87. 42 C.G., app., 479, 484.

88. John Whitney Evans, "Catholics and the Blair Education Bill," *Catholic Historical Review* 46 (Oct. 1960): 273–98, 275–78. Also see Henry Wilson, "The New Departure of the Republican Party," *Atlantic Monthly* 27(159), Jan. 1871, 104–20.

89. 42 C.G., app., 486.

90. 42 C.G., 1326, 1568, 2294–95.

91. Stanley P. Hirshson, *Farewell to the Bloody Shirt: Northern Republicans and the Southern Negro, 1877–1893* (Bloomington: Indiana University Press, 1962), 87; Lee, *Struggle for Federal Aid,* 35–37; Warren, *To Enforce Education,* 58–62; Rush Welter, *Popular Education,* 141–47.

92. 42 C.G., app., 485; *Congressional Globe,* 41st Cong., 3rd sess., vol. 43 (hereafter abbreviated as 43 C.G.), 1041–1042.

93. Their speeches can be found as follows: Bird, 43 C.G., app., 77–81; McNeely, 43 C.G., app., 94–99; Kerr, 43 C.G., 1370–74; and Rogers, 1374–75.

94. Their contributions appear as follows: Degener, 1039; Arnell, 43 C.G., app., 100–101; Clark, 43 C.G., 1072–74; Townsend, 1375–78; McGrew, 1378; and Prosser, 43 C.G., app., 189–93.

95. 43 C.G., 808–9, 1245.

96. 43 C.G., 1246.

97. See chap. 5 for a discussion of the ICC.

98. 43 C.G., 1246.

99. Lee, *Struggle for Federal Aid,* 43–49.

100. 43 C.G., 1379.

101. Kelly, "Congressional Controversy," refers to Perce as a "Mississippi Negro," 543, but Perce's career seems inconsistent and Perce is not listed as an African American in Samuel Denny Smith, *The Negro in Congress, 1870–1901* (1940; rpt., Port Washington, N.Y.: Kennikat Press, 1966), 5–8.

102. Kenneth R. Johnson, "Legrand Winfield Perce: A Mississippi Carpetbagger and the Fight for Federal Aid to Education," *Journal of Mississippi History* 34(4) (Nov. 1972): 331–56, 331–33.

103. Johnson, "Perce," 335–38.

104. Johnson, "Perce," 341–42; Crofts, "Blair Bill and Elections Bill," 10.

105. *Congressional Globe*, 42nd Cong., 2nd sess., vol. 45 (hereafter abbreviated as 45 C.G.), 535–36, 564–70, 791–801, 808–10, 850–64, 881–86, 902–3, 3651.

106. Johnson, "Perce," 348.

107. Lee, *Struggle for Federal Aid*, 66.

108. Crofts, "Blair Bill and Elections Bill," 13–15; Kelly, "Congressional Controversy," 543–44; Johnson, "Perce," 352.

109. Johnson, "Perce," 353.

110. Johnson, "Perce," 353–56.

FIVE: "To Change the Nature of the Government"

1. Stanley P. Hirshson, *Farewell to the Bloody Shirt: Northern Republicans and the Southern Negro, 1877–1893* (Bloomington: Indiana University Press, 1962); Morton Keller, *Affairs of State: Public Life in Nineteenth Century America* (Cambridge: Belknap Press of Harvard University Press, 1977), 268–72; John G. Sproat, *"The Best Men": Liberal Reformers in the Gilded Age* (New York: Oxford University Press, 1968).

2. Crofts, "Blair Bill and the Elections Bill," 48–220; Allen J. Going, "The South and the Blair Education Bill," *Mississippi Valley Historical Review* 44 (Sept. 1957): 267–90; Gordon Canfield Lee, *The Struggle for Federal Aid, First Phase: A History of the Attempts to Obtain Federal Aid for the Common Schools, 1870–1890* (1949; rpt., New York: AMS Press, 1972), 88–162.

3. For the complete text of the bill in its original form in 1882, see *Congressional Record*, 47th Cong., 1st sess., vol. 13 (hereafter abbreviated as 13 C.R.), 4833.

4. David Lane Perkins, *Manchester Up to Date: Story of the City, 1846–1896; Stories, Anecdotes, and Biographical Sketches of Prominent Manchester Men* (Manchester, N.H.: George F. Willey, 1896), 132–34; William Alexander Robinson, "Blair, Henry William," *Dictionary of American Biography*, American Council of Learned Societies, Allen Johnson ed., vol. 2, "Barsotti-Brazer" (New York: Charles Scribner's Sons, 1929), 334–35.

5. 13 C.R., 4821.

6. 13 C.R., 4821.

7. John Bouvier, *A Law Dictionary: Adapted to the Constitution and Laws of the United States of America, and of the Several States of the American Union: With References to the Civil and Other Systems of Foreign Law* (Philadelphia: T. and J. W. Johnson, 1839).

8. The term itself with that particular use dates back to Niccolò Machiavelli at the latest. See generally Alan Harding, "The Origins of the Concept of the State," *History of Political Thought* 15(1) (Spring 1994): 57–72.

9. 13 C.R., 4823–32.

10. See, e.g., I. Bernard Cohen, *The Triumph of Numbers: How Counting Shaped Modern Life* (New York: W. W. Norton, 2005); Daniel J. Boorstin, *The Americans: The Democratic Experience* (New York: Vintage Books, 1973), 165–244.

11. 13 C.R., 4832.

12. 13 C.R., 4821.

13. 13 C.R., 4822.

14. 13 C.R., 4830, 4831.

15. *Congressional Record*, 47th Cong., 2nd sess., vol. 14 (hereafter abbreviated as 14 C.R.), 1014.

16. 14 C.R., 1015.

17. 14 C.R., 1202.

18. Sherwin's explanation of the differences, 14 C.R., 1202; for the full text of the bill 14 C.R., 3253.

19. 14 C.R., 1203.

20. 14 C.R., 1203.

21. 14 C.R., 1204.

22. 14 C.R., 1205.

23. 14 C.R., 3253, 3254.

24. 14 C.R., 3254.

25. 14 C.R., 3254.

26. 14 C.R., 3253–55.

27. 14 C.R., 3257.

28. 14 C.R., 3258.

29. 14 C.R., 3259, app., 172–74.

30. The whole of Wheeler's remarks, 14 C.R., app., 281–87.

31. 14 C.R., app., 282. The capitalized words, as well as other phrases throughout Wheeler's speech, appeared this way in the *Record*. Most likely, it was done to aid the reader of this speech when Wheeler had it printed for campaign use.

32. See, among others, Theda Skocpol, *Protecting Soldiers and Mothers*; and Gaines M. Foster, *Moral Reconstruction: Christian Lobbyists and the Federal Legislation of Morality, 1865–1920* (Chapel Hill: University of North Carolina Press, 2002).

33. 14 C.R., 3259–60.

34. Patricia Wallace Ingraham, *The Foundation of Merit: Public Service in American Democracy* (Baltimore: Johns Hopkins University Press, 1995), 25–26.

35. Ari Hoogenboom, *Outlawing the Spoils: A History of the Civil Service Reform Movement* (Urbana: University of Illinois Press, 1961), 7–11, 13–20, 27–31.

36. Hoogenboom, *Outlawing the Spoils*, 62–63, 55–56.

37. Hoogenboom, *Outlawing the Spoils*, 60–61.

38. Donald R. Harvey, *The Civil Service Commission*, Praeger Library of U.S. Government Departments and Agencies (New York: Praeger, 1970), 6; Jay M. Shafritz et al., *Personnel Management in Government: Politics and Process*, 3rd ed. (New York: M. Dekker, 1986), 13–14; Hoogenboom, *Outlawing the Spoils*, 87, 90–96, 105–10; on scandals, Summers, *Press Gang*, 183–88.

39. Harvey, *CSC*, 5–6.

40. Hoogenboom, *Outlawing the Spoils*, 122–34.

41. Paul P. Van Riper, *History of the United States Civil Service* (Evanston, Ill.: Row, Peterson., 1958), 82. Samuel P. Hays, *The Response to Industrialism, 1885–1914*, 2nd ed.

(Chicago: University of Chicago Press, 1995), documents the professionals' part in reform.

42. Van Riper, *History*, 89–92.

43. Pendleton had offered a bill in the fall of 1881. The debate on that bill has been omitted as duplicative. Hoogenboom, *Outlawing the Spoils*, 200–202, 217–19, 238–47.

44. Van Riper, *History*, 94.

45. Van Riper, *History*, 109.

46. *Congressional Record*, 47th Cong., 2nd sess., vol. 14 (hereafter abbreviated as 14 C.R.), 202.

47. *Members of Congress since 1789* (Washington, D.C.: Congressional Quarterly, 1981), 176.

48. 14 C.R., 204, 205.

49. 14 C.R., 206; Matthew A. Crenson, *The Federal Machine: The Beginnings of Bureaucracy in Jacksonian America* (Baltimore: Johns Hopkins University Press, 1975), 16–17.

50. Phillip S. Paludan, "The American Civil War Considered as a Crisis in Law and Order" *American Historical Review* 77 (1972): 1013; Paludan, *A Covenant with Death: The Constitution, Law, and Equality in the Civil War Era* (Urbana: University of Illinois Press, 1975), 225–31; James S. Ferguson, *Law and Letters in American Culture* (Cambridge: Harvard University Press, 1984), 305–18; Guyora Binder and Robert Weisberg, *Literary Criticisms of Law* (Princeton: Princeton University Press, 2000), 56–57; and William M. Wiecek, *The Lost World of Classical Legal Thought: Law and Ideology in America, 1886–1937* (New York: Oxford University Press, 1998), 79.

51. 14 C.R., 207, 208.

52. See later discussion of the rising professionalization in American life.

53. 14 C.R., 209–10, 275.

54. 14 C.R., 276, 278; italics added.

55. For Brown's biography, see Joseph Parks, *Joseph E. Brown of Georgia* (Baton Rouge: Louisiana State University Press, 1977); Derrell C. Roberts, *Joseph E. Brown and the Politics of Reconstruction* (University: University of Alabama Press, 1973), 1–90.

56. 14 C.R., 281, 319.

57. May Spencer Ringold, "Senator James Zachariah George of Mississippi: Bourbon or Liberal?" *Journal of Mississippi History* 16 (July 1954): 164–83.

58. 14 C.R.; Vest, 461–67; Call, 470–71; Williams, 503–5; Cockrell, 505–9, 510–14, 515–24, 525–27.

59. 14 C.R., 465, 503.

60. 14 C.R., 283.

61. Steven J. Arcanti, "To Secure the Party: Henry L. Dawes and the Politics of Reconstruction," *Historical Journal of Western Massachusetts* 5 (Spring 1977): 33–45.

62. 14 C.R., 467.

63. Dawes had his own, stillborn plan for civil service reform in 1881–82. Dorman B. Eaton to Dawes, Jan. 31, 1882, Henry Laurens Dawes Papers, Library of Congress. I am grateful to Mark Summers for this reference.

64. 14 C.R., 566.

65. 14 C.R., Pugh, 567, 590–91; Garland, 587–88; Morgan, 596–97; Brown, 598–99.

66. Plumb at 14 C.R., 595; Brown at 599.

67. 14 C.R., 602.

68. 14 C.R., 611.

69. 14 C.R., Hawley's, 611–30, 635–44; Blair's, 645–53.

70. 14 C.R., 645, 653.

71. 14 C.R., 661.

72. *Members of Congress since 1789*, 176–77, 170.

73. 14 C.R., 860–61.

74. 14 C.R., 862, 863.

75. Ben H. Procter, *Not without Honor: The Life of John H. Reagan* (Austin: University of Texas Press, 1962), 122–61; Hugh B. Hammett, *Hilary Abner Herbert: A Southerner Returns to the Union* (Philadelphia: American Philosophical Society, 1976), 1–61.

76. 14 C.R., 866.

77. Edward Younger, *John A. Kasson: Politics and Diplomacy from Lincoln to McKinley* (Iowa City: State Historical Society of Iowa, 1955), 7–321.

78. 14 C.R., 867.

79. Mark W. Huddleston and William W. Boyer, *The Higher Civil Service in the United States: Quest for Reform* (Pittsburgh: University of Pittsburgh Press, 1996), 18–20; Ingraham, *Foundation of Merit*, 30–128; Van Riper, *History*, 101.

80. Blair's opening speech on his bill in 1884, *Congressional Record*, vol. 15, 48th Cong., 1st sess. (hereafter abbreviated as 15 C.R.), 1999–2032.

81. 15 C.R., 2062.

82. 15 C.R., 2064–2065; see generally Burton J. Williams, *Senator John James Ingalls: Kansas' Iridescent Republican* (Lawrence: University Press of Kansas, 1972), esp. 79, 90, 99–102.

83. 15 C.R., 2066–67.

84. 15 C.R., 2151.

85. 15 C.R., 2152.

86. For Garland's speech in favor of the constitutionality of the Blair bill, 15 C.R., 2204–7.

87. 15 C.R., 2247; italics added.

88. Louise Horton, *Samuel Bell Maxey: A Biography* (Austin: University of Texas Press, 1974).

89. For one example of a growing field of scholarship in this area, see Gail Bederman, *Manliness and Civilization: A Cultural History of Gender and Race in the United States, 1880–1917* (Chicago: University of Chicago Press, 1995).

90. 15 C.R., 2243.

91. 15 C.R., 2243.

92. 15 C.R., 2255.

93. 15 C.R., 2690–91, 2692.

94. 15 C.R., 2692–93.

95. The amendments included significant word changes regarding reporting as well as minor changes. Though they have some bearing on the second state mind set, their particulars do not add to this analysis. For the relevant pages: 15 C.R., 2706–24.

96. 15 C.R., 2721.

97. Joseph A. Fry, *John Tyler Morgan and the Search for Southern Autonomy* (Knoxville: University of Tennessee Press, 1992), 2–7, 38–45.

98. 15 C.R., 2724.

six: "What Constitutes a State"

1. Leon Fink, *Workingmen's Democracy* (Urbana: University of Illinois Press, 1983), 22–27; Bruce Laurie, *Artisans into Workers: Labors in Nineteenth-Century America* (New York: Hill & Wang, 1989), 141–75; Mark Wahlgren Summers, *The Gilded Age or, the Hazard of New Functions* (Upper Saddle River, N.J.: Prentice Hall, 1997), 139–43; Kim Voss, *The Making of American Exceptionalism: The Knights of Labor and Class Formation in the Nineteenth Century* (Ithaca: Cornell University Press, 1993), 1–14, 72–101.

2. Ewan Clague, *The Bureau of Labor Statistics* (New York: Praeger, 1968), 3–8; Joseph P. Goldberg and William T. Moye, *The First Hundred Years of the Bureau of Labor Statistics* (Washington, D.C.: U.S. Government Printing Office, 1985), 1–4.

3. John A. Garraty, *Labor and Capital in the Gilded Age: Testimony taken by the Senate Committee upon the Relations between Labor and Capital-1883* (Boston: Little, Brown, 1968), vii–xi; Gordon B. McKinney, "The Blair Committee Investigation of 1883," *Appalachian Journal* 26(2) (Winter 1999): 150–66; McKinney, "U.S. Senator Henry William Blair and the 'Labor and Capital Hearings' of 1883: An Industrial Economy in Microcosm," *Historical New Hampshire* 56(1–2) (2001): 20–33.

4. See generally Daniel J. Boorstin, *The Americans: The Democratic Experience* (New York: Vintage Books, 1973), 167–73.

5. *Congressional Record*, vol. 15, 48th Cong., 1st sess. (hereafter abbreviated as 15 C.R.), 1675.

6. Clague, *Bureau of Labor Statistics*, 4–6; Goldberg, Moye, *First Hundred Years*, 2. See later discussion of the Massachusetts railroad commission.

7. 15 C.R., 1675.

8. 15 C.R., 1676.

9. 15 C.R., 1676.

10. 15 C.R., 1677.

11. 15 C.R., 1746–50.

12. "Hopkins, James Herron," *Biographical Directory*, 1235; "The Hopkins Family, p. 32," "Beers Biographical Record On-Line" (text from page 32, J. H. Beers and Co., *Commemorative Biographical Record of Washington County, Pennsylvania* [Chicago: J. H. Beers & Co., 1893]), www.savory.org/chartiers/beers-project/articles/hopkins-32.html; 15 C.R., 3139.

13. 15 C.R., 3139.

14. 15 C.R., 3139.

15. 15 C.R., 3140. The title of the poem is "An Ode in Imitation of Alcaeus," originally published in 1781. *Bartlett Familiar Quotations*, 10th ed., 1919, www.bartleby.com/100/303.html; the full version is available in many locations, including *And Sovereign Law . . .* (painting in the Congressional Reading Room of the Library of Congress), "The Inspiration," Library of Congress, www.loc.og/law/public/asl/htdoc/aslo02.html.

16. 15 C.R., 3140.

17. "Inspiration," www.loc.gov/law/public/asl/htdoc/aslo02.html; italics added.

18. 15 C.R., 3142.

19. "An Ode in Imitation of Alcaeus," "The Inspiration": *And Sovereign Law . . .* (Library of Congress), www.loc.gov/law/public/asl/htdoc/aslo02.html.

20. 15 C.R., 3144.

21. 15 C.R., 3147.

22. 15 C.R., 3148.

23. 15 C.R., 3140, 3144, 3149, 3150.

24. 15 C.R., 3150.

25. 15 C.R., 3152, 3153.

26. 15 C.R., 3153–60.

27. 15 C.R., 3161, 3160, 3161.

28. 15 C.R., 4147–49, 4150–51.

29. 15 C.R., 4153–55.

30. Thomas Adams Upchurch, *Legislating Racism: The Billion Dollar Congress and the Birth of Jim Crow* (Lexington: University Press of Kentucky, 2004), 27; remarks are from 15 C.R., 4156.

31. 15 C.R., 4155, 4157.

32. 15 C.R., 4153.

33. 15 C.R., 4153.

34. 15 C.R., 4281–84.

35. 15 C.R., 4285, 4286.

36. 15 C.R., 4387, 4388.

37. Burton J. Williams, *Senator John James Ingalls: Kansas' Iridescent Republican* (Lawrence: University Press of Kansas, 1972), 5–9.

38. 15 C.R., 4388.

39. U.S. Constitution, art. 2, sec. 2, cl. 2.

40. 15 C.R., 4392–93.

41. 15 C.R., 4393.

42. 15 C.R., 4396; 73 U.S. 385, 18 L. Ed. 830, 1867 U.S. LEXIS 981, 6 Wall. 385 (1867).

43. 15 C.R., 4394–98.

44. 15 C.R., 4428; 99 U.S. 508, 25 L. Ed. 482, 1878 U.S. LEXIS 1569, 9 Otto 508 (1878).

45. 15 C.R., 4427.

46. 15 C.R., 4429, 4430.

47. 15 C.R., 5534.

48. For its first commissioner's, Carroll Wright, career and impact on state-labor relations in Massachusetts and the United States, see James Leiby, *Carroll Wright and Labor Reform: The Origin of Labor Statistics* (Cambridge: Harvard University Press, 1960).

49. Peter Charles Hoffer, *Law and People in Colonial America*, 2nd ed. (Baltimore: Johns Hopkins University Press, 1998); John Brewer, *Sinews of Power: War, Money and the English State, 1688–1783* (Cambridge: Harvard University Press, 1990); Richard B. Morris, *Government and Labor in Early America* (1946; rpt., New York: Harper & Row, 1965).

50. For the relationship between the army and the railroads, see Robert G. Angevine, *The Railroad and the State: War, Politics, and Technology in Nineteenth Century America* (Stanford: Stanford University Press, 2004).

51. Robert E. Cushman, *The Independent Regulatory Commissions* (New York: Oxford University Press, 1941), 22–26; George W. Hilton, "The Consistency of the Interstate Commerce Act," *Journal of Law and Economics* 9 (1966): 87–113, 101–2.

52. Hilton, "Consistency," 94–101; but see Colleen Dunlavy, *Politics and Industrialization: Early Railroads in the United States and Prussia* (Princeton: Princeton University Press, 1994).

53. Tony Allan Freyer, *Forums of Order: The Federal Courts and Business in American History*, Industrial Development and the Social Fabric, vol. 4 (Greenwich, Conn.: JAI Press, 1979), 108–12; Philip L. Merkel, "The Origins of an Expanded Federal Court Jurisdiction: Railroad Development and the Ascendancy of the Federal Judiciary," *Business History Review* 58(3) (Fall 1984): 336–58; on the limited value of land grants, see Lloyd J. Mercer, *Railroads and Land Grant Policy: A Study in Government Intervention* (New York: Academic Press, 1982).

54. Gerald D. Nash, "Origins of the Interstate Commerce Act of 1887," *Pennsylvania History* 24 (1957): 181–90.

55. Procter, *Not without Honor,* 255–56. The amendment anticipated the Supreme Court ruling in *Plessy v. Ferguson* 163 U.S. 537 (1896) that "separate but equal" accommodations in interstate rail carriers was not a violation of the Equal Protection Clause of the Fourteenth Amendment.

56. Scott C. James, *Presidents, Parties, and the State: A Party System Perspective on Democratic Regulatory Choice, 1884–1936* (New York: Cambridge University Press, 2000), 36–122.

57. For the divisions among businessmen on the issue of railroad regulation, see Edward A. Purcell Jr., "Ideas and Interests: Businessmen and the Interstate Commerce Act," *Journal of American History* 54(3) (Dec. 1967): 561–78.

58. James W. Neilson, *Shelby M. Cullom: Prairie State Republican* (Urbana: University of Illinois Press, 1962), 4, 10–17, 28–29, 42.

59. *Congressional Record,* 49th Cong., 1st sess., vol. 17 (hereafter abbreviated as 17 C.R.), 3473, 3474.

60. Peter Charles Hoffer and N.E.H. Hull, *Impeachment in America, 1635–1805* (New Haven: Yale University Press, 1984), 269–70.

61. 17 C.R., 3477.

62. 17 C.R., 3556, 3825, 4184, 4308, 4309, 4354–55, 4421, and 4409; 4184 (Spooner).

63. Their remarks appear as follows in 17 C.R.: Cullom, 3868; Gorman, 3870; Allison, 4229; Blair, 4230; Brown, 4232; and Sewell, 4320.

64. 17 C.R., 4404.

65. See Bradford C. Mank, "Superfund Contractors and Agency Capture," *New York University Environmental Law Journal* (1993): n. 1, www.law.nyu.edu/journals/envtllaw/issues/vol2/1/2nyuelj34.html; Marver Bernstein, *Regulating Business by Independent Commission* (c. 1955; rpt., Westport, Conn.: Greenwood Press, 1977).

66. 17 C.R., 4422.

67. 17 C.R., 4422.

68. But too open-ended a grant of the legislature's constitutional powers to an independent agency was found unconstitutional by a unanimous Supreme Court in *Schechter Poultry Corp v. United States* 295 U.S. 495 (1935).

69. Quotes are from 17 C.R., Cullom, 3723; Teller, 4409; and Saulsbury, 4421; respectively.

70. 17 C.R., 4423.

71. 17 C.R., 7279–80.

72. 17 C.R., 7283.

73. Caldwell at 17 C.R., 7290–93; O'Ferrall at 7293–96.

74. O'Neill at 17 C.R., 7284–87; Hitt at 7289–90; Hepburn at app., 455–58; Rowell at app., 442–44.

75. Hepburn at 17 C.R., app., 455. The vote at 17 C.R., 7755–56.

76. 17 C.R., 7818.

77. *Congressional Record*, 49th Cong., 2nd sess., vol. 18 (hereafter abbreviated as 18 C.R.), 169.

78. 18 C.R., 639, 571, 656.

79. 18 C.R., 643.

80. 18 C.R., 666.

81. 18 C.R., 696; Procter, *Not without Honor,* 263–66.

82. 18 C.R., 784.

83. 18 C.R., 786.

84. 18 C.R., 820, 839, 847.

85. 18 C.R., 881.

86. Hilton, "Consistency," 104–10.

87. For an overview of the Supreme Court rulings that produced this situation, see James W. Ely Jr., *Railroads and American Law* (Lawrence: University Press of Kansas, 2001), 92–96.

SEVEN: "A System Entirely Satisfactory to the Country"

1. *Congressional Record,* 50th Cong., 1st sess., vol. 19 (hereafter abbreviated as 19 C.R.), 2317.

2. 19 C.R., 2319.

3. 19 C.R., 2319–21.

4. 19 C.R., 2321.

5. 19 C.R., 2321–25, 3096.

6. 19 C.R., 4164.

7. 19 C.R., 4500.

8. 19 C.R., 4502, for "class legislation"; 4501, for "money power."

9. 19 C.R., 4503, 4504–5.

10. 19 C.R., 4768, 5371.

11. E.g., Richard Franklin Bensel, *Yankee Leviathan: The Origins of Central State Authority in America, 1859–1877* (1990; rpt., New York: Cambridge University Press, 1995); Heather Cox Richardson, *The Greatest Nation of the Earth: Republican Economic Policies during the Civil War* (Cambridge: Harvard University Press, 1997).

12. Stephen Skowronek's signature term for the first state, *Building a New American State: The Expansion of National Administrative Capacities, 1877–1920* (1982; rpt., New York: Cambridge University Press, 1995), 35, among other pages.

13. For a scholar who has used Max Weber to analyze courts, see John R. Schmidhauser, *Judges and Justices: The Federal Appellate Judiciary* (Boston: Little, Brown, 1979), 2–9.

14. Owen Fiss, "The Bureaucratization of the Judiciary," in Fiss, *The Law as It Should Be* (New York: New York University Press, 2003), 68–72; Kermit L. Hall, *The Magic Mirror: Law in American History* (New York: Oxford University Press, 1989), esp. chap. 10: "Law, Industrialization, and the Beginnings of the Regulatory State: 1860–1920," 189–

210; William J. Novak, "The Legal Origins of the Modern American State," in *Looking Back at Law's Century*, ed. Austin Sarat, Bryant Garth, and Robert A. Kagan (Ithaca: Cornell University Press, 2002), 249–83.

15. See generally Kermit L. Hall, *The Politics of Justice: Lower Federal Judicial Selection and the Second Party System, 1829–61* (Lincoln: University of Nebraska Press, 1979).

16. See generally Stanley I. Kutler, *Judicial Power and Reconstruction Politics* (Chicago: University of Chicago Press, 1968).

17. Kutler, *Judicial Power,* 143–60; William M. Wiecek, "The Reconstruction of Federal Judicial Power, 1863–1875," *American Journal of Legal History* 13(4) (Oct. 1969): 333–59; Felix Frankfurter and James M. Landis, *The Business of the Supreme Court: A Study in the Federal Judicial System* (New York: Macmillan, 1928), 77–78; for a critique of the agenda behind Frankfurter and Landis's presentation, see Edward A. Purcell Jr., "Reconsidering the Frankfurterian Paradigm: Reflections on Histories of Lower Federal Courts," *Law and Social Inquiry* 24 (Summer 1999): 679–750, 693–95, 700–702.

18. See, e.g., Morton J. Horwitz, *Transformation of American Law, 1860–1940: The Crisis of Legal Orthodoxy* (New York: Oxford University Press, 1992); Edward A. Purcell Jr., *Brandeis and the Progressive Constitution* (New Haven: Yale University Press, 2000), 12–17.

19. For the problems increased caseloads can create for the judicial system, see David S. Clark, "Adjudication to Administration: A Statistical Analysis of Federal District Courts in the Twentieth Century," *Southern California Law Review* 55(1) (Nov. 1981): 65–152; Robert A. Kagan, Bliss Cartwright, Lawrence M. Friedman, and Stanton Wheeler, "The Business of State Supreme Courts," *Stanford Law Review* 30(1) (Nov. 1977): 121–56.

20. Frankfurter and Landis, *Business of the Supreme Court,* 57–64.

21. Frankfurter and Landis, *Business of the Supreme Court,* 81, 83–85, 90, 93; Tony Allan Freyer, *Forums of Order: The Federal Courts and Business in American History* (Greenwich, Conn.: JAI Press, 1979), 125–36.

22. Richard E. Ellis, *The Jeffersonian Crisis: Courts and Politics in the Young Republic* (New York: Oxford University Press, 1971), 15, 45–51.

23. *Congressional Record,* 51st Cong., 1st sess., vol. 21 (hereafter abbreviated as 21 C.R.), 3398.

24. *Origins and Development of Congress,* 115–22; Nelson W. Polsby, "The Institutionalization of the House of Representatives," in *Studies of Congress*, ed. Glenn R. Parker (Washington, D.C.: Congressional Quarterly, 1985), 93–95.

25. Blair Bolles, *Tyrant from Illinois: Uncle Joe Cannon's Experiment with Personal Power* (New York: W. W. Norton, 1951), 3–33.

26. 21 C.R., 3398.

27. For the full text of the House version, see 21 C.R., 3402–3.

28. For an introduction to this concept's career in national politics, see Lee J. Alston and Joseph P. Ferrie, *Southern Paternalism and the American Welfare State: Economics, Politics, and Institutions in the South, 1865–1965* (Cambridge: Cambridge University Press, 1999).

29. 21 C.R., 3399.

30. 21 C.R., 3399.

31. 21 C.R., 3399.

32. 21 C.R., 3399.

33. 21 C.R., 3399.

34. 21 C.R., 3400.

35. 21 C.R., 3403, 3404, 3405.

36. 21 C.R., 3403.

37. 21 C.R., 3403.

38. See, e.g., Freyer, *Forums of Order;* Purcell, *Litigation and Inequality.*

39. John D. Hicks, *The Populist Revolt: A History of the Farmers' Alliance and the People's Party* (Minneapolis: University of Minnesota Press., 1931), 147–48, 153–85; Norman D. Pollack, ed., *The Populist Mind* (Indianapolis: Bobbs-Merrill, 1967), xxix–xxxi.

40. 21 C.R., 3404.

41. 21 C.R., 3407.

42. 21 C.R., 3407–8.

43. Some assert that it had little impact at all given that by 1900 there were thirty-two thousand more spoils jobs than 1883, but this was due more to government growth than to the extension of the spoils system. Mark Wahlgren Summers, *The Gilded Age or, the Hazard of New Functions* (Upper Saddle River, N.J.: Prentice Hall, 1997), 191; Donald R. Harvey, *The Civil Service Commission,* Praeger Library of U.S. Government Departments and Agencies (New York: Praeger, 1970), 5–6; Ari Hoogenboom, *Outlawing the Spoils: A History of the Civil Service Reform Movement* (Urbana: University of Illinois Press, 1961); Mark W. Huddleston and William W. Boyer, *Higher Civil Service in the United States: Quest for Reform* (Pittsburgh: University of Pittsburgh Press, 1996), 18–20; Jay M. Shafritz et al., *Personnel Management in Government: Politics and Process,* 3rd ed. (New York: M. Dekker, 1986), 13–14.

44. 21 C.R., 3408–9.

45. 21 C.R., 3409–10.

46. Frankfurter and Landis, *Business of the Supreme Court,* 97–98.

47. Frankfurter and Landis, *Business of the Supreme Court,* 98–100. For the full text of the Evarts proposal, see 21 C.R., 10218.

48. Freyer, *Forums of Order,* 134–36; Purcell, *Litigation and Inequality,* 250–51.

49. Chester L. Barrows, *William M. Evarts: Lawyer, Diplomat, Statesman* (Chapel Hill: University of North Carolina Press, 1941), 3–16; on Lieber, see James Farr, "The Americanization of Hermeneutics: Francis Lieber's *Legal and Political Hermeneutics,*" in Gregory Leyh, *Legal Hermeneutics: History, Theory, and Practice* (Berkeley: University of California Press, 1992), 85, an important influence on Evarts.

50. Barrows, *Evarts,* 28, 46–49, 56–58, 169, 174–75.

51. Barrows, *Evarts,* 253, 183–85, 430.

52. Barrows, *Evarts,* 453, 67, 473–74.

53. 21 C.R., 10217, 10219–20.

54. Administration of justice, 21 C.R., 10220 (twice), 10222, 10223; judicial establishment, 21 C.R., 10220 (twice), 10223.

55. 21 C.R., (twice) 10222.

56. For a discussion of the Democratic Party's central tenets, see John Gerring, *Party Ideologies in America, 1828–1996* (Cambridge: Cambridge University Press, 1998), 161–86.

57. 21 C.R., 10223–24.

58. 21 C.R., 10224.

59. 21 C.R., 10225, 10226.

60. Robert Stevens, *Law School: Legal Education in America from the 1850s to the 1980s* (Chapel Hill: University of North Carolina Press, 1983), 35–56; William M. Wiecek, *The Lost World of Classical Legal Thought: Law and Ideology in America, 1886–1937* (New York: Oxford University Press, 1998), 80–97.

61. 21 C.R., 10226, 10227.

62. For the rise of science and its influence on the national government's development, see, among others, David F. Noble, *America by Design: Science, Technology, and the Rise of Corporate Capitalism* (New York: Knopf, 1977).

63. 21 C.R., 10228, 10230.

64. David W. Blight, *Beyond the Battlefield: Race, Memory, and the American Civil War* (Amherst: University of Massachusetts Press, 2002), 109–10, 178–80.

65. 21 C.R., 10230.

66. 21 C.R., 10278–82.

67. 21 C.R., 10284–85.

68. 21 C.R., 10288.

69. Evarts's response to Daniel, 21 C.R., 10302–3.

70. 21 C.R., 10303–4, 10305.

71. For the legal examination of this mind-set, see Tony Allan Freyer, *Producers versus Capitalists: Constitutional Conflict in Antebellum America* (Charlottesville: University of Virginia Press, 1994); for a different, quasi-Marxist reading, see Charles Sellers, *The Market Revolution: Jacksonian America, 1815–1846* (Oxford: Oxford University Press, 1991).

72. 21 C.R., 10306; Vest at 21 C.R., 10308.

73. 21 C.R., 10311, 10313, 10314, 10316, 10364–65.

74. *Congressional Record*, 51st Cong., 2nd sess., vol. 22 (hereafter abbreviated as 22 C.R.), 3583.

75. 22 C.R., 3584–85.

76. 22 C.R., 3586.

77. 22 C.R., app., 249; 3586.

78. 22 C.R., 3586; akin to Frankfurter's conservation of judicial resources, Felix Frankfurter, *Felix Frankfurter Reminisces: An Intimate Portrait as Recorded in Talks with Dr. Harlan B. Philips* (1960; rpt., Garden City, N.Y.: Reynal, 1962), 348; on Frankfurter and desegregation among other objects of his judicial restraint, see, e.g., Melvin I. Urofsky, *Felix Frankfurter: Judicial Restraint and Individual Liberties* (Boston: Twayne, 1991), 31–32, 134–35; Leonard Baker, *Brandeis and Frankfurter: A Dual Biography* (1984; rpt., New York: Harper & Row, 1986), 465–68, 480–81, 485.

79. 22 C.R., 3586.

80. Both on 22 C.R., 3587.

81. 22 C.R., 3587.

82. 21 C.R., 6083.

83. 21 C.R., 6083.

84. 21 C.R., 6084.

85. 21 C.R., 6084.

86. 21 C.R., 6086.

87. 21 C.R., 6086, 6087. For the full report and the text of the bill, see 21 C.R., 6087–89.

88. 21 C.R., 6333.

89. 21 C.R., 6333.

90. For a more recent overview, see Jerrold M. Packard, *American Nightmare: The History of Jim Crow* (New York: St. Martin's Press, 2002); for the book that accompanied the PBS documentary, see Richard Wormser, *The Rise and Fall of Jim Crow* (New York: St. Martin's Press, 2003).

91. 21 C.R., 6334; italics added.

92. 21 C.R., 6371, 6338.

93. 21 C.R., 6338, 6339.

94. 21 C.R., 6346, 6349.

95. Williams, *Ingalls*, 154.

96. 21 C.R., 6369, 6370, 6371, 6372.

97. 21 C.R., 8828–29.

98. 21 C.R., 8829, 8835.

99. For the history and thought of the Grange, see Solon J. Buck, *The Granger Movement: A Study of Agricultural Organization and Its Political, Economic, and Social Manifestations, 1870–1880* (1913; rpt., Lincoln: University of Nebraska Press, 1963,); D. Sven Nordin, *Rich Harvest: A History of the Grange, 1867–1900* (Jackson: University Press of Mississippi, 1974); Thomas A. Woods, *Knights of the Plow: Oliver H. Kelley and the Origins of the Grange in Republican Ideology* (Ames: Iowa State University Press, 1991); for references to the various Grange groups' interest in the Taylor amendment, see 21 C.R., 8834, 8835.

100. 21 C.R., 8832–34, 8835.

101. 21 C.R., 8836.

102. 21 C.R., 8836–37.

103. 21 C.R., 8839.

104. 21 C.R., 8839, 8874, 9388.

CONCLUSION: "To Answer Our Purposes, It Must Be Adapted"

1. For the article's place in the history of political science, see Jameson W. Doig, "'If I See a Murderous Fellow Sharpening a Knife Cleverly . . .': The Wilsonian Dichotomy and the Public Authority Tradition," *Public Administration Review* 43(4) (July–Aug. 1983): 292–304.

2. "The Science of Administration," *Political Science Quarterly* 2(2) (June 1887): 197–222, 202.

3. For works on American exceptionalism, see Seymour Martin Lipset, *American Exceptionalism: A Double Edged Sword* (New York: W. W. Norton, 1996), 17–19; Dorothy Ross, *The Origins of American Social Science* (1991; rpt., Cambridge: Cambridge University Press, 1997), xiv–xviii; Stephen Skowronek, *Building a New American State: The Expansion of National Administrative Capacities, 1877–1920* (1982; rpt., Cambridge: Cambridge University Press, 1995), 5–10.

Essay on Sources

Debates in the *Congressional Globe* and the *Congressional Record* in the preceding pages provide the vast majority of primary source citations. The usual citation style for them includes not only the volume number but also the date, the Congress, the session, and the part in which the pages appear. Because the citations to the *Globe* and *Record* are so frequent and the text itself refers to the relevant dates and congresses, here only an abbreviated citation follows the initial citation. Because the parts (the individual bounded volumes) are separated by page number, the part number does not appear in the citations. The citation style that appears here is more than sufficient to locate the congressmen's words.

Many have written on the *Congressional Record*'s problems as a source, including Mildred L. Amer, *The Congressional Record: Content, History and Issues* (Congressional Research Service, Library of Congress, Jan. 14, 1993), 1–9; Howard N. Mantel, "The *Congressional Record:* Fact or Fiction of the Legislative Process," *Western Political Quarterly* 12 (Dec. 1959): 981–95; Elizabeth Gregory McPherson, "Reporting the Debates of Congress," *Quarterly Journal of Speech*, in the remarks of Representative Karl E. Mundt, *Congressional Record*, vol. 88 (June 10, 1942), A2182–A2185; Laurence F. Schmeckebier and Roy B. Eastin, *Government Publications and Their Use*, 2nd rev. ed. (1961; rpt., Washington, D.C.: Brookings Institution, 1969), 139–43; and Michelle M. Springer, "The *Congressional Record:* 'Substantially a Verbatim Report?'" *Government Publications Review* 13(3) (1986): 371–78.

For the sake of brevity and efficiency, no citations to general, biographical, or reference works appear in the final version of the manuscript. A copy of the manuscript with all of these citations is on file with the press. Unless the source is otherwise noted, biographical information comes from John A. Garraty and Mark C. Carnes, eds., *American National Biography* (New York: Oxford University Press, 1999); Allen Johnson and Dumas Malone, eds., *Dictionary of American Biography* (New York: Charles Scribner's Sons, 1930); *The National Cyclopedia of American Biography* (New York: James T. White & Co., 1907); and the *Biographical Directory of the American Congress, 1774–1996* (Washington, D.C.: Congressional Quarterly Staff Directories, 1997).

Whenever I quote from or summarize particular ideas from secondary sources, I cite the secondary source in the endnotes. What follows is a more general survey of the literature I read on the subjects. All of these sources informed my thinking in some manner, sometimes merely by forcing me to refine my argument.

This book is not a study of administration or administrative agencies per se. Never-theless, I profited from the classic overviews of the administrative developments in this period: Lloyd Milton Short, *The Development of National Administrative Organization in the United States* (Baltimore: Johns Hopkins Press, 1923); and, for an earlier period, Leonard D. White, with the assistance of Jean Schneider, *The Republican Era: A Study in Administrative History* (New York: Free Press, 1958).

The seminal modern works on the building of the U.S. national state include Richard Franklin Bensel, *Yankee Leviathan: The Origins of Central State Authority in America, 1859–1877* (1990; rpt., New York: Cambridge University Press, 1995); Ballard C. Campbell, *The Growth of American Government: Governance from the Cleveland Era to the Present* (Bloomington: Indiana University Press, 1995); Daniel P. Carpenter, *The Forging of Bu-reaucratic Autonomy: Reputations, Networks, and Policy Innovation in Executive Agencies, 1862–1928* (Princeton: Princeton University Press, 2001); Robert Higgs, *Crisis and Le-viathan: Critical Episodes in the Growth of American Government* (New York: Oxford Uni-versity Press, 1987); William E. Nelson, *The Roots of American Bureaucracy, 1830–1900* (Cambridge: Harvard University Press, 1982); Elizabeth Sanders, *Roots of Reform: Farm-ers, Workers, and the American State, 1877–1917* (Chicago: University of Chicago Press, 1999); Theda Skocpol, *Protecting Soldiers and Mothers: The Political Origins of Social Policy in the United States* (Cambridge: Harvard University Press, 1992); and Stephen Skow-ronek, *Building a New American State: The Expansion of National Administrative Capacities, 1877–1920* (1982; rpt., New York: Cambridge University Press, 1995).

Summaries of the vast literature on the state in the United States appear in Brian Balogh, "Reorganizing the Organizational Synthesis: Federal-Professional Relations in Modern America," *Studies in American Political Development* 5 (Spring 1991): 119–72; Leonard Binder, "The Natural History of Development Theory," *Comparative Studies in Society and History* 28(1) (Jan. 1986): 3–33; Aaron L. Friedberg, *In the Shadow of the Gar-rison State: America's Anti-Statism and Its Cold War Grand Strategy* (Princeton: Princeton University Press, 2000), 9–33; and the more narrowly constructed work by Karen Orren and Stephen Skowronek, *The Search for American Political Development* (New York: Cam-bridge University Press, 2004). For an eminent legal historian's view, see Daniel R. Ernst, "Law and American Political Development, 1877–1938," *Reviews in American History* 26(1) (1998): 205–19.

Michael Adas has recently written on the American ideological contradiction in "From Settler Colony to Global Hegemon: Integrating the Exceptionalist Narrative of the American Experience into World History," *American Historical Review* 106(5) (Dec. 2001): 1692–1720. The intellectual history of Congress's shift from antebellum thinking to the Progressive Era is tracked in Carpenter, *Forging of Bureaucratic Autonomy;* Edward J. Blum, *Reforging the White Republic: Race, Religion and American Nationalism* (Baton Rouge: Louisiana State University Press, 2005); David J. Rothman, *Politics and Power: The United States Senate, 1869–1901* (Cambridge: Harvard University Press, 1966); and Frank Tariello Jr., *The Reconstruction of American Political Ideology, 1865–1917* (Charlottesville: University Press of Virginia, 1982). Richard R. John, "Farewell to the 'Party Period': Po-litical Economy in Nineteenth Century America"; and Julian E. Zelizer, "History and

Political Science: Together Again?" in *Journal of Policy History* 16(2) (2004): 117–25, 126–36, are valuable confirmations of the thesis of the present work.

Although I have not adopted the "rhetorical criticism" school of interpretation, I do emphasize the importance of ideas expressed in public spaces. Kirt H. Wilson, *The Reconstruction Desegregation Debate: The Politics of Equality and the Rhetoric of Place, 1870–1875* (East Lansing: Michigan State University Press, 2002), is an example of this approach and provides a guide to the literature on 206 n. 7.

The impact of lawyers' presence in Congress cannot be disputed, but its precise shape and influence is still debated. Albert P. Melone, "Rejection of the Lawyer-Dominance Proposition: The Need for Additional Research," *Western Political Quarterly* 33(2) (June 1980): 225–32; and Mark C. Miller, *The High Priests of American Politics: The Role of Lawyers in American Political Institutions* (Knoxville: University of Tennessee Press, 1995), 162–63, 171–72, 174, argue that lawyers played a key role. Heinz Eulau and John D. Sprague, *Lawyers in Politics: A Study in Professional Convergence* (Indianapolis: Bobbs-Merrill, 1964), 22–27; Justin J. Green, John R. Schmidhauser, Larry L. Berg, and David Brady, "Lawyers in Congress: A New Look at Some Old Assumptions," *Western Political Quarterly* 26(3) (Sept. 1973): 440–52, maintain that lawyers did not differ appreciably from others. James Willard Hurst, *The Growth of American Law: The Law Makers* (Boston: Little, Brown, 1950), 355, 375, splits the difference, with lawyers being influential but not at odds with the rest of society.

Richard S. Wells, "The Legal Profession and Politics," *Midwest Journal of Political Science* 8(2) (May 1964): 166–90, posits that lawyers had a unique perspective but varied widely within that perspective. Jerome Mushkat and Joseph G. Rayback, *Martin Van Buren: Law, Politics, and the Shaping of Republican Ideology* (DeKalb: Northern Illinois University Press, 1997), esp. 178–81; and Robert A. Ferguson, *Law and Letters in American Culture* (Cambridge: Harvard University Press, 1984), maintain that lawyerly thinking had a special influence over lawmaking, men such as Van Buren, and American literature.

In addition to the works cited in the text on southern attitudes toward the national government, one should consult William J. Cooper, *Liberty and Slavery: Southern Politics to 1860* (New York: Knopf, 1983), on the fear of reform and southern politics; and Ronald G. Walters, *American Reformers, 1815–1860* (New York: Hill & Wang, 1978), on the relationship of reform generally to abolitionism and the South.

In-depth studies of the first Morrill Act include J. B. Edmond, *The Magnificent Charter: The Origin and Role of the Morrill Land-Grant Colleges and Universities* (Hicksville, N.Y.: Exposition Press, 1978); Edmund J. James, *The Origin of the Land Grant Act of 1862 (The So-Called Morrill Act) and Some Account of Its Author Jonathan B. Turner, University Studies* 4(1) (Nov. 1910) (Urbana-Champaign: University of Illinois Press, 1910); John Patrick Murphy, *Congress and the Colleges a Century Ago: A Political History of the First Morrill Act, Other Congressional Support for Educational Purposes, and the Political Climate of the United States as It Involved Education prior to 1862* (Ed.D. diss., Indiana University, 1967); William Edwin Sawyer, *The Evolution of the Morrill Act of 1862* (Ph.D. diss., Boston University, 1948); and John Y. Simon, "The Politics of the Morrill Act," *Agricultural History* 37(2) (1963): 103–11.

More general works on education also deal with the Morrill Act. See Lawrence A. Cremin, *American Education: The National Experience, 1783–1876* (New York: Harper & Row, 1980), 341, calling the act merely the nationalization of a trend; Leonard Curry, *Blueprint for Modern America: Nonmilitary Legislation of the First Civil War Congress* (Nashville: Vanderbilt University Press, 1968), 9, regarding the act as part of the Civil War turning point; Richard Hofstadter and C. DeWitt Hardy, *The Development and Scope of Higher Education in the United States* (New York: Columbia University Press, 1952), 116–17, citing the act as typical of U.S. federalism; Harold M. Hyman, *American Singularity: The 1787 Northwest Ordinance, the 1862 Homestead and Morrill Acts, and the 1944 G.I. Bill* (Athens: University of Georgia Press, 1986), depicting the act as evidence of American uniqueness; Allan Nevins, *The State Universities and Democracy* (Urbana: University of Illinois Press, 1962), 22, lauding the act as a unique and grand project; Roland R. Renne, *Land-Grant Institutions, the Public, and the Public Interest, Annals of the American Academy of Political and Social Science*, special ed., vol. 331, Sept. 1960), 46–51, 48, describing the act as "a whole new concept of higher education"; and Heather Cox Richardson, *The Greatest Nation of the Earth: Republican Economic Policies during the Civil War* (Cambridge: Harvard University Press, 1997), 1–7; and Laurence R. Veysey, *The Emergence of the American University* (1965; rpt., Chicago: University of Chicago Press, 1970) 70, 112, agreeing that the act produced only minor results.

Several works have studied the origin of the Department of Agriculture. See Richardson, *Greatest Nation of the Earth*, 139–69; Charles H. Greathouse, comp., *Historical Sketch of the U.S. Department of Agriculture; Its Objects and Present Organization* (U.S. Department of Agriculture, Division of Publications, Bulletin 3, 2nd rev. ed., Washington, D.C., 1907), 5–14; Wayne D. Rasmussen and Gladys L. Baker, *The Department of Agriculture: Praeger Library of U.S. Government Departments and Agencies* (New York: Praeger, 1972), viii–11; Short, *Development of National Administrative Organization in the United States*, 374–80; Warner W. Stockberger, with Virginia Brand Smith, *Personnel Administration Development in the United States Department of Agriculture: The First Fifty Years* (Washington, D.C.: U.S. Department of Agriculture Office of Personnel, 1947), 1–9; and William L. Wanlass, *The United States Department of Agriculture: A Study in Administration* (Baltimore: Johns Hopkins Press, 1920), 9–24, 110, 113.

Another group of scholars has placed the Department of Agriculture center stage in the story of developing federal administrative capacity but only as a prologue to the New Deal. See Theda Skocpol and Kenneth Finegold, "State Capacity and Economic Intervention in the Early New Deal," *Political Science Quarterly* 97(2) (Summer 1982): 255–78, 271–72; Finegold and Skocpol, *State and Party in America's New Deal* (Madison: University of Wisconsin Press, 1995); David E. Hamilton, "Building the Associative State: The Department of Agriculture and American State-Building," *Agricultural History* 64(2) (Spring 1990): 207–18; and Hamilton, *From New Day to New Deal: American Farm Policy from Hoover to Roosevelt, 1928–1933* (Chapel Hill: University of North Carolina Press, 1991).

Civil War party ideologies are topics in David Montgomery, *Beyond Equality: Labor and the Radical Republicans, 1862–1872* (New York: Knopf, 1969); Richardson, *Greatest Nation of the Earth*. For the Democrats during the war, see Jean Harvey Baker, *Affairs of Party: The Political Culture of Northern Democrats in the Mid-Nineteenth Century* (Ithaca: Cornell University Press, 1983); Leonard P. Curry, "Congressional Democrats, 1861–1863," *Civil War History* 12 (Sept. 1966): 213–29; and Joel H. Silbey, *A Respectable Minority: The Democratic Party in the Civil War Era, 1860–1868* (New York: W. W. Norton, 1977).

Scholars have viewed Reconstruction, the term used to describe the period from 1865 to 1876, as a well-intentioned attempt to provide for justice and civil rights for an oppressed minority; less positively as a capitalist oriented onslaught on a rural proletariat; negatively as the product of a cohort of vengeful, politically motivated Republicans who imposed federal tyranny on a prostrate South; and more ambiguously as an uneven effort to aid the newly freed slaves abandoned when the Republicans lost their nerve. Characterizations of the Bureau of Freedmen, Refugees, and Abandoned Lands—the Freedmen's Bureau—have followed like driftwood on the changing tides of opinion surrounding Reconstruction.

For the *Birth of a Nation* school, see William A. Dunning, *Reconstruction, Political and Economic, 1865–1877* (New York: Harper, 1907); Walter L. Fleming, *The Sequel of Appomattox* (New Haven: Yale University Press, 1919); Robert W. Winston, *Andrew Johnson: Plebeian and Patriot* (New York: Holt, 1926); Howard K. Beale, *The Critical Year: A Study of Andrew Johnson and Reconstruction* (New York: Harcourt Brace, 1930); George R. Bentley, *A History of the Freedmen's Bureau* (Philadelphia: University of Pennsylvania Press, 1955); and E. Merton Coulter, *The South during Reconstruction* (Baton Rouge: Louisiana State University Press, 1968).

For a positive view of the work of the Freedmen's Bureau, see John H. Cox and LaWanda Cox, "General O. O. Howard and the 'Misrepresented Bureau,'" *Journal of Southern History* 19 (Nov. 1953): 427–56; Eric L. McKitrick, *Andrew Johnson and Reconstruction* (Chicago: University of Chicago Press, 1960); W. R. Brock, *An American Crisis* (New York: St. Martin's Press, 1963); Leon F. Litwack, *Been in the Storm So Long: The Aftermath of Slavery* (New York: Knopf, 1979); James M. McPherson, *The Struggle for Equality: Abolitionists and the Negro in the Civil War and Reconstruction* (Princeton: Princeton University Press, 1964); Hans L. Trefousse, *The Radical Republicans: Lincoln's Vanguard for Racial Justice* (New York: Knopf, 1969); and many of the essays in Kenneth M. Stampp and Leon F. Litwack, eds., *Reconstruction: An Anthology of Revisionist Writings* (Baton Rouge: Louisiana State University Press, 1969).

The revisionist view of Reconstruction as an imposition of the industrial system and Yankee Protestantism appears in William S. McFeely, *Yankee Stepfather: General O. O. Howard and the Freedmen* (New Haven: Yale University Press, 1968). A more mixed review forms the basis of Eric Foner, *Nothing but Freedom: Emancipation and Its Legacy* (Baton Rouge: Louisiana State University Press, 1983); and Foner, *Reconstruction: America's Unfinished Revolution, 1863–1877* (New York: Harper & Row, 1988); Kenneth M. Stampp, *The Era of Reconstruction, 1865–1877* (New York: Knopf, 1965); Claude F. Oubre, *Forty Acres and a Mule: The Freedmen's Bureau and Black Land Ownership* (Baton Rouge: Louisiana State University Press, 1978); and Donald G. Nieman, *To Set the Law in Motion: The Freemen's Bureau and the Legal Rights of Blacks, 1865–1868* (Millwood, N.Y.:

KTO Press, 1979). For Radical Reconstruction as a tremendous break from the past examine McPherson, *Ordeal by Fire*, 403.

Radical Reconstruction as a conservative revolution is the central theme of Michael Les Benedict, "Preserving the Constitution: The Conservative Basis of Radical Reconstruction," *Journal of American History* 61 (June 1974): 65–90; Harold M. Hyman, *Lincoln's Reconstruction: Neither Failure of Vision nor Vision of Failure* (Fort Wayne, Ind.: Louis A. Warren Lincoln Library and Museum, 1980). Radical Reconstruction as a little bit of both appears in Foner, *Unfinished Revolution*.

General histories of the federal involvement in education include Edward H. Reisner, *Nationalism and Education since 1789: A Social and Political History of Modern Education* (New York: Macmillan, 1923); Gordon Canfield Lee, *The Struggle for Federal Aid, First Phase: A History of the Attempts to Obtain Federal Aid for the Common Schools* (New York: Bureau of Publications, Teachers College, Columbia University, 1949); Sidney W. Tiedt, *The Role of the Federal Government in Education* (New York: Oxford University Press, 1966); and David Tyack, Thomas James, and Aaron Benavot, *Law and the Shaping of Public Education, 1785–1954* (Madison: University of Wisconsin Press, 1987).

Characterizations of these educational reform efforts are as almost as varied as opinions on Reconstruction. For the spread of capitalism, see Michael B. Katz, *The Irony of Early School Reform: Educational Innovation in Mid-Nineteenth Century Massachusetts* (Cambridge: Harvard University Press, 1968); Samuel Bowles and Herbert Gintis, *Schooling in Capitalist America: Educational Reform and the Contradictions of Economic Life* (New York: Basic Books, 1976); William J. Reese, *The Origins of the American High School* (New Haven: Yale University Press, 1995). For a Yankee Protestant reaction to huddled masses, see Stanley K. Schultz, *The Culture Factory: Boston Public Schools, 1789–1860* (New York: Oxford University Press, 1973). On Yankee Protestantism and centralizing, see David B. Tyack, *The One Best System: A History of American Urban Education* (Cambridge: Harvard University Press, 1974).

Overall surveys of the institutions include H. Warren Button and Eugene F. Provenzo Jr., *History of Education and Culture in America* (Englewood Cliffs, N.J.: Prentice Hall, 1983); and Karl Kaestle, *Pillars of the Republic: Common Schools and American Society 1760–1860* (New York: Hill & Wang, 1983).

The origins and early life of the Department of Justice appear in Homer Cummings and Carl McFarland, *Federal Justice: Chapters in the History of Justice and the Federal Executive* (New York: Macmillan, 1937), 218–21; Albert George Langeluttig, *The Department of Justice of the United States* (Baltimore: Institute for Government Research, 1927), 8–9; Robert M. Goldman, *"A Free Ballot and a Fair Count": The Department of Justice and the Enforcement of Voting Rights in the South, 1877–1893* (New York: Fordham University Press, 2001); Robert J. Kaczorowski, *The Politics of Judicial Interpretation: The Federal Courts, Department of Justice, and Civil Rights, 1866–1876* (Dobbs Ferry, N.Y.: Oceana, 1985), 79–115; William S. McFeely, "Amos T. Akerman: The Lawyer and Racial Justice," in *Region, Race, and Reconstruction: Essays in Honor of C. Vann Woodward*, ed. J. Morgan Kousser and James M. McPherson (New York: Oxford University Press, 1982), 404–11; and Ross A. Webb, "Benjamin H. Bristow: Civil Rights Champion, 1866–1872," *Civil*

War History 15 (Mar. 1969): 39–53, 46–52. Everette Swinney, "Enforcing the Fifteenth Amendment, 1870–1877," *Journal of Southern History* 28 (1962): 202–18; and Richard Zuczek, "The Federal Government's Attack on the Ku Klux Klan: A Reassessment," *South Carolina Historical Magazine* 97 (1996): 47–64, argue that federal efforts were not effective.

In-depth studies of the Blair bill include Daniel W. Crofts, "The Blair Bill and the Elections Bill: The Congressional Aftermath to Reconstruction" (Ph.D. diss., Yale University, 1968), 48–220; Crofts, "The Black Response to the Blair Education Bill," *Journal of Southern History* 37(1) (Feb. 1971): 41–65; John W. Evans, "Catholics and the Blair Education Bill," *Catholic Historical Review* 46 (Oct. 1960): 273–98; Willard B. Gatewood Jr., "North Carolina and Federal Aid to Education: Public Reaction to the Blair Bill, 1881–1890," *North Carolina Historical Review* 40 (Fall 1963): 465–88; Allen J. Going, "The South and the Blair Education Bill," *Mississippi Valley Historical Review* 44 (Sept. 1957): 267–90; Lee, *Struggle for Federal Aid*, 88–162; and Dan M. Robison, "Governor Robert M. Taylor and the Blair Educational Bill in Tennessee," *Tennessee Historical Magazine*, 2nd ser., 2 (Oct. 1931): 28–49.

The basic references on civil service reform are Donald R. Harvey, *The Civil Service Commission* (New York: Praeger, 1970); Ari Hoogenboom, *Outlawing the Spoils: A History of the Civil Service Reform Movement* (Urbana: University of Illinois Press, 1961); Mark W. Huddleston and William W. Boyer, *The Higher Civil Service in the United States: Quest for Reform* (Pittsburgh: University of Pittsburgh Press, 1996); Patricia Wallace Ingraham, *The Foundation of Merit: Public Service in American Democracy* (Baltimore: Johns Hopkins University Press, 1995); Jay M. Shafritz, Albert C. Hyde, and David H. Rosenbloom, *Personnel Management in Government: Politics and Process*, 3rd ed. (New York: M. Dekker, 1986); and Paul P. Van Riper, *History of the United States Civil Service* (Evanston, Ill.: Row, Peterson, 1958).

Introductions to the history of labor-state relations in this period appear in Bruce Laurie, *Artisans into Workers: Labor in Nineteenth Century America* (New York: Hill & Wang, 1989), 113–40; David Montgomery, *The Fall of the House of Labor: The Workplace, the State, and American Labor Activism, 1865–1925* (Cambridge: Cambridge University Press, 1987); Mark Wahlgren Summers, *The Gilded Age, or, The Hazard of New Functions* (Upper Saddle River, N.J.: Prentice Hall, 1997), 79–117, 132–39; Christopher L. Tomlins, *The State and the Unions: Labor Relations, Law, and the Organized Labor Movement in America, 1880–1960* (Cambridge: Cambridge University Press, 1985); and Melvyn Dubofsky, *The State and Labor in Modern America* (Chapel Hill: University of North Carolina Press, 1994), 2–21. The origin of the Bureau of Labor appears in Ewan Clague, *The Bureau of Labor Statistics* (New York: Praeger, 1968), 3–8; Joseph P. Goldberg and William T. Moye, *The First Hundred Years of the Bureau of Labor Statistics* (Washington, D.C.: U.S. Government Printing Office, 1985), 1–4; Jonathan Grossman, *The Department of Labor* (New York: Praeger, 1973), 5–6; Jonathan Grossman, "The Origin of the U.S. Department of Labor," U.S. Department of Labor, Office of the Assistant Secretary for Policy, www .dol.gov/asp/programs/history/dolorigabridge.htm; and W. B. Wilson et al., comp. and ed. O. L. Harvey, with the assistance of Sylvia G. Miller et al., *The Anvil and the Plow: A*

History of the United States Department of Labor (Washington, D.C.: U.S. Government Printing Office, 1963), 259–61.

Works on the Interstate Commerce Commission (ICC) include Gabriel Kolko, *Railroads and Regulation, 1877–1916* (Princeton: Princeton University Press, 1965), 30–44, arguing that the ICC was a conspiracy by the railroads to establish order; Robert W. Harbeson, "Railroads and Regulation, 1877–1916: Conspiracy or Public Interest?" *Journal of Economic History* 27 (1967): 230–42, agreeing with Kolko's characterization of the railroad's motives but not the ICC's actions; as well as Gerald D. Nash, "Origins of the Interstate Commerce Act of 1887," *Pennsylvania History* 24 (1957): 181–90; and Albro Martin, "The Troubled Subject of Railroad Regulation in the Gilded Age—A Reappraisal," *Journal of American History* 61(2) (Sept. 1974): 339–71, opposed to Kolko, arguing the ICC system imposed a bad regime on the railroads to benefit shippers and, ultimately, the automobile. For the divisions among businessmen on the issue of railroad regulation, examine Edward A. Purcell Jr., "Ideas and Interests: Businessmen and the Interstate Commerce Act," *Journal of American History* 54(3) (Dec. 1967): 561–78.

A general overview of Congress and the courts during Reconstruction appears in Michael Les Benedict, *The Blessings of Liberty: A Concise History of the Constitution of the United States* (Lexington, Mass.: D. C. Heath, 1996), 199–213; *A Compromise of Principle: Congressional Republicans and Reconstruction, 1863–1869* (New York: W. W. Norton, 1974); Charles Fairman, *The Oliver Wendell Holmes Devise: History of the Supreme Court of the United States*, vol. 4: *Reconstruction and Reunion, 1864–88*, (New York: Macmillan, 1971), pt. 1, 253–309, 1117–1206; Tony Allan Freyer, *Forums of Order: The Federal Courts and Business in American History* (Greenwich, Conn.: JAI Press, 1979); Stanley I. Kutler, *Judicial Power and Reconstruction Politics* (Chicago: University of Chicago Press, 1968), 48–63; Michael Vorenberg, *Final Freedom: The Civil War, the Abolition of Slavery, and the Thirteenth Amendment* (Cambridge: Cambridge University Press, 2001), esp. 233–39, on enforcement of the Thirteenth Amendment; and William M. Wiecek, "The Reconstruction of Federal Judicial Power, 1863–1875," *American Journal of Legal History* 13(4) (Oct. 1969): 333–59.

For the Congress and the federal court system in the Gilded Age, the foundational work remains Felix Frankfurter and James M. Landis, *The Business of the Supreme Court: A Study in the Federal Judicial System* (New York: Macmillan, 1928), 77–78; but, for a critique of the agenda behind Frankfurter and Landis's presentation, see Edward A. Purcell Jr., "Reconsidering the Frankfurterian Paradigm: Reflections on Histories of Lower Federal Courts," *Law and Social Inquiry* 24 (Summer 1999): 679–750, 693–95, 700–702.

Index

Adams, Charles Francis, Jr., 129, 157, 158
Adams, Henry, 129
Adams, John, 5–6
Adams, John Quincy, 10, 14
administration: in colonies, 10; W. Wilson on, 196
administration of justice: Evarts and, 180; Morgan and, 182; J. Rogers and, 174
administrative state: additions to, 194–95; in 1880s, 168; fears and, 165; Frankfurter and, ix; Interstate Commerce Commission and, 144; lawyers and, 160; opening for, 194; Pendleton Act, Blair bill, and, 118–19; precedents for, 171; second state compared to, 148, 199; transition to, ix–x, 202
adversarial pose, 22
agricultural reformers, 10–12
agriculture, department of: effect of passage of, 50; in House, 43–44; as model, 83, 145; proposal for, 38–43; in Senate, 44–50; sponsorship and, 200
Aiken, David W., 151
Aldrich, Nelson, 147, 156
Allison, William B., 132, 160
American Bar Association, 179, 181
American exceptionalism: first state and, viii; freedmen's bureau debate and, 71; in political speeches and writings, 42; school reform and, 92; W. Wilson and, 197
American Freedmen's Inquiry Commission, 64
American Journal of Education, 91, 99
analogy, arguing by, 53
Anderson, John A., 193
antibureaucracy mindset: Carlisle, Oates, and, 173–74; freedmen's bureau and, 78;

lack of oversight and, 61; Mills and, 177; J. Morrill and, 15; Pendleton Act and, 137; persistence of, 165, 197. *See also* first state ideology
Arnell, Samuel M., 113
Arthur, Chester A., 129
Articles of Confederation, 14
attorney general, 103, 104

Baker, Jehu, 100
Banks, Nathaniel P., 17, 20
Barnard, Henry, 12, 90–91, 99
Barrow, Middleton P., 133–34
Battle of Bull Run, or Manassas, 38
Bayard, James A., Jr., 32, 108
Bayard, Thomas F., Sr.: civil service reform and, 136; justice department and, 108; labor statistics bureau and, 154, 156
Bell, John, 34
Benjamin, John F., 102
Bird, John T., 113
Bismarck Schonhausen, Otto von, vii
Blaine, James G., 101, 112
Blair, Henry W.: civil service reform and, 136; Committee on Education and Labor and, 145–46, 170; on common schools, 187–88; Cullom commission and, 160; federalism and, 190; labor statistics bureau and, 152, 154, 155–56, 157; legislation of, 119, 138; life and career of, 120; oration of, 120–22; Second Morrill Act and, 188–89
Blair bill: debates on, 119; Evarts and, 179; House and, 123–28; opposition to, 122–23, 138–41; reintroduction of, 138–42; second state and, 138, 142–43; support for, 139; third state and, 118–19

Bland, Richard P., 152, 174
block grants, 57
Blount, James H., 151
border states, 66–67
Boutwell, George S., 96
Breckinridge, John C., 21
Breckinridge, William C. P.: bureau of labor and, 169; courts and, 174, 175, 177, 186
Bright, Jesse D., 45
Brooks, Charles, 91
Brooks, James, 70–71
Brown, Benjamin G., 79
Brown, Joseph E.: civil service reform and, 132–33, 135, 136; Cullom commission and, 160, 162; Interstate Commerce Commission bill and, 164
Buchanan, James, 35, 45
Buckalew, Charles R., 79
A Buckeye Abroad (Cox), 69
bureaucracy: definition of, 207n10; as evil, 150; professionalization of, 78–79, 129. *See also* antibureaucracy mindset
bureaucrats, 75
Bureau of Education, Interior Department, 100, 103, 109. *See also* education, department of
Bureau of Freedmen, Refugees, and Abandoned Lands, 87

Caldwell, Andrew J., 162–63
Calkins, William H., 124
Call, Wilkinson: civil service reform and, 133–34; labor statistics bureau and, 147, 152, 154, 155, 156
Cannon, Joseph G., 173, 175
Capitol building, 1–2
Carlisle, John G., 173–74, 180–81
Caruth, Asher G., 193
Caswell, Lucien B., 185, 186
Chandler, Zachariah, 82
Chase, Salmon, 77
Circuit Courts of Appeals Act, 186–87. *See also* Evarts Act
Civil Rights acts of 1866 and 1871, 116
civil rights program, 172
Civil Service Act of 1883, 130. *See also* Pendleton Act

civil service appointments, 128–29
Civil War: Battle of Bull Run, or Manassas, 38; Congress during, 63; Emancipation Proclamation, 65; foreign governments during, 40; House during, 39; Republican Party and, 39–40; secession and, 37–38. *See also* Davis, Jefferson; freedmen's bureau; Lincoln, Abraham
Civil War Sanitary Commission, 64
Clark, William T., 113
Clay, Brutus Junius, 66–67
Clay, Clement C., 32–34
Clay, Henry, 3, 14
Clements, Judson C., 124, 127
Cleveland, Grover, 48, 130, 156
client-oriented departments, 38
Cobb, Williamson R. W., 19–20
Cockrell, Francis, 133–34
Collamer, Jacob: agriculture department bill and, 46; Morrill Act and, 29–30, 34, 54
Committee on Education and Labor: House, 148, 169; Senate, 145–46, 170
Committee on Public Lands, 38, 50, 59
common school movement, 90, 91
Compromise of 1850, 25
Compromise of 1877, 116, 118
Confiscation Act of 1862, 80
Congress: analogy as court, 5, 30; debate in, 2–4; during Civil War, 63; in 1858, 1–2, 8; Forty-seventh, 130; lawyers in, 5–7; localism of, 52, 183; outside counsel, use of, 104, 105; precedents for administrative state and, 171; as public space, 3; supremacy of, and Whig Party, 47–48; Thirty-seventh, 37. *See also* House; Senate
Congressional Globe, x, 4, 130
Congressional Record, x, 4, 130
cooperative federalism, 56, 57, 58
corresponding powers doctrine of borrowing, 160
corruption: freedmen's bureau and, 80–81; judicial branch and, 177; land grants and, 50–51; in New England free schools, 26; scrip and, 52; state building and, 13
courts: analogy of Congress to, 5, 30; caseload of, 172–73, 187; Civil Rights acts of

1866 and 1871 and, 116; civil rights program and, 172; conception of, 171–72; Evarts Act and, 178; forum shopping and, 176; freedmen's bureau and, 76–77; House and, 173–78; labor-management relations and, 145

Cowan, Edgar, 49, 80, 87

Cox, Samuel Sullivan "Sunset": agriculture department and, 41, 44; bureau of labor and, 169; civil service reform and, 138; educational subsidies and, 112; freedmen's bureau and, 65, 68–69; justice department and, 106

Crisp, Charles F., 164–65

Culberson, David B., courts and, 173, 174, 176–77, 185

Cullom, Shelby M., commission plan of, 159–62

Curtis, George W., 129

Daniel, John W., 183–84

Davis, Garrett, 80–81, 85, 98

Davis, Jefferson: Capitol and, 2; Morrill Act and, 28–29, 34; secession and, 37; slave code and, 8; Supremacy Clause and, 29

Davis bill, 172

Dawes, Henry L., 101, 134–35

debates: on Blair bill, 119; consensus in, 197; on education department, 200–201; on freedmen's bureau, 71, 76–80, 200; on justice department, 201; on labor statistics bureau, 145–48; lawyers and, 5–6, 143, 198; on Morrill Act, 24–31, 60–61, 199–200; oratory, in 1860s, 2; personal experience and, 198; procedures for, 3; on Second Morrill Act, xi–xii, 202; in Senate, 21. *See also* House; Senate

Degener, Edward, 113

democracy: essence of American, 3; monarchy compared to, vii

Democratic Party: courts and, 175; freedmen's bureau and, 101; railroad regulation and, 158–59; second state and, 151

de Tocqueville, Alexis, 5

Dibble, Samuel, 165

Dickens, Charles, *A Tale of Two Cities*, 70–71

Dixon, James, 55, 98

Dolph, Joseph N., 180–82

Donnelly, Ignatius, 93–94, 100, 101

Doolittle, James R., 53–54, 80–81, 98

Drake, Charles D., 108

Dunnell, Mark H., 192

Eaton, John, Jr., 103, 109–10, 121

economy, administrative regulation of, 157

Edmunds, George F., 161

education: agricultural reformers and, 10–12; common school movement, 90, 91; direct federal subsidies for, 108–9, 111; foreign models of, 11, 12, 112; illiteracy and, 94, 122–23, 138, 142; J. Morrill and, 15–16; in New England, 26, 90; Perce bill, 114–16; religion and, 127, 141; second state ideology and, 140, 188; state educational reformers, 12–13. *See also* Blair bill; Hoar bill; Morrill Act

education, department of: Barnard and, 99; debates about, 200–201; demotion of, 100–103; Eaton and, 109–10; Garfield and, 92–97; House and, 92–97; push for, 90–92; Senate and, 97–99; support for, 93–94

Eliot, Charles W., 116

Eliot, Thomas D.: freedmen's bureau and, 65–66, 75, 82–83, 84, 87, 88; Pendleton and, 74; second state and, 68

Ellsworth, Henry Leavitt, 39

Emancipation Proclamation, 65

estates, administration of, 7

Europe. *See* foreign governments, as models; Prussia, kingdom of

Evarts, William M.: Interstate Commerce Commission bill and, 164; life and career of, 178–79; oration of, 179–80; outlays to, 106; Second Morrill Act and, 190

Evarts Act (Circuit Courts of Appeals Act): House and, 184–87; Senate and, 178, 179–84; support for, 201–2

exceptionalism, American: first state and, viii; freedmen's bureau debate and, 71; in political speeches and writings, 42; school reform and, 92; W. Wilson and, 197

executive branch, staffing of, 128–29. *See also* Pendleton Act

Farnsworth, John F., 101–3
federalism: cooperative, 56, 57, 58; dual, 13; Second Morrill Act and, 190
Fessenden, William Pitt: agriculture department bill and, 46, 49; Morrill Act and, 53, 55
Field, David, 179
first state ideology: American exceptionalism and, viii; fiscal conservatism and, 188; Mason on, 26; origins of, 9–10; persistence of, 143, 148; transition from, to third state, ix–x, 202. *See also* antibureaucracy mindset
fiscal conservatism, 41, 188
Fitzpatrick, Benjamin, 21
Flower, Roswell P., 123
Foran, Martin A., 150–51, 156
foreign governments, as models: civil service system and, 132; education and, 11, 12, 112; education department and, 96–97; first state and, viii; freedmen's bureau and, 66; history of, 210n1; localist xenophobia and, 52; Sherwin bill and, 126. *See also* Prussia, kingdom of
foreign governments, during Civil War, 40
forum shopping, 176
Foster, Lafayette S., 47–48
fourth state, 202–3
Frank, Nathan, 186
Frankfurter, Felix, ix, 6
Franklin, Benjamin, 10–11
freedmen's bureau: agitation for, 64–65; amendments to, 80–81; Bureau of Education and, 103; conference committee and, 86–87; debates about, 71, 76–80, 200; Democrats and, 101; history of, 87–88; House and, 65–75, 82–85; opposition to, 66–71, 83–84, 85–86; Senate and, 75–82, 84–85; supervision and, 63–64; support for, 71–74
Fugitive Slave Law, 25, 33

Garfield, James A.: assassination of, 129; education department and, 92–97, 101; justice department and, 107
Garland, Augustus H.: civil service reform and, 135, 136, 139; labor statistics bureau and, 147, 155, 156

General Land Office, 16
George, James Z.: civil service reform and, 133, 134, 136; labor statistics bureau and, 145, 152, 153, 155, 156
Godkin, E. L., 129
Gorman, Arthur P., 160
government: first state and, vii–ix; functions of, xi–xii; nature of, C. Clay on, 33; staffing agencies of, 78–79, 81; as trustee, 31, 127. *See also* foreign governments, as models
Granges, 158
Grant, Ulysses S., 103, 109, 129
Gray, George, 180–81
Great Railroad Strike of 1877, 145
Greeley, Horace, vii–ix, 39, 78
Green, James S., 27, 30–31
Grimes, James W.: education department and, 99; freedmen's bureau and, 77, 78, 81, 86; Morrill Act and, 51–52, 55–56, 58–59
Grow, Galusha, 39, 44, 60
guarantee clause, 111
Guiteau, Charles, 129
Gwin, William M., 31–32

Hadley, Arthur T., 158
Hale, John P., 27–28, 48–49, 86
Hamilton, Alexander, 5–6, 10
Hamilton, William T., 108
Hamlin, Hannibal, 31
Hammond, Henry, 8
Harlan, James: freedmen's bureau and, 80; Morrill Act and, 26–27, 31, 56–57, 62
Harris, Jedidiah, 14–15
Harrison, Benjamin, 140–41, 175, 194
Harrison, William Henry, 34
Hawley, Joseph R., 132, 136, 191
Hayes, Rutherford B., 179
Hendricks, Thomas A., 77–78, 80–82
Hepburn, William P., 163
Herbert, Hilary A., 137
hermeneutics, principles of, 6
Hitt, Robert R., 163
Hoar, Ebenezer Rockwood, 110
Hoar, George F.: Blair bill and, 141; civil service reform and, 132, 136; constitutional arguments of, 117; Evarts Act and,

180–81, 184; Interstate Commerce Commission bill and, 163–64; labor statistics bureau and, 146–47, 148, 155–56; life and career of, 110–11; oration of, 111–12; Perce bill and, 116; Second Morrill Act and, 188; second state and, 119

Hoar bill: House and, 114; introduction of, 108; opposition to, 112–14; support for, 113

Holman, William S.: agriculture department and, 40–41, 42, 44; bureau of labor and, 169; freedmen's bureau and, 65, 66–67, 84; Morrill Act and, 60

Hopkins, James H., 139, 148–50, 151

House: after southern secession, 39; agriculture department bill and, 43–44; Blair bill and, 123–28; chambers of, 2; Committee on Education and Labor, 148, 169; courts and, 173–78; education department and, 92–97; Evarts Act and, 184–87; freedmen's bureau and, 65–75, 82–85; Hoar bill in, 114; Interstate Commerce Commission bill and, 162–63, 164–66; labor department bill and, 169–70; labor statistics bureau and, 148–52; Morrill Act and, 18–20, 59–60; Pendleton Act and, 137–38; procedures of, 17, 60, 173–74; Second Morrill Act and, 191–94; speaker of, 17

Howard, Jacob M., 86

Howe, Timothy O.: freedmen's bureau and, 86; Morrill Act and, 54, 56, 57, 58

Hutchins, John, 40

illiteracy: Blair bill and, 138, 142; Donnelly and, 94; Logan and, 122–23

industrialization, 145

information gathering and second state ideology: Bureau of Labor, 169; labor statistics bureau, 146; statistics, power of, 121, 141

Ingalls, John James: Blair bill and, 139; courts and, 183; labor department bill and, 154–55; Second Morrill Act and, 191

Interior Department, Bureau of Education, 100, 103, 109

Internal Revenue Service, 61

Interstate Commerce Act of 1887, 158, 176, 201–2

Interstate Commerce Commission: administrative state and, 144; conference committee and, 163–66; House and, 162–63, 164–66; legal status of, 166; second state and, 166–67; Senate and, 157–62, 163–64

Jackson, Andrew, 82

Jacksonian ideology, viii, 10, 199

Jefferson, Thomas: agriculture and, 10–11; C. Clay on, 34; as lawyer, 5–6; state building and, 13

Jeffersonian ideology: Cowan and, 49; Cox and, 69; description of, viii, 199. *See also* republicanism

Jenckes, Thomas Allen: education department and, 102; justice department and, 104–5, 106, 107; oration of, 117; second state and, 119

Johnson, Andrew: education department and, 99; Evarts and, 106; freedmen's bureau and, 87; impeachment trial of, 179; Reconstruction and, 128

Johnson, Reverdy, 77–78, 86

Joint Committee on the Conduct of the War, 38

Jones, Charles W., 139

Jones, William, poem of, 148–49, 150

Jordan, Edward, 61

Judiciary Act of 1789, 173

Judiciary Act of 1801, 10

Jurisdiction and Removal Act of 1875, 172

justice, department of: Congress and, 103; debates about, 201; in Senate, 107–8; support for, 104–8

Kalbfleisch, Martin, 67–68, 69–70

Kasson, John A., 137–38

Keifer, J. Warren, 137

Keit, Lawrence, 39

Kelley, William D., 71–72, 75

Kerr, Daniel, 192

Kerr, Michael C., 113

Knapp, Anthony, 66–68, 72–74

Knights of Labor, 145, 156

labels, stickiness of, 151
labor, department of, 169–71, 201–2
labor-management relations, 145–48
labor statistics, bureau of: debate on, 145–48; House and, 148–52; second state and, 156–57, 166–67; Senate and, 152–57
land confiscation, 80
Land Grant College. *See* Morrill Act
Land Grant College Act of 1862, 116
land grants, 14, 50–51
Lane, James H., 50–51, 57, 58–59
Langdell, Christopher Columbus, 181
Lanham, Samuel W. T., 192
law enforcement: local power and, 103; Secret Service Division, 61; U.S. marshals, 16, 104
Lawrence, William: Hoar bill and, 113–14; justice department and, 104, 106, 107; oration of, 117; second state and, 119
lawyers: administration of estates and, 7; administrative state and, 160; agriculture department and, 40; appeal of professional opinion of, 141–42; argument by analogy and, 53; congressmen as, 5–7; consistency, uniformity, and, 105; debate and, 143, 198; debates and, 5–6; education of, 22, 181; Evarts bill and, 194; freedmen's bureau and, 79–81, 88; as general practitioners, 40; as governing class, 23; Interstate Commerce Commission bill and, 165–66; justice department and, 107; land disputes and, 67; Morrill Act and, 21–22, 36; public service and, 22–23; as representatives of people, 57; second state ideology and, 171, 198–99; use of, by Congress, 104, 105
Leverett, William, 120
Lieber, Francis, 6
Lincoln, Abraham: agriculture department bill and, 39, 50; freedmen's bureau and, 65, 87; Wade and, 38
localism: agricultural colleges and, 193; Congress and, 52, 183; B. Harrison and, 140–41; Vest and, 181. *See also* regionalism
localist xenophobia, 52
Logan, John: Blair bill and, 122–23, 139; civil service reform and, 136; justice department and, 107
Lovejoy, Owen: agriculture department and, 41–42, 43, 44, 50; freedmen's bureau and, 75
Lynch, John R., 116, 124–25

machinery metaphor, 125, 181–82
Madison, James, 34
Mallory, Robert, 66–67
Manassas, Battle of, 38
Mann, Horace, 12, 90, 141
Martin, William T., 115
Maryland Agricultural Society, 39
Mason, James M., 25–26, 34, 58
Massachusetts Board of Agriculture, 39
Maxey, Samuel B., 140
Maynard, Horace, 42, 106–7
McClellan, George B., 77
McComas, Louis E., 192
McGrew, James C., 113
McNeely, Thompson W., 113
Miller, John F., 141–42
Miller, Warner, 134
Mills, Roger Q., 177
misprision, 121
Morgan, John T.: Blair bill and, 141, 142; civil service reform and, 135; Cullom commission and, 161, 162; Evarts Act and, 182; Interstate Commerce Commission bill and, 164; labor statistics bureau and, 152–54; Second Morrill Act and, 189–90
Morrill, Justin Smith: Blair and, 122; civil service reform and, 136; freedmen's bureau and, 75; Interstate Commerce Commission bill and, 164; labor statistics bureau and, 146, 155–56; life and career of, 14–16; oration of, 18–19; Perce bill and, 116; proposal of, 16, 17–18. *See also* Second Morrill Act
Morrill, Lot M., 85–86
Morrill Act: Blair bill compared to, 121; debate on, 24–31, 60–61, 199–200; description of, 8–9, 16; in House, 18–20, 59–60; lawyers and, 21–22, 36; opposition to, 19–20, 24–26, 30–31, 38; pas-

sage of, 60–62; perspectives of, 17–18; reconsideration of, 31–34, 59–60; re-introduction of, 50; in Senate, 20–31, 50–54; sponsorship and, 14; support for, 20, 26–27, 29–30; veto of, 35; Wilkinson amendment to, 52–53, 55. *See also* Second Morrill Act

Moulton, Samuel W., 95, 116–17

National Agricultural Society, 48
National Association of School Superintendents, 92, 114
National Civil Service Reform League, 129
National Education Association, 12, 91–92, 114
National Teachers Association, 12–13, 91–92
Native American tribes, 72
Neill, Edward, 99
"The New Departure of the Republican Party" (H. Wilson), 112
New England region: education and, 26, 90; Republican ideal and, 66; views of, 18, 29
Nimmo, John, Jr., 152
Northwest Ordinance of 1787, 14, 26
Norton, Daniel S., 98

Oates, William C.: courts and, 173, 174, 176–77, 186; Interstate Commerce Commission bill and, 165–66
O'Donnell, James, 192
O'Ferrall, Charles T., 162–63
Office of the Controller of the Currency, 61
O'Hara, James, 158
O'Neill, Charles, 163, 165
O'Neill, John J.: labor department and, 169, 170; labor statistics bureau and, 150, 152, 156
oratory, in 1860s, 2

Packard, Frederick A., 96
Palmer, Thomas W., 160
patronage, 128–29
Patterson, James W., 108
Peabody Fund, 109
Pendleton, George H.: freedmen's bureau and, 74–75; legislation of, 129, 136; life and career of, 130–31; rhetoric of, 131–32
Pendleton Act: amendments to, 135–36; in House, 137–38; impact of, 132; opposition to, 132–34, 137; second state and, 142–43; in Senate, 132–36; support for, 134–35, 137–38, 201–2; third state and, 118–19
People's, or Populist, Party, 176
Perce, Legrand W., 114–15, 116
Perce bill, 114–16
Pierce, Cyrus, 12, 90
Pierce, Franklin, 24, 28, 35
Pike, Frederick A., 95–96, 101
Platt, Orville H., 161, 164
Plumb, Preston B., 135, 191
political culture, uniqueness of, x
political science, as academic discipline, 196–97
Pomeroy, Samuel C., 53, 56
Potter, John F., 59–60
Powderly, Terence, 145, 156
Powell, Lazarus W., 79, 86
power: control and, 99; of lawyers, 22
pragmatism, 71
Price, Hiram, 74, 75
professionalization of bureaucracy, 78–79, 129
Progressive Era state: opening for, 194; second state ideology compared to, 148. *See also* administrative state
Prosser, William F., 113
Prussia, kingdom of: higher education in, 11; school system in, 90, 91, 112; J. Wright and, 46–47
Pruyn, John V.S.L., 100
public dialogue, analysis of, xii–xiv
public service, and lawyers, 22–23
public space, Congress as, 3
Pugh, George E.: as lawyer, 22; Morrill Act and, 21, 23, 24–25, 28, 31, 32, 34
Pugh, James L.: civil service reform and, 135; Evarts Act and, 184; labor statistics bureau and, 145; Second Morrill Act and, 191

qualification for office, 78–79, 81

race: expansion of state and, 69; impact on governing, 153; Second Morrill Act and, 189–90; second state and, 125
radical, use of term, 175
Radical Reconstruction, 115–16
railroad regulation, 157–62. *See also* Interstate Commerce Commission
Randall, Samuel J., 94–95, 96
Reagan, John H.: civil service reform and, 137; Evarts Act and, 183; Interstate Commerce Commission and, 158, 162–63, 164; labor department bill and, 170–71; Second Morrill Act and, 188, 189; Sherwin bill and, 127
Reconstruction agencies, 89–90, 103
Reed, Thomas B., 173, 186
regionalism: Blair and, 122; labor statistics bureau and, 153; Lane and, 58; West and East, 55. *See also* localism; New England region; sectional animosity
regulatory commission, advent of, 157
religion and education, 127, 141
republicanism: agriculture department bill and, 49; description of, 199; freedman's bureau and, 63; Wade and, 23–24. *See also* Jeffersonian ideology
Republican Party: after southern secession, 39–40; courts and, 172; freedmen and, 67; freedmen's bureau and, 84; A. Johnson and, 128; proposals of, 116–17
Rice, Henry M., 57, 58, 59
Richardson, William A., 76–77
riding circuit, 172
Robeson, George M., 127–28
Rockefeller, John D., 158
Rogers, Anthony A. C., 113
Rogers, John H., circuit court bill and, 174–75, 176, 177–78, 185
Rowell, Jonathan H., 163

Saulsbury, Eli, 161–62
Saulsbury, Willard, Sr., 78, 141
Schenck, Robert C., 83, 84
Schurz, Carl: as activist, 118; Bismarck and, vii; civil service reform and, 129; first state and, viii–ix

"The Science of Administration" (W. Wilson), 196
Scofield, Glenni W., 101, 103, 107
scrip, 52, 55
secession of southern states, 37–38
Second Morrill Act: debate on, xi–xii, 202; in House, 191–94; introduction of, 187–88; opposition to, 191–93; in Senate, 188–91; support for, 193
second state ideology: administration of estates and, 7; administrative state compared to, 148, 199; Blair bill and, 138, 142–43; conservatism of, 83; contestation and, xiii; Democratic Party and, 151; early approaches to, 59; education and, 140, 188; education department and, 93; T. Eliot and, 68; evidence of, x–xi; Fessenden and, 49; freedman's bureau and, 63–64; Harlan and, 27; at high-water mark, 144; G. Hoar and, 119; Hopkins and, 149; information gathering and, 121, 141, 146, 169; Interstate Commerce Commission and, 166–67; Jenckes and, 104–5, 119; justice department and, 103, 105–6, 108; labor statistics bureau and, 156–57, 166–67; Lawrence on, 114, 119; lawyers and, 171, 198–99; legislation and, 81; Pendleton Act and, 142–43; Progressive Era ideology compared to, 148; racialism and, 125; Second Morrill Act and, 187; Sherwin bill and, 124; sponsorship and, 9; standardization and, 90; as state of mind, xii; Wade and, 27; war experience and, 89–90, 102; W. Wilson and, 197
Secret Service Division, 61
sectional animosity: civil service reform and, 136; in 1858, 1, 8; Hoar bill and, 112
segregation, 191
Senate: agriculture department bill in, 44–50; chambers of, 2; Committee on Education and Labor, 145–46, 170; debates in, 21; education department and, 97–99; Evarts Act and, 178, 179–84; freedmen's bureau and, 75–82, 84–85; Interstate Commerce Commission bill in, 157–62,

163–64; justice department and, 107–8; labor department bill in, 170–71; labor statistics bureau and, 152–57; Morrill Act in, 20–31, 50–54; Pendleton Act and, 132–36; procedures of, 20–21, 33; Second Morrill Act and, 188–91

Seward, William, 8, 21

Sewell, William J., 160

Sherman, John: Blair bill and, 138–39, 141; civil service reform and, 132; Interstate Commerce Commission bill and, 164; labor statistics bureau and, 155–56

Sherman, Roger, 110

Sherwin, John C., 123, 125–27

Sherwin bill, 123–28

Simmons, James F.: agriculture department bill and, 44–45, 46, 48–50; use of word *colleges*, 47

slaveocracy, 13

slippery slope rhetoric, 44–50, 186, 218n37

Smith, Caleb Blood, 39

social economy, 73

social sciences, 150–51

sources, handling, sifting, and selection of, xii–xiv

speaker of the House, 17

speculators, 52, 59

spoils system, 82, 177

sponsorship: agriculture department bill and, 49, 200; evolution of thought on, 193; as function of government, xi–xii; Morrill Act and, 14, 35, 36, 54, 199–200; secession of southern states and, 37–38; second state and, 9; supervision and, 50, 75–82; J. Wright on, 45

Spooner, John C., 160, 180–81

Springer, William M., 123–24

staffing government agencies, 78–79, 81. *See also* Pendleton Act

standardization: civil service reform and, 136; description of, 118–19; as function of government, xi–xii; Hoar bill and, 112–13; justice department and, 201; second state and, 90

Stanford, Leland, 161

state: as leviathan, 208n18; twin pillars of, 90; use of, as term of art, 121

state building, ideological aversion to, 13

state educational reformers, 12–13

state sovereignty, 29

states' rights ideology, 121. *See also* Jeffersonian ideology; republicanism

Sterne, Simon, 158

Stevens, Thaddeus: education department and, 91, 97, 100; view of South by, 71

Stewart, Charles, 151–52

Story, Joseph, 22, 49

Stowe, Calvin E., 12, 90

Stuart, Charles E.: as lawyer, 22; Morrill Act and, 21, 23, 32, 34

Sumner, Charles: agriculture department bill and, 46, 48; civil service reform and, 128; courts and, 172; education department and, 98; freedmen's bureau and, 65, 75, 77, 78, 79, 80, 83, 84–86; as lawyer, 22; as orator, 21

supervision: freedman's bureau and, 64, 88; as function of government, xi–xii; Hoar bill and, 112–13; Knapp and, 72–73; labor statistics bureau and, 156–57; Morrill Act and, 54–55; G. Pugh and, 25; secession of southern states and, 37–38; sponsorship and, 50, 75–82

Supreme Court, 172

system, Trumbull on, 97–98

A Tale of Two Cities (Dickens), 70–71

Tarbell, J., vii

Taylor, Ezra B., 177, 185

Taylor, Joseph D., 192

Taylor, Zachary, 77–78

Teller, Henry M., 161–62

Ten Eyck, John, 57–58

third state. *See* administrative state

Thirteenth Amendment, 63

Townsend, George Alfred, 3

Townsend, Washington, 113

treasury, department of: Bureau of Statistics, 147; freedmen's bureau and, 75; Secret Service Division, 61

Trumbull, Lyman: civil service reform and, 129; Confiscation Act and, 80; courts and, 172; education department and, 97–98; freedmen's bureau and, 86, 87, 88; justice department and, 104, 108
trustee, government as, 31, 127
trusteeships, court-based, 117
Tuskegee Institute, 191

Upson, Charles, 101
U.S. Agricultural Society, 39
U.S. Department of Agriculture. *See* agriculture, department of
U.S. Department of Education. *See* education, department of
U.S. marshals, 16, 61, 104
U.S. Treasury Department. *See* treasury, department of

Van Wyck, Charles H., 154
Vaux, Richard, 186
Vest, George G.: civil service reform and, 133–34, 136; Evarts Act and, 180–81, 184
Villard, Henry, 129
Voorhees, Daniel W., 141, 156

Wade, Benjamin Franklin: agriculture department bill and, 46; Lincoln and, 38; Morrill Act and, 23–24, 32, 50, 51, 53,

54; second state and, 27; Wilkinson amendment and, 52, 55
Wadsworth, William H., 75
War Department, 64, 86
Washburn, Emory, 110
Washburne, Elihu B., 100, 101
Washington, George, 10, 34
Watson, James H., 158
Weaver, James B., 165
Webster, Daniel, 3
Webster, Noah, 10–11
Wheeler, Joseph, 127
Whig Party, 34, 47–48, 65
White, Edward Emerson, 92, 93, 114
Whittemore, Benjamin F., 101
Wilkinson, Morton S., 52–53
Willey, Waitman T., 78
Williams, John S., 133–34
Willis, Albert S., 124
Wilson, Henry, 112
Wilson, James (founding father), 5–6
Wilson, James F. (R-Iowa), 83–84
Wilson, Woodrow, 196
Wood, Fernando, 101
Wood, William P., 61
Wright, Carroll, 169, 170
Wright, Joseph A., 45–47, 50

Yates, Richard, 98–99, 117
Young, Hiram C., 150, 151

Books in the Series

Washington County: Politics and Community in Antebellum America
Paul Bourke and Donald DeBats

Bennington and the Green Mountain Boys: The Emergence of Liberal Democracy in Vermont, 1760–1850
Robert E. Shalhope

An Army of Women: Gender and Politics in Gilded Age Kansas
Michael Lewis Goldberg

Fireside Politics: Radio and Political Culture in the United States, 1920–1940
Douglas B. Craig

Red Feminism: American Communism and the Making of Women's Liberation
Kate Weigand

Beyond Party: Cultures of Antipartisanship in Northern Politics before the Civil War
Mark Voss-Hubbard

The Price of Progress: Public Services, Taxation, and the American Corporate State, 1877 to 1929
R. Rudy Higgens-Evenson

Against Obscenity: Reform and the Politics of Womanhood in America, 1873–1935
Leigh Ann Wheeler

The Big Vote: Gender, Consumer Culture, and the Politics of Exclusion, 1890s–1920s
Liette Gidlow

Black Power: Radical Politics and African American Identity
Jeffrey O. G. Ogbar

To Enlarge the Machinery of Government: Congressional Debates and the Growth of the American State, 1858–1891
Williamjames Hull Hoffer